THE TEMPLE

OTHER BOOKS AND AUDIO BOOKS
BY ED J. PINEGAR

Turn It Over to the Lord
Leadership for Saints
Love One Another
Come Unto Me
Press Forward Saints
Living By the Word
Your Patriarchal Blessing
A Prophet's Voice: Inspiring Quotes by Joseph Smith
Choose Ye This Day
A Woman's Heart
I Will Follow Thee
Look to the Temple
Rejoice in Christ
Blessed from on High
On the Bright Side
All Is Well
Living the Gospel
Pleasing God
Overcoming Twelve Tough Temptations
Personal Success
Hope in Christ
Happily Ever After
Raising the Bar
Clearing the Bar
Preparing for a Mission
Missionary Essentials
Ultimate Missionary Companion
Words of Wisdom for Missionaries
Especially for Missionaries, Six Volumes
More Especially for Missionaries, Two Volumes
Power Tools for Missionaries, Four Volumes
After Your Mission
Lengthen Your Shuffle

Series of Latter-Day Commentaries, Teachings and Commentaries, Unlocking, and Who's Who—Old Testament, New Testament, Book of Mormon, and Doctrine and Covenants

THE TEMPLE

Gaining Knowledge and Power in the House of the Lord

ED J. PINEGAR

Covenant Communications, Inc.

Cover Image: *Everlasting* © Robert A. Boyd. For information on art prints by Robert A. Boyd, please call 1-801-373-2787 or visit www.RobertABoyd.com.

Published by Covenant Communications, Inc.
American Fork, Utah

Printed in the United States of America
First Printing: April 2014

20 19 18 17 16 15 14 10 9 8 7 6 5 4 3 2 1

ISBN-13: 978-1-62108-713-7

List of Abbreviated Sources

Teachings of Ezra Taft Benson—TETB
Teachings of Howard W. Hunter—THWH
Teachings of the Prophet Joseph Smith—TPJS
Teachings of Harold B. Lee—THBL
Discourses of Brigham Young—DBY

Table of Contents

Acknowledgments

I am indebted to many friends and colleagues who have taught, mentored, and helped me in this undertaking. All are dear friends. The safest way to introduce them is alphabetically:

Randy Bryson, my former student, helped so much with the family history section of this book.

Andrew Ehat introduced me to many scriptures and insights regarding the Lord's holy house.

Alonzo Gaskill helped me understand symbolism and the Fall and answered my continual questions, always with patience and love.

Don Norton, an editor and temple scholar, worked long and faithful hours to bring this book to its present state. I am forever indebted to his editorial skills, excellent insights, and devoted friendship. Without him, this book would have struggled to be born.

Donald Parry, the luminous scholar of the Hebrew Bible and editor of the Dead Sea Scrolls, has a great listening ear and a humble heart and introduced me to the temple hymns.

John Welch, an insightful scholar, brought me knowledge of chiasms in the Book of Mormon as well as the temple text the Savior included in the Sermon on the Mount, both in Jerusalem and at the Nephite temple site. He was kind enough to write his thoughts on the temple as a template for teaching our families for this book.

To these great brothers and countless others, I am eternally indebted. I am grateful to the editors at Eschler Editing—especially Noelle Perner for her timely suggestions. Thanks to my wonderful counselors, Dennis Slack and Dewey Bennett, and to my coworkers in the Manti Temple, whom I dearly love with all my heart. Deep gratitude to my eternal sweetheart, Pat, who carefully listened each time I excitedly explained an insight I had just gained. She has been patient with me and my "book time" and has always supported my efforts.

To Covenant Communications, I express my gratitude for asking me to undertake this project. I am particularly grateful to my editors, Kathy Gordon and Samantha Millburn, for their support and editorial skills. Kathy, in her ever wonderful and insightful way, made dramatic changes in the order of the book that brought understanding and clarity to the doctrines of the temple.

Explanation of References

I often add italics to parts of scriptures and other quoted material for emphasis. Unless otherwise indicated, italics do not occur in the original texts. The bibliography for all references begins on page 255.

Introduction

The Temple, the Only Way—Through Christ the Lord

It is with great reverence that I approach the task of writing about the sacred and holy house of the Lord. I begin by testifying that the ordinances and covenants we enter into in the temple are the only way to return to the presence of the Father and the Son and the only way families become eternal. No other place on Earth testifies with such clarity of the goodness and mercy of our Heavenly Father and our beloved Savior, Jesus Christ. The temple is where we see Their glory and feel Their presence, where the Savior is manifest and typified in every doctrine, principle, ordinance, covenant, and action. The temple is also where we receive the power and the fulness of the Holy Ghost, which should help us go about doing good as the Savior did (see Acts 10:38).

I gladly witness that the grace of God affords us the opportunity to be empowered in His holy house. It is there that we receive the mysteries of the kingdom—the knowledge of God, the power of godliness, and the ordinances and covenants that enable us to truly become the sons and daughters of God and enjoy the blessings of exaltation.

In the years I have spent as a temple patron, a temple ordinance worker, a temple sealer, and a temple president, I have learned that the temple is a house of hope—hope of eternal life through Jesus Christ our Lord and His infinite Atonement. I have also come to understand that the temple is the panacea for many of life's challenges. Most of all, I have learned that when it comes to the temple, I am never finished learning. I suspect it is the same for each of Heavenly Father's children. I pray that each of us will continually look to the temple, worship in the temple, and learn and receive revelation in the temple, where we become more holy, sanctified, and justified through the Lord Jesus Christ by the power of the Holy Ghost.

In writing about the temple, I have taken great pains to adhere to the counsel of the Brethren in every way. I have not written of those things we covenant not to discuss outside the temple walls. I have confined my text to the scriptures; the teachings of the prophets, seers, and revelators; and trusted LDS authors. I am grateful to those who have written concerning the Lord's holy house and thank them for their insights.

Throughout this book, I will ask questions that will lead you to the scriptures; I hope they will cause you to reflect on the doctrines, covenants, and ordinances of the temple. As Nephi counseled, we are to feast together on the word of God: "Wherefore, I said unto you, feast upon the words of Christ; for behold, the words of Christ will tell you all things what ye should do" (2 Ne. 32:3). As we ponder and pray and ask and knock, we will receive great blessings. Our study will take us to greater depths, and the heavens will open to us as they have for so many prophets and righteous men and women before us. President Joseph F. Smith's vision of the spirit world teaches us the process:

> I sat in my room pondering over the scriptures; And reflecting upon the great atoning sacrifice that was made by the Son of God, for the redemption of the world; And the great and wonderful love made manifest by the Father and the Son in the coming of the Redeemer into the world; That through his atonement, and by obedience to the principles of the gospel, mankind might be saved. . . . As I pondered over these things [1 Peter chapters 3 and 4] which are written, the eyes of my understanding were opened, and the Spirit of the Lord rested upon me, and I saw the hosts of the dead, both small and great. (D&C 138:1–4, 11)

There is a price for revelation, and it begins with pondering and mighty prayer.

The questions of conscience I pose will help you examine whether you understand and truly appreciate the blessings of the temple. I hope they will prick your conscience and create a greater desire within you to keep your covenants and truly go about doing good.

Each section or subsection in this book will build on one another. I will use repetition to show how all of the doctrines, covenants, ordinances, and principles of the Atonement are integrally connected to and reflected in the temple. Forgive me if the repetition feels cumbersome at first, but it is purposeful because I have come to understand that repetition is one of the Lord's ways of teaching and is a divine principle of learning. Consider how often a doctrine or principle is repeated in the standard works, in general conferences, and in lesson manuals. Consider, too, that each verse may have many facets, so a single scripture may be used to teach several different doctrines.

The principle of learning through repetition becomes especially clear as we return to the temple repeatedly to participate in vicarious work and to worship. The endowment doesn't change, yet through inspiration, we see things we didn't see before. Through careful attention to the words and actions of temple ordinances, we learn more each time we attend the temple—*if* we prepare ourselves. *If* we seek and knock and prepare, the Lord will pour forth His blessings upon us and lead us home.

The intent of this book is not to lay out every possible doctrine and principle taught in the temple but rather to encourage each of us to open our eyes, ears, mind, and heart in understanding and appreciation for the great blessings of the temple. As that change occurs in me, I am able to see clearly and feel deeply the goodness and love of God. This experience is available to all; it comes to us from a God who wants, more than anything, for His children to return home to Him. The gratitude we feel as this miracle unfolds in our lives is at the heart of true worship of our Heavenly Father and our Savior Jesus Christ. It is the catalyst for all spiritual growth.

The observations I make throughout this book have led me to recognize the goodness and mercy of God; as a result, I have an overwhelming desire to do good—to be more kind and loving. I have come to desire what the people of the Book of Mormon achieved following the visit of our beloved Savior: "There was no contention in the land, because of the love of God which did dwell in the hearts of the people. And there were no envyings, nor strifes, nor tumults, nor whoredoms, nor lyings, nor murders, nor any manner of lasciviousness; and surely there could not be a happier people among all the people who had been created by the hand of God" (4 Ne. 1:15–16).

Through studying about the temple, attending the temple, worshipping in the temple, and officiating in its ordinances, I have come to enjoy a portion of the power of the Holy Ghost—the power God bestows on each of us as we harness it through our actions. Each of us has the responsibility to study, ponder, and pray to better understand and appreciate the symbolism and doctrines of the temple as well as the ordinances and covenants, all of which culminate in the endowment and sealing ceremonies. In the ordinances thereof, the greater priesthood, the power of godliness is made manifest (see D&C 84:21).

My intent in sharing the temple insights I have gained throughout my life is to ignite in you a desire to look deeply into the scriptures and the doctrines of the temple and thereby realize that the scriptures speak constantly of the Atonement, as symbolized in the temple ordinances. I, like you, am a child of God who seeks to please our Heavenly Father as I follow His Beloved Son and become perfected in Him. As evidenced in the temple, all things are done through Christ the Lord; He is "the way, the truth, and the life; no man cometh unto the Father, but by me" (John 14:6). He is the only way back into the presence of our Heavenly Father. In all things, He typifies the Father, just as the temple ordinances typify the Savior and His Atonement.

I testify that we can truly feel and recognize the glory and presence of the Lord in the temple. Temple worship can and will bring great joy into our lives, as the Lord has promised, and sanctify our very beings. The Atonement will come alive as we see Christ in the symbols and covenants, and we will see how the Father and the Son are intimately involved from on high in every aspect of the endowment, which includes all of the ordinances and covenants of the temple.

I am not trying to provide a complete treatise but instead a setting in which we can come to better understand and appreciate the magnificent and perfect plan of our Father. I hope what I have written shows the need for the Savior's infinite Atonement and how His Atonement is inseparably connected to the temple. As you come to learn and accept these truths, you will experience profound gratitude that will in turn inspire you to become Christlike and to go about doing good.

My approach in writing this book represents a highly personal journey of discovery that I wish I had taken, or at least been introduced to, earlier in my life. My purpose in writing this book is to please my Heavenly Father and bless my brothers and sisters. I alone am responsible for its contents; in no way should it be considered an official Church publication. I pray that it will uplift and edify you, that it will inspire you to undertake a deeper study of the doctrines of the temple as you commit to keep your covenants, to prayerfully prepare for temple worship, and to have an increased desire to serve and to participate in vicarious work.

CHAPTER 1

Temple Eyes—Temple Ears—Temple Heart—Temple Soul

FOR A LONG TIME, I did not realize the depth of the temple doctrines because I was afraid to talk about them. But over the years, I have come to realize there is so much we *can* discuss about the temple that will enlighten our minds. In fact, we *can* discuss much more about the temple than we cannot discuss.

For example, I never realized how important it is to see, feel, understand, and appreciate that *all* things typify—that is, symbolize—Christ and center on His infinite Atonement: "And all things which have been given of God from the beginning of the world, unto man, are the typifying of him" (2 Ne. 11:4). "All things" surely includes the temple and all of the ordinances and covenants of the greater priesthood. As you attune your senses to the temple, you will come to understand how the Atonement and endowment are inseparably connected. You will see that "He [Christ] . . . ascended up on high, as also he descended below all things, in that he comprehended all things, that he might be in all and through all things, the light of truth" (D&C 88:6). "And the light which shineth, which giveth you light, is through him who enlighteneth your eyes, which is the same light that quickeneth your understandings" (D&C 88:11). In essence, you will come to see the Savior in all things.

When we enter the temple for the first time, we are often told not to worry about understanding the symbolism right away—and rightfully so. However, this is an admonition to be patient with ourselves and our understanding, not encouragement to ignore or shy away from this symbolism. We must come to embrace symbolism and tune our eyes, ears, and hearts to seek its meaning, for the Lord uses it in *all* of His teachings, whether in the temple or the scriptures. As a young man, I unfortunately shied away from symbolism. But as I grew older and gradually saw and understood the symbols in the temple, my increased understanding brought greater appreciation and a greater desire to learn and become better. The experience was enlightening, but it also required work. I have learned that whether it be figurative language or symbols in the temple, the process of discovery is the same: we must search out the meaning.

Recognizing Symbols

The Atonement is the central focus of the temple; as such, it is typified in all aspects of the temple ordinances. However, we must train our eyes, ears, and hearts to recognize the significance and meaning behind the symbols related to the Atonement. As we do, we will gain access to its enabling power, including forgiveness of sins, the restoration of all things, and even the resurrection of every living soul ever born.

The word *atonement* (at-one-ment) means "to return to the presence of" or "be at one with": *at*—"the place or condition of," *one*—"being united with," and *ment*—"the act of." The Atonement is literally the act of being united to the place or condition where we were previously—in the presence of our Heavenly Father. This oneness with the Father and the Son occurs as we come back into Their presence. Our Savior's Intercessory Prayer takes on greater significance when we understand that the Atonement is the power that enables that oneness.

The Greek word for *atonement* refers to "reconciliation." We are indeed reconciled to God through Christ the Lord. We see this concept in the temple ceremony itself as well as in the covenants we make.

As we look for understanding regarding the symbols of the temple, particularly those related to the Atonement, it is significant to note that the scriptures call Christ the *Anointed One* (in fact, the word *Christ* means "anointed one") who redeems all mankind through the enabling power of the Atonement—His infinite sacrifice. We learn that the Atonement is the focus and central event of the plan of redemption and exaltation and is indeed the foundation of The Church of Jesus Christ of Latter-day Saints. Likewise, many of Christ's other titles carry with them great symbolic meaning; an example is *Messiah*, which in Hebrew also means "anointed one." Just as Christ was anointed with healing oil, He in turn anoints us to exaltation. That is why we take upon us the name of Christ. Even using the title *Christian* to define who we are makes us "anointed ones" with Him. The scriptures literally use hundreds of titles to describe the Savior and His mission, each bearing deep symbolic meaning and each representing one of the Savior's many saving roles (see Bible Dictionary, Christ, names of). Whenever we see the words *Christ, Savior, Redeemer, Mediator, Advocate,* or any other word or title that describes Christ in any way, our minds should turn to the temple and the blessings promised to us there through our obedience.

We gain further understanding about the temple's symbols of the Atonement by looking at the Hebrew word for *atonement,* which comes from the word *kaphar,* meaning "to cover, to embrace, to forgive." The Atonement "embraces" and "covers" us, enabling us to see ourselves in our fallen state and giving us an added desire to be embraced by the Lord as we pass into His presence.

We can also gain understanding of temple symbolism by studying the very words that describe the temple ceremony. For example, we often think of the word *endow* or the phrase *receiving our endowment* as receiving a "gift" from God or "power" from on high. However, as we look more closely at the meanings of these words, we gain additional insight. The Greek word *enduein*—the root of the word *endow*—means "to clothe, to put on garments or attributes of virtue and righteousness" and expresses a connection between the Atonement and the endowment. In becoming endowed, we are "covered" and brought symbolically back into the presence of God. As we begin to look for and seek an understanding of symbolism, we will come to see and feel supernal truths that will lead us to righteousness.

Understanding of temple symbolism also comes through the Holy Ghost. Because God's holy house is a house of revelation, the Holy Ghost can quicken our eyes, ears, hearts, and minds and can teach us the truth of all things.

Let us attune our eyes, ears, and hearts to the glory and presence of the Father as well as the Son in the symbols of the temple. Remember, this is Their house. We build temples so They may come and dwell therein, that Their children can feel Their glory and presence. Our Father's ultimate purpose is our happiness, immortality, and eternal life. He seeks to give us all that He has (see D&C 84:38), a promise we symbolically receive in His holy house as we attune ourselves to meanings and engage more fully in the process of coming into the presence and glory of the Father.

The greater priesthood holds the keys to the mysteries of the kingdom and to the knowledge of God, and in its ordinances the "power of godliness is manifest" (D&C 84:20). It is only through the ordinances and covenants of the temple that we can come to know the "mysteries of godliness" and receive our exaltation and eternal lives. Without these ordinances and our subsequent faithfulness, we cannot see the face of God.

Further Study

The following study resources will help us have temple eyes, temple ears, temple hearts, and temple souls. Though not exhaustive, these resources provide a wonderful beginning. Remember, studying the doctrines and ordinances of the temple is the work of a lifetime—but a critical step is to begin!

From the scriptures:

- We are temples of God—see 1 Cor. 3:16, 6:19; D&C 93:35; Mosiah 2:37.
- The temple is a house of God—see Isa. 2:3; Ezek. 43:6; Matt. 21:13; Rev. 7:15; D&C 110:7.
- The temple is "a house of prayer, a house of fasting, a house of faith, a house of learning, a house of glory, a house of order, a house of God"—D&C 109:8.
- The temple is where we are endowed with power from on high—see D&C 38:32, 38; 43:16; 105:11.
- The temple is where we receive exalting ordinances—see D&C 84:19–22.
- The temple is where we are given to understand the power of godliness, the mysteries of the kingdom, and the knowledge of God—see D&C 84:19–22.

From the prophets, General Authorities, and officers of the Church:

- "Quotes," Temples of The Church of Jesus Christ of Latter-day Saints, accessed January 6, 2014, http://www.ldschurchtemples.com/articles/quotes/.
- "Articles," Temples of The Church of Jesus Christ of Latter-day Saints, accessed January 6, 2014, http://www.ldschurchtemples.com/articles/.

CHAPTER 2
The Perfect Plan

IN OUR FATHER'S INFINITE GOODNESS, He created a plan that would provide a way for us to return to His presence—a plan centered on His Son, Jesus Christ. It has been called the plan of happiness, the plan of salvation, the plan of exaltation, and the plan of redemption, among many other names. The purpose of our Father's plan was to provide a way—through the infinite Atonement of His Only Begotten Son in the flesh—for His children to learn, grow, and prove themselves (see Abr. 3:25) so they might, through the grace of God and their obedience, return to the presence of the Father and the Son and enjoy never-ending happiness.

The plan is based on many eternal truths, which, when understood, inspire reverence and honor for our Father and bring meaning to all aspects of our lives. *What* we need to do and *why* and *how* to do it are taught throughout the temple ordinances and in the covenants. It is in these that the plan of exaltation unfolds figuratively or, in other words, symbolically.

Some of these eternal truths become evident as we participate in the initiatory ordinances, others in the endowment ceremony, and still others in the sealing ordinance. The scriptures and the words of the prophets also teach eternal truth. Knowledge of these truths helps us understand and appreciate the grand plan of happiness and empowers us as we respond to the direction of the Spirit. I bear witness that we not only agreed to this plan, but we also rejoiced in it—and now we have the opportunity to live it. As we do, we are better prepared for the test of life and for our return to meet God.

Understanding the Plan

The plan of happiness that leads to exaltation for the faithful focuses on our Heavenly Father's Beloved Son, Jesus Christ. It began in the premortal realms as we became spirit children of our Heavenly Parents. Then came the Creation, which Christ—the premortal Jehovah—brought about at the command and request of His Father. Next came the foreordained Fall, which was essential so mankind could receive all-important bodies and progress, through obedience, toward eventually becoming like God Himself. Becoming like God is made possible through the infinite Atonement of our Savior and Redeemer, the Lord Jesus Christ.

The Creation, the Fall, and the Atonement are the three pillars of the plan:

The Creation—so that we, the spirit children of God and mortal descendants of Father Adam and his wife, Eve, would have a place to dwell and rear our families (the family of God).

The Fall—so that we could experience mortality and prepare to return to our Heavenly Father.

The Atonement—so that we could be redeemed from our fallen state and—through Christ the Lord, the only way—return to the presence of the Father.

Along with those three pillars are three other important elements of the plan:

Opposition—so that we might experience both good and evil.

Temptation—so that we can be tried and tested.

Agency—so that we can choose, be held accountable, and grow through our choices.

The plan is the strait and narrow path laid out for us to follow so we can, through obedience, partake of the love of God and thus gain eternal life. Holding to the iron rod (the word of God) will keep us on the path that leads to the tree of life, which represents the love of God, even Christ the Lord, and eternal life. Holding to the iron rod and feasting upon the word of God, then, are essential to our eternal life:

> And I now give unto you a commandment to beware concerning yourselves, to give diligent heed to the words of eternal life.
>
> For you shall live by every word that proceedeth forth from the mouth of God.
>
> For the word of the Lord is truth, and whatsoever is truth is light, and whatsoever is light is Spirit, even the Spirit of Jesus Christ.

> And the Spirit giveth light to every man that cometh into the world; and the Spirit enlighteneth every man through the world, that hearkeneth to the voice of the Spirit.
>
> And every one that hearkeneth to the voice of the Spirit cometh unto God, even the Father. (D&C 84:43–47)

The word of God leads us to the temple, and in the temple we are taught the things we need to do through words that testify of Christ and open our minds to eternal truths, empower us with knowledge, and instill in us a desire to do the will of God.

The endowment ceremony itself presents the plan of redemption.

The Beginning

In the beginning, we were with God as intelligences (see D&C 93:29). Because God is the Father of our spirits, we understand that we are indeed divine and eternal children; as Paul wrote, "The Spirit itself beareth witness with our spirit, that we are the children of God" (Rom. 8:16).

The plan was presented in our premortal state, where we, exercising our moral agency, chose to accept it—when we and "all the sons of God shouted for joy" (Job 38:7). Then war ensued (see Rev. 12, beginning with verse 7), and Lucifer was cast out with a "third part of the hosts of heaven" (D&C 29:36), and he became Satan, even the devil, the "father of all lies" (Moses 4:4) and "an enemy to all righteousness" (Alma 34:23).

Not knowing the mind of God, Satan began to act as a source of temptation. Without that temptation, we could not be "agents unto ourselves," able "to act . . . and not to be acted upon" (2 Ne. 2:26). Just as agency is an eternal verity, "it must needs be, that there is an opposition in all things" (2 Ne. 2:11); in other words, we must be tempted in order to become agents unto ourselves. We learned in our preparation to come to Earth that by our being tried in all things, we could prove ourselves worthy to "keep [our] second estate," even life here upon the Earth, "and they who keep their second estate shall have glory added upon their heads for ever and ever" (Abr. 3:26). The Creation and the very plan hinge on these pivotal doctrines laid out to us before we came to this Earth; otherwise, the eternal purposes of God could not come to pass.

We must come to understand and appreciate each doctrine and principle of the perfect plan of our Father in Heaven as presented in the premortal existence and reiterated now in the temple. They will help us understand who we are, where we came from, and how we can return to our Father.

The Creation

Accounts of the Creation are given in the books of Abraham, Moses, and Genesis and in the temple endowment ceremony. Though there are some differences between these accounts, all express the majesty and power of God, explain the purposes of the Creation, and include the same basic doctrine:

- All things were created in spirit before they were created physically.
- God the Father accomplished the Creation through His Beloved Son, Jehovah, the God of the Old Testament.
- The Earth was created near Kolob, the presence and throne of God (see Abr. 3:9).
- The Earth and all things on it, including Father Adam and Mother Eve, did not begin their journey in the fallen mortal state that we know but in a higher state while yet in the presence of God (see Moses 4:14).

All things were created, organized, or physically formed in seven "days"; according to the scriptures, these are seven periods of time whose length we do not know, for all things were done in a timeless state, not the temporal state by which we mortals perceive time.

I will not rehearse what was created on each day; suffice it to say that all things were organized, and Adam and Eve were then placed in the Garden of Eden. When the Lord comes again, He will teach us the specifics concerning the Creation: "Yea, verily I say unto you, in that day when the Lord shall come, he shall reveal all things—Things which have passed, and hidden things which no man knew, things of the earth, by which it was made, and the purpose and the end thereof—Things most precious, things that are above, and things that are beneath, things that are in the earth, and upon the earth, and in heaven" (D&C 101:32–34).

As we seek to understand the Creation in both a figurative and literal manner, we must remember that God did it all for us. The Earth in all its splendor and beauty was created as a dwelling place for us. All the planning and execution that went into the Creation happened to bring us closer to God. This is why Moroni said, "Behold, I would exhort you that when ye shall read these things, if it be wisdom in God that ye should read them, that ye would remember how merciful the Lord hath been unto the children of men, from the creation of Adam even down until the time that ye shall receive these things, and ponder it in your hearts" (Moro. 10:3).

Pondering on the goodness of God helps us appreciate the Creation and evokes gratitude in our souls. The Earth was created as a place where families would live, learn, grow, and make covenants so they could prove themselves worthy to return to the presence of our Father. We see how much God loves us through His effort to organize every needful thing for His children. How we should reverence the Father and the Son in blessing our lives so completely! How we should seek to obey Their words and keep Their commandments! As we appreciate the magnitude of what went into the Creation for our benefit, we are drawn to our Father and our Savior, and our desire becomes to please Them.

Opposition, Temptation, and Agency

All things to perpetuate the plan of exaltation began in the Garden of Eden; through that experience, we learn that "all things have been done in the wisdom of him [God] who knoweth all things" (2 Ne. 2:24). This included the introduction of the law of opposition as Lucifer was allowed to tempt Adam and Eve. Through this, Adam and Eve gained the right to exercise their agency, which led to their fall from an innocent state to that of mortality: "Adam fell that men might be; and men are, that they might have joy" (2 Ne. 2:25).

God had to introduce opposition. God had to allow temptation. God had to provide an opportunity to choose between different alternatives so agency could be exercised. It is not coincidental that it is called the law of opposition in *all things,* for that is exactly what it is.

Opposition touches everything in our lives. Our very bodies operate through the great principle of opposition. Almost every muscle in the body has an antagonist opposing it so the muscle does not atrophy or waste away. The magnificent heart, the muscle of muscles, is constantly under opposition (it's called *blood pressure*) as it pushes blood through the circulatory system to all parts of the body. The same principle applies to all things. This Earth is in constant opposition within the solar system as the gravitational pull of universal bodies keeps the solar system in order. We as individuals are drawn to the Earth by the magnetic force of gravity, or we would be unstable. Without resistance, there would be no stability. Without opposition, there would be no power to act. Without opposition, nothing would exist. Even the tiny atom, with a positively charged nucleus and negatively charged electrons, bears witness that the law of opposition is at work all things, from the most massive to the most microscopic.

Can we see that opposition is absolutely necessary for life?

Do we realize that without opposition everything would be a "compound in one," unable to act? (see 2 Ne. 2:11).

Do we realize that without opposition there is no opportunity for growth and no opportunity for agency to be exercised—therefore, there is no hope for life eternal?

Lehi teaches us this doctrine clearly and succinctly in 2 Nephi 2:10–18. Opposition is placed before us. The adversary tempts us to do evil, and the Holy Spirit entices us to do good (see Mosiah 3:19; D&C 11:12–13). The opposite ends of the spectrum are extreme: When we yield to the enticings of the Holy Spirit, we put off the natural man and become a saint through the Atonement of our Savior Jesus Christ (see Mosiah 3:19). But when we yield to the devil and his temptations, we reap destruction, darkness, and hell (see 2 Ne. 26:10). It is our choice.

Temptation is ever present in mortality. The Lord has declared, "And it must needs be that the devil should tempt the children of men, or they could not be agents unto themselves; for if they never should have bitter they could not know the sweet" (D&C 29:39). This temptation or enticement is ongoing so we can continually exercise our agency. Eternal verities are always in place; they do not turn on and off. Opposition is always there. Temptation to do evil and enticement to do good are ever present. The only variable is what we choose.

What determines who yields to temptation? Some are able to resist temptation because they have on the armor of God (see Eph. 6:11–18; D&C 27:15–17), are in a state of righteousness (see Alma 11:23), pray constantly to not yield to temptation (see 3 Ne. 18:18), and have the habit of feasting upon the word of God (see 1 Ne. 15:24), which protects them. Throughout it all, they exercise agency.

God will never take away this right and privilege to the gift of agency. We fought the War in Heaven over this very principle. Because agency carries with it a responsibility, it is described as *moral agency*, which implies accountability for our choices—"That every man may be accountable for his own sins in the day of judgment" (D&C 101:78). If we think it unfair that the tempter challenges our agency at every turn, we need to remember that we *must* be tempted, else men could not be "agents unto themselves" (D&C 29:39).

Agency is the supreme power to act and not be acted upon. It is the power to protect ourselves from Satan because the war between Satan and the Savior for our souls still rages. Satan's purpose is to drag us down to hell, "that all men might be miserable like unto himself" (2 Ne. 2:27). He especially seeks "to destroy the agency of man" (Moses 4:3). And as he goes about his destructive work, he wants us to believe he does not exist: "I am no devil, for there is none" (2 Ne. 28:22).

In sharp contrast, on Christ's side of the war, He and our Father act out of love to give Their children an opportunity to become like Them. Our relationship to and dependence on God are evident in all things we see, feel, and experience here on Earth—something that becomes even more clear as we carefully observe what goes on in the temple.

Until we truly recognize that we are at war for our very lives, we may never act with decisiveness in keeping the commandments and may never realize the importance of agency, the Atonement, and the temple. Without that recognition, we may become casual about the gospel. But we must be diligent, anxiously engaged in doing good, as the scriptures counsel us to do: "Men should be anxiously engaged in a good cause, and do many things of their own free will, and bring to pass much righteousness; for the power is in them, wherein they are agents unto themselves" (D&C 58:27–28).

God designed this eternal verity, which Lehi explained: "Wherefore, men are free according to the flesh; and all things are given them which are expedient unto man. And they are free to choose liberty and eternal life, through the great Mediator of all men, or to choose captivity and death, according to the captivity and power of the devil; for he seeketh that all men might be miserable like unto himself" (2 Ne. 2:27).

Adam and Eve were the first to face opposition and the first to yield to temptation. This act introduced mortality and the opportunity for them and all humankind to make choices that could result in righteousness or sin.

The Fall

The Fall was foreordained; because it was part of the plan, it did not occur by chance. The prophet Brigham Young taught, "It was necessary that sin should enter into the world; no man could ever understand the principle of exaltation without its opposite; no one could ever receive an exaltation without being acquainted with its opposite. How did Adam and Eve sin? Did they come out in direct opposition to God and to His government? No. But they transgressed a command of the Lord, and through that transgression sin came into the world. The Lord knew they would do this, and He had designed that they should" (*JD*, 10:312).

We do not have the complete details regarding what happened in the Garden of Eden. President Joseph Fielding Smith wrote, "The simple fact is, as explained in the Book of Mormon and the revelations given to the Prophet Joseph Smith, the fall was a very essential part of the divine plan. Adam and Eve therefore did the very thing that the Lord intended them to do. If we had the original record, we would see the purpose of the fall clearly stated and its necessity explained" (*Answers to Gospel Questions*, 80).

One of the purposes of the Fall was to bring about mortality, an essential step in the plan and in man's progress toward exaltation. It was necessary that we have mortal bodies and that we pass through mortality with the ability to choose either good or evil: "Behold, he [God] created Adam, and by Adam came the fall of man. And because of the fall of man came Jesus Christ, even the Father and the Son; and because of Jesus Christ came the redemption of man" (Morm. 9:12).

The separation of mankind from the presence of God planted in fallen humans a desire to return to God's presence and led to the need for a Savior, whose magnificent Atonement makes that return possible. He is the only way back to the Father. In fact, without the Savior's Atonement, the effects of the Fall would be catastrophic:

We would be separated from God.

There would be no resurrection.

Our spirits would become subject to the devil—in fact, we would be angels to the devil.

Graves and spirit prison would not deliver up their dead.

We would not be delivered from the awful monster we know as the devil.

I encourage you to read the words of the Book of Mormon prophet Jacob, who offers more insights concerning the conditions of the plan and the great blessings of the Atonement (see 2 Ne. 9).

Mortality

Man is a divine being born in innocence, yet because he is born into a fallen state, he is subject to trials and temptations. Though mortal, he is not inherently evil—but he certainly has the moral agency to *choose* to become "carnal, sensual and devilish" (Moses 5:13) or to *choose* to become a saint, led by the "enticings of the Holy Spirit" (Mosiah 3:19).

King Benjamin clearly defines the "natural man" as being an enemy to God—*if* he "repenteth not, and remaineth and dieth an enemy to God, the demands of divine justice do awaken his immortal soul to a lively sense of his own guilt, which doth cause him to shrink from the presence of the Lord, and doth fill his breast with guilt, and pain, and anguish, which is like an unquenchable fire, whose flame ascendeth up forever and ever" (Mosiah 2:38). We come to understand that the "natural man" who is an enemy to God is one who does not repent.

Other prophets use the terms *natural* or *by nature* without reference to being sinful or unrepentant. This is also a correct use of the word; however, the term *natural man* refers to those who come to love Satan so much more than God that they become carnal, sensual, and devilish: "And Satan came among them, saying: I am also a son of God; and he commanded them, saying: Believe it not; and they believed it not, and they loved Satan more than God. And men began from that time forth to be carnal, sensual, and devilish" (Moses 5:13). When we yield to the enticings of the Holy Spirit, we put off that "natural man" and become "as a child, submissive, meek, humble patient, full of love, willing to submit to all things which the Lord seeth fit to inflict upon [us]" (Mosiah 3:19; see also Maxwell, *Notwithstanding My Weakness*, 70–88).

Temptation is a necessary part of the great plan: "And it must needs be that the devil should tempt the children of men, or they could not be agents unto themselves; for if they never should have bitter they could not know the sweet—Wherefore, it came to pass that the devil tempted Adam, and he partook of the forbidden fruit and transgressed the commandment, wherein he became subject to the will of the devil, because he yielded unto temptation" (D&C 29:39–40). Verse 40 teaches a transcendent truth. We see that when we yield to the temptations of the devil, we become subject to him. That is *our* choice, *our* decision. We are responsible and accountable for the consequences.

When we become subject to the devil, it is not the fault of mortality or the flesh, for the flesh in and of itself does not sin. It is our spirit—our desires—that dictate the choices we make. If our spirit is not in tune with the things of God and is not being directed by the Spirit, we are left to ourselves—and then, indeed, the flesh becomes weak because of our spiritual weakness. On our own, we are nothing; only in the strength of the Lord can we overcome the trials and vicissitudes of life. The Book of Mormon prophet Ammon confessed such dependence: "Yea, I know that I am nothing; as to my strength I am weak; therefore I will not boast of myself, but I will boast of my God, for in his strength I can do all things" (Alma 26:12).

When we do not have the Spirit to direct our flesh, the appetites of the flesh can seem overpowering, beyond our control. We may fall short of our desires to do good things when our bodies are weak. They need sleep, nourishment, and exercise, but these needs are not the seat of our battle in mortality; the battle is in not yielding to the desires of the flesh—hence the continual admonition of the Lord to "watch and pray always, lest ye enter into temptation" (3 Ne. 18:18). This is where the Lord comes to our aid through the infinite Atonement:

> And he shall go forth, suffering pains and afflictions and temptations of every kind; and this that the word might be fulfilled which saith he will take upon him the pains and the sicknesses of his people.
>
> And he will take upon him death, that he may loose the bands of death which bind his people; and he will take upon him their infirmities, that his bowels may be filled with mercy, according to the flesh, that he may know according to the flesh how to succor his people according to their infirmities.
>
> Now the Spirit knoweth all things; nevertheless the Son of God suffereth according to the flesh that he might take upon him the sins of his people, that he might blot out their transgressions according to the power of his deliverance; and now behold, this is the testimony which is in me. (Alma 7:11–13)

It is the *entering*, the *yielding*, that brings about our problems and sins. Our focus should be on not entering, not yielding to the desires of the flesh. And in all things, we must remember that the temptation that so plagues us is a welcome part of a plan that was designed specifically with us in mind. We need to remember that in our eagerness to come to the Earth, we once shouted for joy over mortal trials, that we might prove ourselves worthy by being obedient to the commandments of God.

The Purpose of Earth Life

How will we respond to the principles, doctrines, and truths we learn here on Earth related to the plan of salvation? Will we embrace them and grow toward our eternal potential? Or will we push them aside and suffer the consequences of allowing the natural man to take hold? Mortal men and women came here to be tested and proved, "to see if they will do all things whatsoever the Lord their God shall command them" (Abr. 3:25).

A number of principles help us understand why we entered mortality:

- We came to Earth to learn self-mastery, to yield to the enticings of the Spirit, and to become a saint through the Atonement of Christ (see Mosiah 3:19).
- We came here to learn to whom we should look for a remission of our sins (see 2 Ne. 25:26).
- We came here to learn that it is by grace we are saved after all we can do (see 2 Ne. 25:23).
- We came here to start the process of taking upon ourselves the divine nature of Christ (see 2 Pet. 1:3–10) and becoming perfect, as our Father and our Savior Jesus Christ are perfect (see 3 Ne. 12:48).
- We came here to receive truth and light from our Father and our Savior through the Holy Ghost and through all of God's messengers, including living prophets, seers, and revelators (see Alma 38:9; 3 Ne. 12:2, 28:34–35; Ether 4:12).
- We came here to worship our Father through our beloved Savior by the power of the Holy Ghost as we pray, make and keep sacred covenants, and seek to build up the kingdom of God (see John 4:23; Jacob 4:5; Alma 34:38; 3 Ne. 13:33; D&C 42:67).
- We came here to take upon ourselves the name of the Lord Jesus Christ and to receive the Holy Ghost, the blessings of the priesthood, and all the ordinances and covenants of the gospel, including those in the temple (see 2 Ne. 31:13; Mosiah 5:8; 3 Ne. 27:5; D&C 84:19–22).
- We came here to live by every word that proceeds forth from the mouth of God (see D&C 84:43–46).
- We came here to prepare to meet God (see Alma 12:24; 34:32).
- We are ourselves a temple of God, as well as a vital part of a body of Saints who are a temple of God (see 1 Cor. 3:16–17, 6:19; D&C 93:35). As such, we are stewards of our temples and stewards of all the gifts of God (see 1 Pet. 4:10).

We are brothers and sisters, sons and daughters of the most high God; as such, we have a responsibility to one another (see Matt. 5:44, 25:40; 3 Ne. 14:12).

Those of us who are parents have children who must be cared for, nurtured, and taught the gospel (see D&C 68:25–27; Moses 5:11–12).

Our physical needs must be met and our lives balanced. We need to attend to the practical demands of daily life: attending to our employment, maintaining a household, getting children to their various appointments and commitments, helping with homework, engaging in service projects—the list could go on and on. The scriptures, the living prophets, caring friends, and, above all, counsel from the Lord and inspiration from the Holy Ghost can help us organize our daily lives (see Jacob 4:10; 2 Ne. 32:5). In short, we came here to learn how to organize "every needful thing" (D&C 88:119); we came here to learn how to unclutter life by relying on the Lord. The Lord and His gospel teach us a practical approach to all things (see Prov. 3:5–6).

We came here not to compartmentalize the activities of our lives but to use gospel teachings to bring unity and harmony to all we do (see 2 Ne. 31:13; Alma 37:45; Moro. 7:11).

We came here to learn that all things are possible for those who believe (see Mark 9:23).

We came here to learn of the Lord and His words that we might receive peace (see D&C 19:23).

We came here to do hard things, to offer a living sacrifice by our reasonable service (see Rom 12:1–2).

We came here to find God, follow His Son, and go about doing good, that all might come unto Christ and enjoy the blessings of exaltation (see Acts 10:38; Jacob 1:7; Omni 1:26; 2 Ne. 33:4, 10; Mosiah 5:2; Alma 41:14, 63:2; Hel. 14:31; Ether 8:26; Moro. 7:13).

We came here to worship the Lord in His holy house, where we may find peace and perspective away from the noises of the world (see D&C 109:24).

And as mortality draws to a close for each, we must never forget that death is a part of life. The transfer to the spirit world prior to the Resurrection is a vital part of the plan. We literally live to die, that we might return to the presence of our Father through Christ's Atonement (see Hel. 14:17).

This list of why we came to mortality is certainly not exhaustive but is intended to give us eyes to see, to give us a better perspective on life, to prompt some introspection: *Can I perhaps do better than I'm doing?*

How could I better integrate these many principles into my life? Your list of the purposes of mortality may be different from mine. There is nothing wrong with that because mortality is an individual journey, and your daily commitments and priorities may be different from mine. Yet for all of us, life is to be lived joyously and happily—that is the design of our existence.

I am sensitive to life and all of the things we have to do, but above all, I take great joy in searching the scriptures and being reminded of the ways I can improve my relationship with God and my faithfulness in the gospel. We will find lasting joy in doing what matters most.

The Atonement

The Atonement of Christ, the redemptive force of our Savior, is *the* great and holy act, an infinite and redemptive sacrifice. It is the central theme, the culminating power of the gospel, and the very plan of exaltation—because it delivers us from death and hell. The Savior paid the price to reconcile us from the debt we've incurred through our sins and to bring us back to the presence of God. This great plan of redemption covers both the living and the dead—which is how worship in the temple ultimately reunites families. This plan of redemption is what we teach our children, just as Father Adam and Mother Eve taught their children: where to look for a remission of their sins and how to retain that remission. Indeed, the redemption of all humankind comes only in and through the Savior Jesus Christ, a point that God our Father makes clear to all the world.

There is nothing that is not anchored to our Savior's Atonement; everything is an appendage to it. The Atonement is the empowering and enabling power of the magnificent plan of our Heavenly Father and the ultimate expression of our Father's love: "For God so loved the world, that he gave his only begotten Son" (John 3:16). It is the foreordained act of the Anointed One: "I am the way, the truth, and the life: no man cometh unto the Father, but by me" (John 14:6).

Everything hinges on the great and infinite Atonement. It brings forth the power to be cleansed from our sins so we can be forgiven. It is the power by which we are drawn back to God. It nurtures and succors us, as the great high priest Alma so eloquently explained (see Alma 7:11–12). Through this great act, we enter the waters of baptism, receive the Holy Ghost, perform the temple ordinances, and become sealed for all eternity to our families.

It is impossible to write here all that the Lord has done or will yet do for us to make it possible to receive all the blessings of exaltation. Please don't stop here; I encourage you to read and study all you can about this sublime act and gift—and more importantly, to take the time to ponder on your feelings and gratitude as your understanding grows deeper. I especially recommend to you the book *The Infinite Atonement* by Elder Tad R. Callister.

What a joy to live on this beautiful Earth and walk the path set out for us by a loving Heavenly Father and Savior Jesus Christ. I hope this chapter has provided a launching pad for evaluating our lives and considering how we might best use our time here. Despite our mortal frailties, *we can live with hope*, looking to our Savior Jesus Christ and His infinite Atonement and the covenants we make with Him in the temple. We can receive strength through our Savior, through whom we can, as Ammon testified, "do all things" (Alma 26:12). Through worship in the temple, we can receive a fulness of the Spirit and the promised blessings of the everlasting covenant and thus be empowered to go about doing good.

The *Guide to the Scriptures* contains an excellent summary of the Father's perfect plan, the plan of redemption, under the heading "Plan of Redemption." I encourage you to read it slowly and take time to search out the scriptures referenced within it:

> The fulness of the gospel of Jesus Christ is designed to bring about man's immortality and eternal life. It includes the Creation, Fall, and Atonement, along with all God-given laws, ordinances, and doctrines. This plan makes it possible for all people to be exalted and live forever with God (2 Nephi 2:9). The scriptures also refer to this plan as the plan of salvation, the plan of happiness, and the plan of mercy. He was wounded for our transgressions (Isa. 53:5; Mosiah 14:5). There is none other name under heaven by which man can be saved (Acts 4:12). "As in Adam all die, even so in Christ shall all be made alive" (1 Cor. 15:22). "By grace are ye saved through faith" (Eph. 2:8; see also 2 Nephi 25:23). God promised eternal life "before the world began" (Titus 1:2). Jesus is the author of eternal salvation (Heb. 5:8–9). The plan of redemption was extended to the dead (1 Peter 3:18–20; 4:6; D&C 138). Death fulfills the merciful plan of the great Creator (2 Nephi 9:6). How great is

the plan of our God! (2 Nephi 9:13). The plan of redemption brings to pass the Resurrection and a remission of sins (Alma 12:25–34). Aaron taught the plan of redemption to Lamoni's father (Alma 22:12–14). Amulek explained the plan of salvation (Alma 34:8–16). Alma explained the plan of salvation (Alma 42:5–26, 31). The doctrines of the creation, fall, atonement, and baptism are affirmed in modern revelation (D&C 20:17–29). The plan was ordained before the world (D&C 128:22). My work and my glory is to bring to pass the immortality and eternal life of man (Moses 1:39). This is the plan of salvation unto all men (Moses 6:52–62). We will prove them herewith (Abr. 3:22–26). (See lds.org; Study Helps; Guide to the Scriptures, P–R; "Plan of Redemption")

As we read in Moses 5:11–12, we come to understand that Adam and Eve first taught this plan of redemption in mortality. Each of us would do well to ask ourselves the following questions as we study such passages of scripture:

Do I understand and appreciate the plan of redemption?

Do I joy in that plan?

Am I grateful enough for the plan that I am moved to action by it?

Further Study

As I have increased my own efforts to study the doctrines of the temple and of eternal life, I have come to increasingly appreciate the great resource of the Church's website. I encourage you to spend time familiarizing yourself with the many wonderful resources found there. The following are a few starting places I enjoyed searching from at www.lds.org:

- Scriptures—Study Helps—Guide to the Scriptures—Plan of Redemption
- Scriptures—Study Helps—Topical Guide (you are then able to read the entries on plan, redemption, exaltation, salvation, and happiness. All of these entries give us insight into and understanding of the great and perfect plan of our Heavenly Father)
- Teachings—Gospel Topics—Select the following: plan of salvation, creation, Satan, fall of Adam, death, spiritual, atonement, gospel, and related topics

It amazes me that all of this information is at our fingertips. We need only pay the price to search these things diligently; we will then find our hearts filled with deep gratitude for the perfect plan of our Father, which Christ the Lord fulfilled, that we may have life eternal.

CHAPTER 3

Partaking of the Goodness of God and Christ

THE GOODNESS AND MERCY OF GOD and our beloved Savior are evidenced by the purpose of Their work: to enable us to attain immortality and eternal life. God willingly gave His Son as a sacrifice because He loved us (see John 3:16). As far as Christ is concerned, everything He does is for the benefit of the world because He loves us; He even gave His life that we might have eternal life (see 2 Ne. 26:24). As we accept and receive the Atonement, we are actually empowered to partake of the goodness of our Heavenly Father and Savior—empowered to exercise greater faith, be more diligent in our efforts, be ever patient in the process of becoming like Them.

Through that process, we also begin to learn the doctrines of the temple and come to understand and appreciate the Lord's holy house, where our Father and Christ gather us so we can partake of Their goodness and mercy. As that process unfolds, the doctrines, ordinances, and covenants of the temple will begin to take root in us, for, as Alma wrote, "Because of your diligence and your faith and your patience with the word in nourishing it . . . it may take root in you" (Alma 32:42).

Earlier in my life, I was not diligent. I wasn't patient, either—I wanted to know everything *now*. I wanted my Heavenly Father to give me understanding simply because I asked for it. I didn't exercise the necessary faith, make the necessary mental exertion, or do the actual works; I thought that simply asking the question was enough. I have since learned that faith, diligence, and patience lead to a greater understanding and appreciation of not only the Atonement but the doctrines of the temple, too. It is through faith, diligence, and patience that revelation opens to us and we partake of the tree of life.

Faith

When the prophet Enos wrestled before God to receive a remission of his sins, his guilt was swept away through his faith (see Enos 1:4–8). The vehicles that made such a thing possible were the goodness of God and the Atonement of our Savior Jesus Christ.

Gaining insights into the full endowment (the initiatory and ceremony) and the new and everlasting covenant of marriage (the completion of the endowment) requires faith. Honoring the inward voice that prompts us to exercise faith and to change our lives helps us gain further insight into the covenants of the temple. This expression of conscience leads to a soul-searching evaluation. Do we ask ourselves the questions that really matter, or do we choose to set them aside, avoiding that kind of introspection?

The great prophet Alma, while admonishing his people to choose to change and become better sons and daughters of God, likened that process to awakening from a "deep sleep," becoming "illuminated by the light of the everlasting word" (Alma 5:7; see also all of chapter 5). That very process occurs when we exert ourselves to understand temple ordinances and covenants; such exertion is an initial step toward exercising faith. When I finally started to really seek to understand, I began to learn by exercising my faith.

In his words to the people in Gideon, Alma further described the process of "awakening" as he admonished the people to figuratively keep their garments clean that they might partake of the blessings of Abraham, Isaac, and Jacob:

> And now I would that ye should be humble, and be submissive and gentle; easy to be entreated; full of patience and long-suffering; being temperate in all things; being diligent in keeping the commandments of God at all times; asking for whatsoever things ye stand in need, both spiritual and temporal; always returning thanks unto God for whatsoever things ye do receive.
>
> And see that ye have faith, hope, and charity, and then ye will always abound in good works.
>
> And may the Lord bless you, and keep your garments spotless, that ye may at last be brought to sit down with Abraham, Isaac, and Jacob, and the holy prophets who have been ever since the world began, having your garments spotless

> even as their garments are spotless, in the kingdom of heaven to go no more out. (Alma 7:23–25)

As we speak of faith, we must also speak of mercy, even the tender mercies of God made manifest in all things (including the very breath we breathe and the beating of our hearts). We can exercise faith in God and Christ because of their omniscience, omnipotence, and omnipresence—and especially because of Their perfectness in character, including Their mercy. We begin to see and understand the goodness and long-suffering—the tender mercy—of God as Moroni admonished us in closing the Book of Mormon: "Behold, I would exhort you that when ye shall read these things, if it be wisdom in God that ye should read them, that ye would remember how *merciful* the Lord hath been unto the children of men, from the creation of Adam even down until the time that ye shall receive these things, and ponder it in your hearts" (Moro. 10:3).

Jacob expressed the enabling power of the Atonement beautifully, reminding us what we would be without the mercy and grace of God as realized in the infinite Atonement:

> For as death hath passed upon all men, to fulfill the merciful plan of the great Creator, there must needs be a power of resurrection, and the resurrection must needs come unto man by reason of the fall; and the fall came by reason of transgression; and because man became fallen they were cut off from the presence of the Lord.
>
> Wherefore, it must needs be an infinite atonement—save it should be an infinite atonement this corruption could not put on incorruption. Wherefore, the first judgment which came upon man must needs have remained to an endless duration. And if so, this flesh must have laid down to rot and to crumble to its mother earth, to rise no more.
>
> O the wisdom of God, his mercy and grace! For behold, if the flesh should rise no more our spirits must become subject to that angel who fell from before the presence of the Eternal God, and became the devil, to rise no more. (2 Ne. 9:6–8)

While teaching religion at Brigham Young University, I asked my students to read 2 Nephi 9 once each day for an entire month. It was an exercise in faith. At first, there was some resistance; they wondered why reading it once was not enough. (Some students even thought they could accomplish the assignment by reading the chapter thirty times in one day.) I continually encouraged them to be patient in the learning process. I talked about repetition in learning. I spoke of savoring the words and praying about a single sentence or verse; I talked about pondering and praying over the chapter each night so they could come to an understanding of and an appreciation for the goodness of God and how merciful our Father and our Savior are to us.

The results were amazing. A change took place in the hearts of those students who did the assignment. Their understanding, appreciation, and gratitude grew as they recognized the magnificence of the great plan of happiness and exaltation, which centers in the mercy and grace exemplified by the Savior's sacrifice and infinite Atonement.

May we never forget the gift we have been given through this sacrifice. We are made clean through the blood of the Lamb (see Morm. 9:6) and are saved through the gift of mercy after all we can do, "for we know that it is by grace that we are saved, after all we can do" (2 Ne. 25:23).

Only through faith can we grasp the power of the Atonement in relationship to the temple. The temple ordinances show that everything in the temple will bring us back into the presence of God only through the power of our Savior and Redeemer Jesus Christ. If we ponder with faith, we understand why the Lord wants to gather His people to His house, where He may empower them to return to His presence. These blessings, which come to God's children as they exercise faith and partake of His mercy, are the blessings of exaltations—temple blessings brought forth by the goodness of God according to our faithfulness in keeping our covenants.

Faithfulness is simply the result of exercising our faith. If we observe carefully—with our temple eyes—*while thanking God for His mercy and exercising faith*, we will see and experience the awakening process Alma speaks of.

Diligence

Diligence is an expression of our persistence, dedication, and effort as expressed through our works. To partake of all of God's blessings and goodness and mercy, we must honor our covenants through our diligence, which reflects our faithfulness.

law of Sacrifice
law of chastity
law of consecration

As we are diligent, we seek to do good. Good works always follow those who receive the fullness of the Holy Spirit in the temple, "which leadeth to do good—yea, to do justly, to walk humbly, to judge righteously" (D&C 11:12).

This process of being made clean, having our garments made spotless, and becoming forgiven partly depends on our diligence—our works: "And may God grant, in his great fulness, that men might be brought unto repentance and good works, that they might be restored unto grace for grace, according to their works" (Hel. 12:24). The Lord reminds us, "And no unclean thing can enter into his kingdom; therefore nothing entereth into his rest save it be those who have washed their garments in my blood, because of their faith, and the repentance of all their sins, and their faithfulness unto the end" (3 Ne. 27:19). The Apostle James confirmed this principle of faithfulness: "Ye see then how that by works a man is justified, and not by faith only. . . . Let him know, that he which converteth the sinner from the error of his way shall save a soul from death, and shall hide a multitude of sins" (James 2:24; 5:20).

Diligence based on faith has to do with actively serving others. Serving others as we keep our temple covenant to build up the kingdom of God has everything to do with sharing the gospel of Jesus Christ. And when we share the gospel, our garments are made spotless. Of the early missionaries, we read, "Let them journey and declare the word among the congregations of the wicked, inasmuch as it is given; And inasmuch as they do this they shall rid their garments, and they shall be spotless before me" (D&C 61:33–34), that the souls of the people to whom they preach "may escape the wrath of God, the desolation of abomination which awaits the wicked, both in this world and in the world to come. Verily, I say unto you, let those who are not the first elders continue in the vineyard until the mouth of the Lord shall call them, for their time is not yet come; their garments are not clean from the blood of this generation" (D&C 88:85). These principles are exemplified every day throughout the world as missionaries bring hundreds of thousands of our Heavenly Father's children into the Church and kingdom of God.

The work of our Father is the happiness, joy, and eternal life of His children. We are *His* work. We are *His* glory. We become partakers of these—immortality and eternal life—as we go about doing good, for we will be judged by our works and the desires of our hearts.

Patience

Learning the things of God takes patience. Think about times when you have had to learn a new skill, grasp a new concept, study for a major exam, or complete a significant project. Now consider whether you have ever put that much effort into your study of the gospel and the word of God? That's a sobering thought, isn't it?

We have been counseled to seek wisdom so the mysteries of God can be unfolded to us (see D&C 6:7). One meaning of the word *unfold* implies a gradual disclosure—or, as the scriptures say, "line upon line." We learn as we seek to live by every word that proceeds forth from the mouth of God: "Give diligent heed to the words of eternal life" (D&C 84:43). To truly understand requires desiring the knowledge, being easily entreated and humble, and having purity of heart. It also takes a great deal of patience.

Ammon explained the process of coming to know the mysteries of God: "Yea, he that repenteth and exerciseth faith, and bringeth forth good works, and prayeth *continually* without ceasing—unto such it is given to know the mysteries of God; yea, unto such it shall be given to reveal things which never have been revealed; yea, and it shall be given unto such to bring thousands of souls to repentance, even as it has been given unto us to bring these our brethren to repentance" (Alma 26:22). Do the words *faith* and *works* sound familiar? Following faith and diligence, we gain *patience* as we pray continually.

As we seek to understand the scriptures or to appreciate what happens in the temple, the task to know the mysteries of God may seem overwhelming. After all, there is much to learn and understand. But remember this: we're not expected to learn it all at once. We learn through studying hour by hour, a page here and there in quiet moments, a day at a time—not by leaping in and expecting immediate insight. We're not in a race; the process is the point, and time is our ally. What can be more rewarding than to realize we are on the journey of becoming like our Savior, joint heirs of the kingdom, eventually to receive all that the Father has and to enjoy the blessings of exaltation? The journey of learning is, in fact, the joy of learning.

Patient progress is what life is all about. Let's not miss this purpose of Earth life because of distractions Satan would have us focus on, including immediate gratification. The father of lies fosters turmoil, confusion, the worship of idols and possessions, and an obsession with titles, stations, and positions. And where is God in all of this? God is in the beautiful and the peaceful and the patient process. While Satan would have us demand immediate answers and blessings, God patiently points us home little by little: "For behold, this life is the time for men to prepare to meet God; yea, behold the day of this life is the day for men to perform their labors" (Alma 34:32). This is what life is truly about. We can't miss the real purpose of preparing to meet God, or we will miss the real joy. Patient progress toward understanding the mysteries of godliness will help us see life for what it should be; then we can set out to do the things that will help us become all that our Father intends us to become—even as He and our Savior are.

Introspection also helps foster patience. Have you ever searched the scriptures to find verses about the words *atonement*, *redeemer*, *reconciled*, *mediator*, and *advocate*? Have you seriously studied words that relate to *power*, *empowered*, *endowment*, and *gifts of God*? When we take the time to do that, we find that the concepts unfold line upon line. The blessings of gratitude await us as we come to understand and appreciate the doctrines of the temple and the mysteries of God. As patient and grateful receivers of this gift—knowledge, ordinances, and covenants—we become bound to the givers, Christ the Lord and God the Father.

Gratitude

As we read in the scriptures about the tender mercies of God, what do we feel concerning our Savior's Atonement? I hope we feel *gratitude*. We feel gratitude when we understand that it is through the symbols and covenants of the temple endowment that we may, through the Atonement, symbolically enter into the Father's presence. These ordinances lead to the blessing of literally sitting down with Abraham, Isaac, and Jacob in the hereafter. We will sit together again in the heavenly council and "inherit thrones, kingdoms, principalities, and powers, dominions, all heights and depths . . . and a continuation of the seeds forever and ever. . . . Then shall [we] be gods" (D&C 132:19–20, 37).

As the mysteries of the kingdom unfold to us, we begin to understand and appreciate the doctrines of the temple; we become filled with gratitude as the Spirit witnesses to us. We then begin to feel an overwhelming desire to follow our Savior and become as He is (see 3 Ne. 27:27). We desire to become perfect, even as we have been commanded (see 3 Ne. 12:48). We truly want to follow Moroni's counsel to deny ourselves of all ungodliness (see Moro. 10:32). We come to understand the power of godliness as we are taught and make covenants and receive the sacred ordinances in the house of the Lord.

We are also filled with gratitude when we recognize that after all we can do, we literally are perfected through Christ; only through Him can we come into the presence of the Father. Moroni's closing words eliminate any misunderstanding:

> Yea, *come unto Christ*, and *be perfected in him*, and deny yourselves of all ungodliness; and if ye shall *deny yourselves of all ungodliness*, and *love God with all your might, mind and strength*, then is *his grace sufficient for you*, that *by his grace ye may be perfect in Christ*; and if by the grace of God ye are perfect in Christ, *ye can in nowise deny the power of God.*
>
> And again, if ye by the grace of God are perfect in Christ, and deny not his power, then are *ye sanctified in Christ by the grace of God, through the shedding of the blood of Christ*, which is in *the covenant of the Father unto the remission of your sins*, that *ye become holy, without spot.* (Moro. 10:32–33)

There are at least eleven specific doctrines and principles taught in those two verses (shown by the italicized words and phrases), and they will be quoted repeatedly in the pages that follow. Remember, repetition is good. Read carefully each time you see these verses, just as you worship in the temple with an attentive spirit.

The word of God permeates every covenant, ordinance, and teaching in the temple. The scriptures and the words of our living prophets invite us to the Lord's house so we can partake of the blessings there: "I gave unto you the commandment that ye should go to the Ohio; and there I will give unto you my law; and there you shall be endowed with power from on high" (D&C 38:32). It is in the Lord's house that He leads us to light, truth, and exaltation. If we are not moved by these promises, we may be guilty of one of the greatest sins—the sin of ingratitude. President Ezra Taft Benson reminded us:

> "Thou shalt thank the Lord thy God in all things" (D&C 59:7–8). . . .
>
> The Prophet Joseph said at one time that one of the greatest sins of which the Latter-day Saints would be guilty

> is the sin of ingratitude. I presume most of us have not thought of that as a great sin. There is a great tendency for us in our prayers and in our pleadings with the Lord to ask for additional blessings. But sometimes I feel we need to devote more of our prayers to expressions of gratitude and thanksgiving for blessings already received. We enjoy so much. (*God, Family, Country*, 199)

How can we overcome the sin of ingratitude? Take a moment to ponder and thank the Lord. Dedicate a notebook or journal as a "gratitude journal," and write down at least one thing a day that fills your heart with gratitude. Occasionally share your book with family and special friends. Several years ago, as I wrote regularly in my "gratitude journal," it amazed me to see how my attitude and actions became increasingly more reflective of the Savior as time went by. To be grateful is a choice we make every moment of every day. And when we are grateful, we are moved to action through the desire to help others and to build up the kingdom of God.

Further Study

Consider the following to better understand and appreciate the goodness and mercy of God our Father and our Savior Jesus Christ.

From the scriptures:

- Topical Guide—God—Mercy of
- Topical Guide—God—Works of
- Topical Guide—Feast on the scriptures about faith, diligence, patience, and gratitude

From the prophets, General Authorities, and officers of the Church:

- David A. Bednar, "The Tender Mercies of the Lord," *Ensign*, May 2005.
- W. Jeffrey Marsh, "Remember How Merciful the Lord Hath Been," *Ensign*, April 2000.
- Lds.org—under Teachings—Gospel Topics—select a topic to study; I recommend grace, faith, mercy, patience, gratitude, and other similar topics.

CHAPTER 4
The Lord's Holy House

THE WORD *TEMPLE* COMES FROM the Latin word *templum*, which is the equivalent of the Hebrew words *beth Elohim*, signifying the abode of Deity—a place specially reserved for religious activity. As associated with divine worship, *temple* means, literally, the sacred house of the Lord.

Man's quest since the beginning of time has been to commune with God, who has taught us that His work and glory is our immortality and eternal life, our return to His presence. Our loving Heavenly Father prepared a way for all mankind to commune with Him in the temple, where He blesses us, His children, through His perfect plan.

Latter-day prophets and leaders have provided insights that give a broad perspective of the Lord's house while explaining why temple worship is so important to gaining our exaltation.

Elder Bruce R. McConkie:

> What is a temple? It is a house of the Lord; a house for Deity that is built on earth; a house prepared by the saints as a dwelling place for the Most High, in the most literal sense of the word; a house where a personal God personally comes. It is a holy sanctuary, set apart from the world, wherein the saints of God prepare to meet their Lord; where the pure in heart shall see God, according to the promises; where those teachings are given and those ordinances performed which prepare the saints for that eternal life which consists of dwelling with the Father and being like him and his Son. The teachings and ordinances here involved embrace the mysteries of the kingdom and are not now and

never have been heralded to the world, nor can they be understood except by those who worship the Father in spirit and in truth, and who have attained that spiritual stature which enables men to know God and Jesus Christ, whom he hath sent. (*The Mortal Messiah*, 1:98)

President Harold B. Lee:

From the beginning of time the chosen people of the Lord in the various dispensations have, under his direction, designated sacred places and structures as temples of worship. Such temples have not been the usual meeting places for congregational worship. They have been structures specially set apart for service regarded as sacred . . . and exclusively devoted to sacred rites and ceremonies. (*Decisions for Successful Living*, 132)

President Ezra Taft Benson:

Temples are built and dedicated so that, through the priesthood, parents can be sealed to their children and children can be sealed to their parents. These sealing ordinances apply to both the living and the dead. If we fail to be sealed to our progenitors and our posterity, the purpose of this earth, man's exaltation, will be utterly wasted so far as we are concerned. (*TETB*, 248)

President Gordon B. Hinckley:

Surely these temples are unique among all buildings. They are houses of instruction. They are places of covenants and promises. At their altars we kneel before God our Creator and are given promise of his everlasting blessings. In the sanctity of their appointments we commune with him and reflect on his Son, our Savior and Redeemer, the Lord Jesus Christ, who served as proxy for each of us in a vicarious sacrifice in our behalf. Here we set aside our own selfishness and serve for those who cannot serve themselves. Here we are bound together in the most sacred of all human relationships—as husbands and wives, as children and parents, as families under a sealing that time cannot destroy and death cannot disrupt. ("Why These Temples?" 41)

Elder Joseph B. Wirthlin:

> The House of the Lord is a place where we can escape from the mundane and see our lives in an eternal perspective. We can ponder instructions and covenants that help us understand more clearly the plan of salvation and the infinite love of our Heavenly Father for his children. We can ponder our relationship to God, the Eternal Father, and his Son, Jesus Christ. ("Seeking the Good," *Ensign*, May 1992, 88)

Elder John A. Widtsoe:

> The temple is a place of peace. Here we may lay aside the cares and worries of the outside, turbulent world. Here our minds should be centered upon spiritual realities, since here we are concerned only with things of the spirit. ("Looking Toward the Temple," 56)

Elder Robert L. Simpson:

> The temple is a house of commitment and sacrifice, for it is truly stated that there can be no true worship without sacrifice; indeed, as the saints sing, sacrifice brings forth blessings of heaven. The temple is a house of solemn covenant where one appropriately commits himself to live a more Christlike life. Oh, that four billion [now more than 7 billion] people on earth could enter into that kind of covenant! ("The House of the Lord," *Ensign*, Nov. 1980, 10)

The Prophet Joseph Smith:

> The Church is not fully organized, in its proper order, and cannot be, until the Temple is completed, where places will be provided for the administration of the ordinances of the Priesthood. (*HC*, 4:603)

The Prophet Joseph continued:

> God gathers together His people in the last days, to build unto the Lord a house to prepare them for the ordinances and endowments, washings and anointings, etc. . . . If a man gets a fulness of the priesthood of God, he has to get it in the same way that Jesus Christ obtained it, and that was by keeping all the commandments and obeying all the ordinances of the house of the Lord. . . . These things are revealed in the most holy place in a Temple prepared for that purpose. . . . Why gather the people together in this place? For the same purpose that Jesus wanted to gather the Jews—to receive the ordinances, the blessings, and the glories that God has in store for His Saints. (*HC*, 5:424, 427)

The prophets have taught us well in these matters. Let's now summarize the key points that describe the Lord's holy house. The temple is:

- A place where our Father and our Savior can come to dwell, where Their glory and presence may be seen and felt.
- A place of holiness, consecrated to the service of the Lord, where we can show our devotion to Him. It is a place set aside to worship and reverence the Lord.
- A place where the Lord gathers his Saints and endows them with power and the Holy Ghost.
- A house of prayer, where we come to call upon the holy name of God and commune with Him, thus showing our gratitude and seeking His blessings.
- A house of fasting. We leave behind the world and prepare our spirits that we might receive the blessings of God.
- A house of faith. The temple is where we center our hope and belief in the eternities. It is where we come to act symbolically upon the works of God. It is where we are empowered by God through our faith.
- A house of learning. It is where we are taught the way, the truth, and the light of life. It is where we learn of God, where we receive sacred ordinances, and where we commit ourselves to Him through sacred covenants. It is where we learn how to return to the presence of God.

- A house of glory. Because the personage of God has glory, His house is a house of glory. His light is in all things there.
- A house of order. Every needful thing is in place. Everything is in harmony. All blessings are prepared specifically for God's children.

Indeed, the Lord's house is a place where revelation is given that all men might understand the things of God and prepare themselves to return to His presence. Elder Richard H. Winkle of the Seventy reminds us, "The temple is a place to know the Father and the Son. It is a place where we experience the divine presence. The Prophet Joseph Smith made this plea: 'I advise all to . . . search deeper and deeper into the mysteries of Godliness. And where shall we search? In the house of God" ("The Temple Is about Families," *Ensign*, Nov. 2006, 9–11).

I have many times sat contemplating in the celestial room the goodness and mercy of God and the infinite Atonement of the Savior. I have there pondered the way in which the holy endowment is so life-giving and exalting. I testify that I have felt the glory and presence of the Lord. As I have sealed couples for time and all eternity, I have witnessed the sealing power come down into their very souls. The power of God is manifested in His holy house, and it is real.

All of these aspects of the Lord's house point to the majesty, glory, and power of God. The questions then remain: Why wouldn't all of God's children seek to come to His holy house as often as possible? Why do we not center our plans and our hearts on His house instead of on the things of the world? Oh, my heart aches when I realize that I fully comprehended these eternal verities so late in my life. I feel as Nephi must have felt when he composed his psalm (see 2 Ne. 4:17). My version would be something like this: "O wretched man that I am! I could have learned so much sooner in my life that would have empowered me to do good. I could have redeemed more souls and researched more of my kindred dead. Yea, my heart sorroweth because of my flesh; my soul grieveth because of mine iniquities." Yet, like Nephi, I rejoice that I *did* come to the knowledge of these things. I rejoice, too, as I seek to share the things I have learned and felt with the Saints so we can have joy together in the kingdom of heaven.

As we ponder our relationship with the temple, we must ask ourselves the following questions. We must meditate on it and determine how we will improve our lives based on the answers we find:

Do I take advantage of every facet of the Lord's house?

Do I understand and appreciate the ordinances and covenants I made in the temple?

What is my part in keeping the temple holy?

The temple is the only way back to God's presence—through Christ the Lord. What does this mean to me?

Chapter 5
Holiness to the Lord

Holiness to the Lord—The House of the Lord

These words, chiseled in stone and overlaid with gold, appear on the dedication stone on the east end of the Salt Lake Temple, testifying that the edifice has been dedicated and consecrated to the service of the Lord. As the words imply, the purpose of the gospel is to enable us to walk "in holiness before the Lord" by entering the temple (D&C 20:69).

Through repentance and by the power of the sacrifice and infinite Atonement of Christ the Lord, we can be forgiven and find ourselves in a state of being holy, clean, without spot, virtuous, and sanctified, as Moroni explains: "Ye become holy, without spot" (Moro. 10:33). The temple and the endowment provided therein are all about becoming holy, binding ourselves to act in all holiness, as the Lord reminds us: "And thus ye shall become instructed in the law of my church, and be sanctified by that which ye have received, and ye shall bind yourselves to act in all holiness before me" (D&C 43:9). In our quest to become holy, we covenant to do the will of God: "Know ye not that ye are the temple of God, and that the spirit of God dwelleth in you?" (1 Cor. 3:16–17). We become holy as we bind ourselves by covenants in the temple, and thus we become *justified* and *sanctified.*

Justification comes through the grace of our Lord and Savior Jesus Christ. Elder Bruce R. McConkie explained:

> What then is the law of justification? It is simply this: "All covenants, contracts, bonds, obligations, oaths, vows, performances, connections, associations, or expectations" (D&C 132:7), in which men must abide to be saved and exalted, must be entered into and performed in righteousness

> so that the Holy Spirit can justify the candidate for salvation in what has been done. . . . An act that is justified by the Spirit is one that is sealed by the Holy Spirit of Promise, or in other words, ratified and approved by the Holy Ghost. This law of justification is the provision the Lord has placed in the gospel to assure that no unrighteous performance will be binding on earth and in heaven, and that no person will add to his position or glory in the hereafter by gaining an unearned blessing. (*Mormon Doctrine*, 408)

I cannot thank the Lord enough, for it was through His suffering and sacrifice that justice was paid. He sweat blood from every pore. He paid for our sins. It is personal to me and for me. When we think about the price He paid, our sense of debt swells within our souls and the ensuing gratitude to the Lord causes a great change in our hearts. We somehow want to let the Lord know of our love.

Sanctification also comes through the grace of our Lord and Savior Jesus Christ, as Moroni explained: "Yea, come unto Christ, and be perfected him, and deny yourselves of all ungodliness; . . . then is his grace sufficient for you, that by his grace ye may be perfect in Christ. . . . And again, if ye by the grace of God are perfect in Christ, and deny not his power, then are ye sanctified in Christ by the grace of God, through the shedding of the blood of Christ" (Moro. 10:32–33). This process of sanctification, like all other blessings, depends on our individual righteousness. It is the oil in our lamps (our righteousness and holiness) that we are to bring to meet the Bridegroom, the Lord Jesus Christ (see Matt. 25).

In seeking the blessing of sanctification, trust in the Spirit, "which leadeth to do good—yea, to do justly, to walk humbly, to judge righteously," for it shall "enlighten your mind, which shall fill your soul with joy" (D&C 11:12–13). To be such a person connotes exemplifying truth and righteousness, having high moral standards, and being fair and upright. The Spirit testifies to us those things that we should do: "And that which the Spirit testifies unto you even so I would that ye should do in all holiness of heart, walking uprightly before me, considering the end of your salvation, doing all things with prayer and thanksgiving" (D&C 46:7).

We are sanctified when we receive the Holy Ghost (see 3 Ne. 27:20). The Spirit is the key to living a Christlike life. It purges our soul and makes us spotless before the Lord. We are clean and holy, and thus we desire the fruits of the Spirit, "love, joy, peace, longsuffering, gentleness, goodness, faith, Meekness, temperance: against such there is no law" (Gal. 5:22–23). I, like you, have felt these wonderful feelings, which bring about such wonderful results. And let us remember why the Father gave us the Holy Ghost: "Father, I pray thee that thou wilt give the Holy Ghost unto all them that shall believe in their words. Father, thou hast given them the Holy Ghost because they believe in me" (3 Ne. 19:21–22).

Does the Lord expect too much of us? Is the task too overwhelming to hope to ever accomplish? The answer is a resounding *no*. As the Savior told the prophet Jeremiah, "Behold, I am the Lord, the God of all flesh: is there any thing too hard for me?" (Jer. 32:27). Our Savior has commanded us to be *perfect*—that is, to be "complete" (3 Ne. 12:48). Becoming holy through obedience and through the temple ordinances is part of becoming perfect, or "complete."

We are told, "Ye are complete in him [Jesus Christ], which is the head of all principality and power" (Col. 2:10). It is through the Lord and through receiving our temple ordinances that we can be made complete and worthy to enter our Father's presence. The key is seeking to become a little better each day—offering a kind thought, a tender smile, an uplifting phone call to a friend or family member, a prayer of gratitude to Heavenly Father in a quiet moment. We have plenty of time to perform these acts; we simply need to prioritize them and think about becoming holy and pure before the Lord. In so doing, we begin the process.

There will be distractions, but reminders can help us stay on track. They can be as simple as a beautiful sign or card bearing the word *remember* that we can place where we will see it often. Achieving holiness then becomes a matter of practice: "And let every man esteem his brother as himself, and practice virtue and holiness before me" (D&C 38:24). What a wonderful aspiration! There are many scriptures, phrases, or thoughts that can help us along the way. Let us especially remember that the greatest reminders are the sacred clothing we wear and the sacred ordinance of the sacrament.

Know that we will have some good days and some bad days. Perfection is a process, and sometimes we simply fall short of our own hopes and expectations. On the bad days, we may say to ourselves, "Why can't I be good all the time?" Welcome to the club. When we become distracted from righteousness by lack of patience or by seeking the things of the world, we can become unholy. It happens to me, and rest assured, it occurs far too often. Even seemingly little things can take us off track.

I'd like to share an example from my own life that shows how easily this can happen. I played ball all my life. I loved athletics. I enjoyed the thrill of the contest. The BYU years under the tutelage of the legendary basketball coach Stan Watts were a thrill for a young boy who loved to play ball. There was just one problem: the men in the striped shirts—the referees. They were the judges, the jury, and often the ones who decided the outcome of the game. We as players and spectators were the ones who yelled and screamed for our team—and at the men with the whistles. After my playing days, I became a true "fan"—you know, protecting the home team by yelling at the referees.

As my children grew, they too became athletes—competing in state championships with all of the excitement—and I was their personal protector, so I continued to scream at the referees. It often embarrassed the children. I would be quiet for a while, and then I would get upset and lose my self-control—not really bad, never shouting obscenities, mind you, just riding the referees and telling them to do better. It showed a lack of dignity, manners, true compassion, and love for my fellowmen. I was wrong. I needed to change. I needed to gain self-control. I needed to truly love all of my brothers, even the ones in the striped shirts!

So I made a commitment. I set a goal—I would exercise good sportsmanship and compassion for all, especially the referees at ball games. My desire was strong. My plan was to pray before each game to be a good sport and be dignified at all times—even to be a holy man. After all, I was fifty-three years old.

Well, it worked! My wife and my children couldn't believe the change. I became a true gentleman. I gained self-control. I was so pleased. There was joy in confession and change!

One day I attended a basketball game in which our youngest daughter, Tricia, was playing. I was doing just fine until the referee made a horrible mistake—at least in my eyes—and I yelled out, "Come on, ref!" My older daughter, Traci, looked at me and said, "Dad, did you forget to pray?" I dropped my head, realizing I *had* forgotten. I left the game, found a quiet place outside, and said a prayer. I returned to the game—and, sure enough, I behaved like a true gentleman again, dignified in every way in the strength of the Lord. The scripture I had taught for many years came to strengthen me in my hour of need:

"Behold, verily, verily, I say unto you, ye must watch and pray always lest ye enter into temptation; for Satan desireth to have you, that he may sift you as wheat" (3 Ne. 18:18). When we choose to pray with real intent and then act in faith, believing, we will conquer.

So here is what we have to do to gain self-mastery: set a goal, make a plan, get the support of family and friends, and pray with all our hearts. Then we can repent. Trust me, confession is good for the soul. We feel better when we choose to be more Christlike and holy. The weaknesses and setbacks that impede the process are many; some are small, and some are massive. Regardless, God will help us overcome them all as we turn toward Him and exert our best effort.

We must never give in and never—no *never*—give up. Does this sound like a pep talk on a highly spiritual topic? Well, it is, because we all need it. We are all in this together—to help each other become sanctified and holy through the Savior by the power of the Holy Ghost. It was the Lord Himself who said, "F [illegible] am able to make you holy, and your sins are forgiven you" (D&C [illegible] [illegible]eed, all things can be accomplished through Christ the Lor[illegible]

Christ is our Advocate and M [illegible] dvocate, He speaks for us and pleads our case befor[illegible] [illegible]e Mediator, through the power of His Atonement, [illegible] separation from God. It is *through Him that we ca*[illegible] *and do all things.* Lest we forget, He is "the way th[illegible] [illegible]fe: no man cometh unto the Father, but by me" (Jo[illegible] [illegible]ophets also speak of being reconciled: "Be reconcile[illegible] *[illegible]gh the atonement of Christ*" (Jacob 4:11); then we "[illegible] *[illegible]rough the atonement of Christ and the power of his re*[illegible] [illegible]aised unto life eternal, and this because of your fait[illegible] [illegible]7:41). "There shall be no other name given nor an[illegible] [illegible]neans whereby salvation can come unto the children [illegible] *and through the name of Christ,* the Lord Omnipote[illegible]

In his grea[illegible] Benjamin spoke of how all things are done through [illegible]rist: "Therefore, I would that ye should be steadfast an[illegible] [illegible]ys abounding in good works, that Christ, the Lord Go[illegible] [illegible]may seal you his, that you may be brought to heaven, that ye may [illegible] [illegible]erlasting salvation and eternal life, through the wisdom, and power, and justice, and mercy of him who created all things, in heaven and in earth, who is God above all" (Mosiah 5:15).

We "have eternal life through Christ, who has broken the bands of death" (Mosiah 15:23), "and remember that only in and through Christ ye can be saved" (Mosiah 16:13), for "redemption cometh through Christ the Lord" (Mosiah 16:15). This plan of redemption was "prepared from the foundation of the world, through Christ, for all whosoever would believe on his name" (Alma 22:13). God the Father "may bring about, through his most Beloved, his great and eternal purpose" (Morm. 5:14). Alma's counsel to his son Shiblon expands on this principle: "My son, I have told you this that ye may learn wisdom, that ye may learn of me that there is no other way or means whereby man can be saved, only in and through Christ. Behold, he is the life and the light of the world. Behold, he is the word of truth and righteousness" (Alma 38:9).

As Moroni's closing address in the Book of Mormon reminds us, the necessity of our perfection through Christ is clear: "And again, if ye by the grace of God are perfect in Christ, and deny not his power, then are ye sanctified in Christ by the grace of God, through the shedding of the blood of Christ, which is in the covenant of the Father unto the remission of your sins, that ye become holy, without spot" (Moro. 10:33).

We know from the scriptures that the blessings of justification and sanctification—of being made holy and pure—come from the Lord: "Justification through the grace of our Lord and Savior Jesus Christ is just and true; And we know also, that sanctification through the grace of our Lord and Savior Jesus Christ is just and true, to all those who love and serve God with all their mights, minds, and strength" (D&C 20:30–31).

The word *through* as a preposition in this quote brings to mind such concepts as *the instrumentality of, our relationship and dependence on*. Therefore, we pray in the name of and *through* the Savior Jesus Christ. We are redeemed, reconciled, made clean, made pure, and sanctified *through* Jesus Christ. We are ultimately perfected *through* Christ. The scriptures in this chapter explain the transcendent truth of how in mortality, and especially in the temple, we symbolically and then literally in the Resurrection return to the presence of the Father and receive the blessings of exaltation. That happens only *through* our Savior Jesus Christ.

In Mosaic times, only the high priest was allowed to go into the Holy of Holies, the holiest place in the tabernacle and later in the temple. The veil precluded all others from entering. When the Lord and Savior offered His infinite sacrifice, the way opened to us *through Him* to enter that holiest of chambers, for "the veil of the temple was rent in twain from the top to the bottom" (Mark 15:38). This passage has great implications to each of us: each of us may now enter the temple if we are worthy.

Jesus Christ is called our Great High Priest, for He has made it possible for us to enter into the presence of God. As the Apostle Paul wrote, "Seeing then that we have a great high priest, that is passed into the heavens, Jesus the Son of God, let us hold fast our profession" (Heb. 4:14). In his epistle to the Hebrews, Paul further clarifies this doctrine: "Having therefore, brethren, boldness to enter into the holiest by the blood of Jesus, By a new and living way, which he hath consecrated for us, through the veil, that is to say, his flesh; And having an high priest over the house of God" (Heb. 10:19–21).

Because of the Savior's Atonement, we no longer live in fear but with a hope of life eternal, which He has provided. Because of our faith in Jesus Christ, we become bold, not hesitant or fearful, in living our lives and striving to return to God. We come into His holy house by the power and blessings of His Atonement. The new and living way is through the greater priesthood; the law of Moses, which the Lord fulfilled, no longer restricts the fulness of the gospel: "And my Father sent me that I might be lifted up on the cross; and after that I had been lifted up upon the cross . . . even so should men be lifted up by the Father" (3 Ne. 27:14).

The Lord has ordained, set apart, and sanctified the way for us to pass through the veil, which was rent symbolically by His broken flesh. Thus we see the significance of our Savior's statement: "I am the way, the truth, and the life: no man cometh unto the Father, but by me" (John 14:6). This brings great meaning to the endowment and the way in which we symbolically enter the holiest of sanctuaries—the celestial room—through Christ and come into the presence of the Father.

Our Heavenly Father seeks that all of His children, through His Son, may return to His presence and enjoy the blessings of exaltation. This is the purpose of the temple, which, for that reason, has been designated *the house of the Lord.*

Chapter 6

The Glory and Presence of God

In our fallen state, we have been cut off, as were Adam and Eve, from the presence of God. Coming back into God's presence is made possible through the Savior:

> Wherefore, redemption cometh in and through the Holy Messiah; for he is full of grace and truth.
>
> Behold, he offereth himself a sacrifice for sin, to answer the ends of the law, unto all those who have a broken heart and a contrite spirit; and unto none else can the ends of the law be answered.
>
> Wherefore, how great the importance to make these things known unto the inhabitants of the earth, that they may know that there is no flesh that can dwell in the presence of God, save it be through the merits, and mercy, and grace of the Holy Messiah, who layeth down his life according to the flesh, and taketh it again by the power of the Spirit, that he may bring to pass the resurrection of the dead, being the first that should rise. (2 Ne. 2:6–8)

We must also realize that if we do not repent, the "lively sense of [our] own guilt will cause [us] to shrink from the presence of the Lord" (Mosiah 2:38).

This pattern of redemption plays out symbolically in the drama we witness in the temple endowment ceremony and in the covenants we make in the Lord's holy house. God our Father loves us, and we love Him. That is why we seek to enjoy the glory of His presence and receive the blessings of exaltation and eternal lives in a state of never-ending happiness. We, through God's sealing power, seek to become like our Heavenly Parents. Moses reached for this same goal. He "sought diligently to sanctify his people that they might behold the face of God" (D&C 84:23), but the Israelites hardened their hearts and did not endure His presence. As a result, they could not enter His *rest*, which is the fulness of His glory. The prophets labor diligently to persuade their people "to come unto Christ, and partake of the goodness of God, that they might enter into his rest" (Jacob 1:7). If we but repent and do not harden our hearts, we can, through our faithfulness, likewise enter into that rest and glory of the Lord (see Alma 12:34).

Because we have been blessed with the greater priesthood, we (whether male or female) can be endowed and receive the blessings available in the house of the Lord. Those blessings allow us, if worthy, to partake of His glory and His holy presence—and as was promised in the dedication of the Kirtland Temple, "all people who shall enter upon the threshold of the Lord's house may feel thy power, and feel constrained to acknowledge that thou hast sanctified it, and that it is thy house, a place of thy holiness" (D&C 109:13).

For our part, we must help protect the temple from being defiled or made unclean, else His glory and presence cannot be there: "And ye shall not suffer any unclean thing to come in unto it; and my glory shall be there, and my presence shall be there" (D&C 94:8).

Glory refers to greatness, exaltations, honor, praise, majesty, triumphal power, and goodness—definitions that describe our Heavenly Father, for He is a personage of glory. The glory of God is expressed in many ways. It is "intelligence, or in other words, light and truth" (D&C 93:36).

The word *glory* is also used to describe a condition or state of resurrected beings, such as the degree of glory with which individuals are endowed upon resurrection. It's also a word that describes the Lord's house, because it is a house of glory.

God's very *presence* is in His holy house: "Yea, and my presence shall be there, for I will come into it [the temple], and all the pure in heart that shall come into it shall see God" (D&C 97:16). The greater priesthood holds the keys of the spiritual blessings through which we receive all the ordinances and mysteries of the kingdom of heaven that permit us to enjoy God's presence symbolically in the temple (see D&C 107:18–19)—and, ultimately, to literally be in His presence.

If we want to enjoy the presence of God in our lives and in the temple, we must practice charity and virtue. We read, "Let thy bowels also be full of charity towards all men, and to the household of faith, and let virtue garnish thy thoughts unceasingly; then shall thy confidence wax strong in the presence of God; and the doctrine of the priesthood shall distil upon thy soul as the dews from heaven. The Holy Ghost shall be thy constant companion, and thy scepter an unchanging scepter of righteousness and truth; and thy dominion shall be an everlasting dominion, and without compulsory means it shall flow unto thee forever and ever" (D&C 121:45–46). The fruits of charity and virtue are obedience and the actual works of love and compassion.

Only through our beloved Savior and based on our personal righteousness can we partake of God's glory and presence. There is no other way. So let us go forward with an eye single to the glory of God: "And if your eye be single to my glory, your whole bodies shall be filled with light, and there shall be no darkness in you; and that body which is filled with light comprehendeth all things. Therefore, sanctify yourselves that your minds become single to God, and the days will come that you shall see him; for he will unveil his face unto you, and it shall be in his own time, and in his own way, and according to his own will" (D&C 88:67–68).

Can this really be so? Can we actually, in our mortal state, partake of the glory and presence of God? The scriptures promise us that we can: "And again, verily I say unto you that it is your privilege, and a promise I give unto you that have been ordained unto this ministry, that inasmuch as you strip yourselves from jealousies and fears, and humble yourselves before me, for ye are not sufficiently humble, the veil shall be rent and you shall see me and know that I am—not with the carnal neither natural mind, but with the spiritual" (D&C 67:10).

This promise was not given to only prophets and apostles. God is no respecter of persons. All can qualify to receive this blessing through worthiness and according to the will of God. But we must first overcome our jealousies with charity and love. This is the love that helps us become like Christ: "That ye may be filled with this love, which he hath bestowed upon all who are true followers of his Son, Jesus Christ; that ye may become the sons of God; *that when he shall appear we shall be like him*" (Moro. 7:48). We overcome our fears with faith, love, preparation, knowledge, the Holy Spirit, prayer, and experience. We humble ourselves as we come to understand our relationship with God and our dependence on Him. These are the things we do to qualify to come into the presence of the Father. All can receive the blessings of exaltation, even all that the Father has. We are reminded, "And it shall come to pass afterward, that I will pour out my spirit upon all flesh; and your sons and your daughters shall prophesy, your old men shall dream dreams, your young men shall see visions" (Joel 2:28; Acts 2:17).

In November 1831, the Lord revealed the following to the Prophet Joseph Smith in Hiram, Ohio:

> And this is the ensample unto them, that they shall speak as they are moved upon by the Holy Ghost.
>
> And whatsoever they shall speak when moved upon by the Holy Ghost shall be scripture, shall be the will of the Lord, shall be the mind of the Lord, shall be the word of the Lord, shall be the voice of the Lord, and the power of God unto salvation.
>
> Behold, this is the promise of the Lord unto you, O ye my servants.
>
> Wherefore, be of good cheer, and do not fear, for I the Lord am with you, and will stand by you; and ye shall bear record of me, even Jesus Christ, that I am the Son of the living God, that I was, that I am, and that I am to come.
>
> *This is the word of the Lord unto you*, my servant Orson Hyde, and also unto my servant Luke Johnson, and unto my servant Lyman Johnson, and unto my servant William E. McLellin, *and unto all the faithful elders of my church.*" (D&C 68:3–7)

I ask again: Can we *really* enjoy these blessings in the flesh? Such a thing seems almost unfathomable, but listen to the Lord: "Neither is man capable to make them [the mysteries] known, for they are only to be seen and understood by the power of the Holy Spirit, which God bestows on those who love him, and purify themselves before him; To whom he grants this privilege of seeing and knowing for themselves; That through the power and manifestation of the Spirit, while in the flesh, they may be able to bear his presence in the world of glory" (D&C 76:116–118). I testify that this privilege awaits in the temples of the Lord.

The goodness and mercy of God is extended to all of His children if they but believe and exercise faith. But all too often, like the Israelites, we look beyond the mark. We may think we must have a First Vision–type experience to say we have received these blessings. If not an experience like the First Vision, what must we see and feel to partake of the Lord's glory and presence? We will not experience it through our natural mind but only by our spiritual mind (see D&C 67:10). And when can we expect it? We cannot force the Spirit or make demands of it.

So how do we partake of these promised blessings? How do we experience the presence of the Lord while we are still in the flesh? The Spirit will bear witness of truth to our hearts if we seek that witness. To begin, the Spirit must quicken our flesh (see D&C 67:11). We must have eyes to see, ears to hear, minds to understand, and hearts to feel, and we must not allow ourselves to be distracted by the things of the world. As the Spirit accompanies us, we find ourselves in the presence of God, and we partake and feel of His glory. Then we begin to see His glory and power in all things: "He is above all things, and in all things, and is through all things, and is round about all things" (D&C 88:41).

Two people sitting next to each another in the same endowment session can have totally different experiences depending on their individual preparation and desire. We cannot be casual about our ability to see with temple eyes. Both Nephi and President Joseph F. Smith pondered deeply before receiving the spiritual experiences and revelations each experienced (see 1 Ne. 11; D&C 138). We must also ponder deeply, enjoying the outpouring of the Spirit available in the house of the Lord.

Don't give up if you think it hasn't happened for you. Remember that it is possible to be influenced by the glory and presence of God without initially realizing it. Just as we need to know what to look for when feeling the Holy Spirit, we also need to understand how to recognize the glory and presence of God. As such understanding occurs, our gratitude for our Father and His Son will increase to the point that we will be consumed with light and will begin to comprehend all things. Then we will see the glory of God and feel His presence.

Chapter 7

Grace and the Mysteries, Knowledge, and Power

Grace is the love, goodness, mercy, power, and infinite benevolence of God the Father and Jesus Christ. The enabling power of the infinite Atonement through the Lord Jesus Christ continually expresses grace to the children of God, and grace permeates the temple experience. It is what empowers us to do all things.

The scriptures are clear: it is through grace that we are saved (see 2 Ne. 10:24). We are justified by grace (see Rom. 3:24). His grace is sufficient for us (see 2 Cor. 12:9). We have hope through His grace (see 2 Thes. 2:16). Grace brings us salvation (see Titus 2:11). "And again, if ye by the grace of God are perfect in Christ, and deny not his power, then are ye sanctified in Christ by the grace of God, through the shedding of the blood of Christ, which is in the covenant of the Father unto the remission of your sins, that ye become holy, without spot" (Moro. 10:33).

A gift from Heavenly Father and the Savior, grace covers everything because the Atonement covers everything. Grace, as expressed through the Atonement, *pays for our sins*; it is our salvation, justification, and perfection. We cannot repay the debt for our sins—but the grace of God has paid the debt not only for our sins but also for our salvation. If you look carefully, you will see the manifestations of grace in the temple—in the entire endowment, in every ordinance, and in every covenant.

We become empowered as we accept the grace of God. We are made holy as *we come unto Christ* and deny not His power; we become sanctified in Christ by the grace of God and become free from our sins. As we accept grace through our temple worship, we become endowed with its amazing power to do good. "Nevertheless, the Lord God showeth us our weakness that we may know that it is by his grace, and his great condescensions unto the children of men, that we have power to do these things" (Jacob 4:7).

A key doctrine teaches that we are saved by grace and empowered by grace to do good, and then we are judged by our works: "But by the grace of God I am what I am: and his grace which was bestowed upon me was not in vain; but I laboured more abundantly than they all: yet not I, but the grace of God which was with me" (1 Cor. 15:10). We become strong in the grace of the Lord (see 2 Tim. 2:1). Through His grace, we choose to serve Him (see Heb. 12:28), and as we repent and do good works, we are restored to that grace we once enjoyed in the presence of our Father (see Hel. 12:24).

Grace becomes sufficient for those of us who humble ourselves before God and then, through our faith, become strong (see Ether 12:27). As the Prophet Joseph prayed, "Help thy servants to say, with thy grace assisting them: Thy will be done, O Lord, and not ours" (D&C 109:44).

The grace of God and the Atonement of the Savior are the enabling power of all things; it is this power that draws us to Christ and inspires us to become like Him. Our hope through the Atonement of Christ is to be raised up to eternal life, a hope exemplified through our faithfulness and personified in our works, which are merely an expression of our accepting the Savior's Atonement.

There must be a way that can help all of us get grace, accept grace, and act upon grace. Long ago there was a council held in which the plan was presented, detailing how we could become perfect like our Heavenly Father. We readily accepted God the Father's perfect plan. Jehovah, our elder brother, would pay for our sins so we could become perfect through Him. We came to Earth to partake of the gift of God the Father's only Begotten Son in the flesh, even Christ the Lord, the Anointed One. Through this great plan, we receive the grace of God.

Now here we are: the Savior provided us the way back into the presence of our Father, which has been our greatest desire from the very beginning. Christ paid for everything, and we do not have the power to repay. So the question begs: Does grace take care of everything, and we don't have to do anything? Quite the contrary. Because it is impossible to pay the debt, there is a stipulation: we are to accept Jesus as our Savior and receive the principles and ordinances of the gospel. We are to come unto

Christ and seek to become like Him by keeping the commandments and enduring to the end (see John 14:15, 21; 2 Ne. 31:20). We are to exercise faith unto repentance. We honor our covenants and endure to the end. We never give in. We never give up. We cheerfully endure all things. In other words, we are to work to become worthy of the presence of our Father, who will judge us according to our works and the desires of our hearts (see Alma 41:3; D&C 137:9).

To take full advantage of the transcendent gift of grace, we must receive it and make it a part of our very souls: "For what doth it profit a man if a gift is bestowed upon him, and he receive not the gift? Behold, he rejoices not in that which is given unto him, neither rejoices in him who is the giver of the gift" (D&C 88:33). *Receiving* means we actually obtain the gift. It becomes part of us.

Again, we do not earn grace. We do not merit it. Its fruits are expressed in our righteousness. We become what we are through Christ the Lord. Here's a scripture that describes perfectly how grace operates and what happens as we receive it into our lives: "For by grace are ye saved through faith; and that not of yourselves: it is the gift of God: Not of works, lest any man should boast. *For we are his workmanship, created in Christ Jesus unto good works, which God hath before ordained that we should walk in them*" (Eph. 2:8–10).

Sometimes we feel as if we work out our own salvation, but look how Paul helps us understand how God works within us: "Wherefore, my beloved, as ye have always obeyed, not as in my presence only, but now much more in my absence, work out your own salvation with fear and trembling. *For it is God which worketh in you both to will and to do of his good pleasure*" (Philip. 2:12–13).

Christ exemplified this very principle of God's power within us when He was anointed by His Father: "How God anointed Jesus of Nazareth with the Holy Ghost and with power: *who went about doing good*, and healing all that were oppressed of the devil; *for God was with him*" (Acts 10:38). God was with Him, and God is with us by the power of His Spirit. These scriptures surely demonstrate that our works follow our faith and conversion to Christ and that the good we do comes from God and the power He puts into us.

To work out our salvation does not mean that *we* work it out or earn it; rather, when we come to the Lord with all our hearts—that is, when we accept His infinite Atonement—we are empowered to work out our salvation through our faithfulness (see Morm. 9:27). Working out our salvation is really part of enduring to the end. Our love of God and our gratitude for His goodness motivate us. Instead of being a check-off list of things to do, the commandments become a joyful expression of the love of God, the empowerment of the Atonement, and the grace of God in our lives. Keeping the commandments becomes a natural thing to do. We not only obtain a hope in Christ, but Christ empowers us, perfects us, and becomes our strength, too, "for in his strength [we] can do all things" (Alma 26:12).

The Grace and Mercy of God

To be reconciled to God, to come unto Christ, implies that we, through Christ and His Atonement, can be brought back into the presence of God as we follow Christ and accept Him as our Savior and Redeemer. We are to reconcile (align) our lives to the will of God, as Nephi instructs us: "Reconcile yourselves to the will of God, and not to the will of the devil and the flesh; and remember, after ye are reconciled unto God, that it is only in and through the grace of God that ye are saved" (2 Ne. 10:24).

This reconciliation is symbolically realized in the temple as we receive the ordinances with a promise to be faithful in keeping our covenants. The realization of all our blessings comes to us as we keep all of the commandments, which include our covenants, and enjoy a state of happiness: "I would desire that ye should consider on the blessed and happy state of those that keep the commandments of God. For behold, they are blessed in all things, both temporal and spiritual; and if they hold out faithful to the end they are received into heaven, that thereby they may dwell with God in a state of never-ending happiness. O remember, remember that these things are true; for the Lord God hath spoken it" (Mosiah 2:41).

As we come unto Christ through His Atonement and in His holy house to be perfected in Him—and as we are made clean, holy, and sanctified and deny ourselves of all ungodliness, we receive the power of godliness: "Therefore, in the ordinances thereof [the greater priesthood], the power of godliness is manifest" (D&C 84:20). What an empowering verse! (Even though I had taught Doctrine and Covenants and had written two commentaries on it, I never really understood the eternal verities of that verse until I was in my seventies; consider the power of repetition combined with new eyes to see!)

After denying all ungodliness, we show our love to God by our willingness to "serve him with all [our] heart, might, mind and strength, that [we] may stand blameless before God at the last day" (D&C 4:2). Then by the grace of God, we become perfect in Christ, for He is "the way, the truth, and the life: no man cometh unto the Father, but by me" (John 14:6). All of this comes through the grace of God, through the Atonement of His Beloved Son, "which is in the covenant of the Father" (Moro. 10:33).

One of the sweetest manifestations of the grace of God, expressed through His Son, is the fact that the Savior so willingly suffered for us:

> And he shall go forth, suffering pains and afflictions and temptations of every kind; and this that the word might be fulfilled which saith he will take upon him the pains and the sicknesses of his people.
>
> And he will take upon him death, that he may loose the bands of death which bind his people; and he will take upon him their infirmities, that his bowels may be filled with mercy, according to the flesh, that he may know according to the flesh how to succor his people according to their infirmities. (Alma 7:11–12)

This scripture is often quoted, but it needs to be embedded in our hearts.

Through the goodness of the Father, the Lord will come to us, and He too will be "full of grace, equity, and truth, full of patience, mercy, and long-suffering, quick to hear the cries of his people and to answer their prayers" (Alma 9:26). Through His suffering and sacrifice, the Savior will not only nurture us but will also empower us to everlasting life in the resurrection.

The plan of redemption encompasses everything a Savior would do for us—and it is the doctrine of the temple. It is expressed in the endowment. We cannot separate the Atonement from the endowment. We worship in the temple to understand the things of God—to learn to look to God and live.

I personally know of the Lord's enabling power and tender mercy because my family and I experienced the tender mercies of God in a life-threatening situation, as have so many others. What we learned of God's goodness and His word in the temple became reality as we grappled with an unexpected and tragic event. It happened in October 1986 while I was serving as president of the England London South Mission. President Wendell Ashton of the London England Mission had invited our family to a special youth morningside where President Thomas S. Monson would be speaking. We were all excited and looking forward to the day.

Just before the meeting, we met for a short time with President Monson and other Church leaders. During that meeting, President Ashton's secretary rushed up to me and said, "President, you have an urgent call from the States." I took the call in the room and learned that our son Cory, who was attending his senior year of high school in Provo, had been in a serious car accident and was in a coma. Upon hearing the news, President Monson quickly took his airline ticket out of his pocket, gave it to my wife, Pat, and told his traveling companion—a security guard—to take Pat home to Utah on the next flight. (This was back when airline tickets were interchangeable.) President Monson then turned to me and said, "You may need to go home if things do not improve shortly." In shock, we all agreed, and Pat headed for home.

The following day, Cory's condition worsened, so I hurried back to Provo with my daughters Traci and Tricia. When we arrived at the hospital, I offered a prayer and pleaded with the Lord to spare our beloved son. The answer came the next morning. I remember holding his hand as the life-support systems were turned off. His hand became cold, and Cory Matthew Pinegar passed on to the other side of the veil.

Ever the servant, President Monson called several times to get a report on Cory's condition. When he heard of Cory's passing, President Monson called, expressed his sorrow, and asked how he might help. I asked if he would speak at Cory's funeral, and he responded with loving-kindness, "I hoped you would ask."

At the funeral, President Monson spoke with great empathy and power. He said, "Don't ask why. That is a negative comment. Cory had his mission call early and has been transferred to the spirit world, where a great deal of work is going on." He smiled, then added, "I can see him with his new companion. Yes, Elder LeGrand Richards—they would be a great twosome." We all chuckled, and the idea brought joy to a somber family. Then, with the power of the Melchizedek Priesthood, he bestowed an apostolic blessing upon our family and spoke of how we would be healed by the enabling power of the Atonement and would continue to serve the Lord in England.

We carried back to England the pain of a lost loved one. My entire body felt as though it had been ripped from its moorings. My soul retched in pain. The very innards of my body and mind were racked with sorrow. My beloved son, who had faced such a bright future, flesh of my flesh, was dead. I was so weak that I wondered how could I ever preach and teach with enough power to inspire the missionaries. I'd lost my father when I was twelve, but this was different—very different. Might this opposition be too much for me to handle?

And then the miracle happened. The power of the Atonement entered into my very being and spread throughout our family, and the pain was swept away. There were moments of tenderness when our thoughts turned to our son, but we were healed. I prayed to my Father about Cory's condition, and feelings of sweet peace came into my soul; I knew what Cory was doing and how he felt. The perfect plan of my Heavenly Father was in place, and my son was happy serving his mission in the spirit world. The power of godliness was made manifest for me in that situation, just as we learn in the temple.

When I spoke with the missionaries the week after we returned from Cory's funeral, they were amazed. Greater power filled my soul. Inspiring words came by the power of the Holy Ghost. Through a living prophet, the Lord in His goodness made me into something I cannot describe, save it were to become an instrument to do His work. I knew who I was serving and who was helping me at every turn. I can testify with great power that the Lord and His goodness are ever present as He succors and blesses His children.

In the pain of this great trial, greater knowledge of the infinite Atonement and its power came to me. It was real. I felt it. I now know it works. I know I was healed from my grief and sorrow. And I know I teach with greater faith, conviction, and power, all through the goodness and mercy of God. There is a difference in my heart. I am more grateful to my Father and my Savior. I acknowledge my nothingness and joy in my dependence upon the strength of the Lord in my life. My empathy and compassion have increased. I am better able to help someone who is struggling. I never would have understood and appreciated their sorrow or grief had I not known such sorrow and been healed myself. The pain of opposition was the requirement for me to suffer so I could better appreciate the Atonement and the life of my beloved son—so I could move from pain to peace, from brokenheartedness to joy. Only through suffering can we grow.

Let us ponder and enjoy the Lord's nurturing in all of our trials and tribulations. That is why we find such peace and healing within the walls of the temple; it is there that we come to feel the fulness of the Lord's comfort through the Holy Ghost.

At a time when the Nephites were on the brink of destruction, the prophet Mormon gave one of the most earnest sermons on grace and mercy in all the scriptures: "But may Christ lift thee up, and may his sufferings and death, and the showing of his body unto our fathers, and his mercy and long-suffering, and the hope of his glory and of eternal life, rest in your mind forever. And may the grace of God the Father, whose throne is high in the heavens, and our Lord Jesus Christ, who sitteth on the right hand of his power, until all things shall become subject unto him, be, and abide with you forever. Amen" (Moro. 9:25–26).

The Mysteries of the Kingdom

The mysteries of God are the doctrines and truths of the gospel that are taught in His holy house. The Greek word translated as *mystery* in the New Testament often means quite literally the "sacred" or "secret." However, the colloquial use of the word *mystery*—"something that cannot be understood"—is what often leads us astray. The *mysteries*, as defined by the scriptures and also by dictionaries as "something secret or sacred," are the knowledge of God. And this knowledge is not always understood by mankind—which is why it is called a mystery. The Lord will reveal through His Melchizedek Priesthood all spiritual blessings, including these mysteries—knowledge, light, and truth—through the ordinances of the temple, according to His good pleasure and by the power of His Spirit (see D&C 76:5–10; 107:19). Such mysteries, or sacred truths, can come to us through our faith, diligence, and patience as we seek greater understanding and knowledge of the Atonement and endowment.

It is important to remember that the Lord reveals the mysteries only to those who ask in faith: "If thou shalt ask, thou shalt receive revelation upon revelation, knowledge upon knowledge, that thou mayest know the mysteries and peaceable things—that which bringeth joy, that which bringeth life eternal" (D&C 42:61; compare D&C 76:5–10). God reveals eternal truths to those who truly seek the knowledge of God; Paul describes the Apostles and prophets as "stewards of the mysteries of God" (1 Cor. 4:1).

We, like the prophets and Apostles, should seek to understand the mysteries by exercising patience and faith through fervent prayer and diligent study and especially by coming to the Lord's house—which is why temple worship is key to gaining the true knowledge of God. But it is not enough to simply *expect* a revelation of the mysteries: "Behold, you have not understood; you have supposed that I would give it unto you, when you took no thought save it was to ask me" (D&C 9:7). We must pay a price.

The mysteries of God are not intellectual knowledge; they are knowledge we gain through the covenants and symbols of the endowment, which reflect the glory and presence of God. The process of gaining the knowledge of God and the power of godliness happens line upon line and precept upon precept: "And if your eye be single to my glory, your whole bodies shall be filled with light, and there shall be no darkness in you; and that body which is filled with light comprehendeth all things. Therefore, sanctify yourselves that your minds become single to God, and the days will come that you shall see him; for he will unveil his face unto you, and it shall be in his own time, and in his own way, and according to his own will" (D&C 88:67–68). If our focus is the glory of God, the blessings of light and truth can be ours, and we will be filled with light.

The mysteries of God—light and truth—come as we worship in the temple and keep the commandments (see D&C 63:23). We also learn of them in the scriptures: "The glory of God is intelligence, or, in other words, light and truth" (D&C 93:36). This is not secular knowledge but the revealed word of God—the same light and truth we learn about in the temple.

We also read that "light and truth forsake that evil one" (D&C 93:37). In other words, through obtaining further light and truth, we become empowered to withstand temptation. Receiving our own endowment gives us protection from evil and temptation.

Perhaps the most important point regarding the mysteries of God is that the Savior is the light and truth (see D&C 88:6). He is the only way. The doctrines of truth and light unto salvation come from the word of God through the Savior, angels, the Holy Spirit, and our living prophets, who are the stewards of the mysteries of God. In the Lord's university—His holy house—we learn all things concerning life everlasting.

Christ is in all the doctrines and eternal truths (the mysteries) having to do with the plan of God. In fact, the mysteries really come down to understanding Christ. We must learn the doctrines of Christ, the truths of His gospel, the word of God (which is Christ—see John 1; Rev. 19:13), and the doctrines taught in the temple. We can then live the doctrines and become like Christ, which He has commanded us to do (see 3 Ne. 12:48; 27:27).

The Power of Godliness

We receive the power of godliness through the ordinances of the greater priesthood (see D&C 84:19–22). This power helps us possess a godlike behavior and countenance that enables us to return to the presence of our Father. This priesthood power is exactly what the churches in the days of the Prophet Joseph Smith were lacking: "They draw near to me with their lips, but their hearts are far from me, they teach for doctrines the commandments of men, having a form of godliness, but they deny the power thereof" (JS—H 1:19).

The priesthood of God and its ordinances are what empower us. And everything we receive from the greater priesthood—in fact, everything in the gospel, the good news—has to do with Christ. Every blessing we receive from the Father comes because we believe in His Son and follow Him (see 3 Ne. 19:22; Moro. 7:48) The authority to act for God is His priesthood; even as Christ did the Father's will, He was acting with the full authority or priesthood of His Father.

We see in all things the connection to Christ. The priesthood allows us to take His name upon us through baptism and thus receive the Holy Ghost and look forward to the endowment from on high. Let us endure to the end through steadfastness in Christ, drawing upon His strength through the enabling power of the Atonement and eventually becoming perfect as He is.

As part of the perfection process, the ordinances of the temple empower us to become godly. Godliness is all about becoming like God, which is the essence and purpose of the temple. This is why Moroni speaks of this doctrine as he closes the Book of Mormon. We become perfected as we deny every form of ungodliness and become godly; then His grace is sufficient for us.

We receive the fulness of the Spirit in the temple. With godliness, we will have "a godly walk and conversation, that [we] are worthy of it, that there may be works and faith agreeable to the holy scriptures—walking in holiness before the Lord" (D&C 20:69). The power of godliness is a gift of grace; it comes to us individually as we prepare ourselves to receive it through the ordinances of the priesthood in the temple.

We must remember as we seek to understand all these truths that they come by revelation. Elder John A. Widtsoe taught, "The endowment is so richly symbolic. . . . It is so packed full of revelations to those who exercise their strength to seek and see, that no human words can explain or make clear the possibilities that reside in the temple service. The endowment which was given by revelation can best be understood by revelation" ("Why Symbols?" *Ensign*, Feb. 2007, 12–17). The Prophet Joseph counseled us to "search deeper and deeper in the mysteries of Godliness" (Joseph Fielding Smith, *TPJS*, 364). Surely this requires us to come to the house of the Lord to worship and receive revelation, which is the key to understanding.

Godliness is a cardinal virtue we should seek as we serve in the Church and kingdom of God (see D&C 4:6; 107:30). Godliness is holiness, righteousness, and saintliness; it is taking upon oneself the divine nature of Christ, the true process of becoming godly. Peter describes the process:

> According as his divine power hath given unto us all things that pertain unto life and godliness, through the knowledge of him that hath called us to glory and virtue:
>
> Whereby are given unto us exceeding great and precious promises: that by these ye might be partakers of the divine nature, having escaped the corruption that is in the world through lust [unrighteous desire].
>
> And beside this, giving all diligence, add to your faith virtue; and to virtue knowledge;
>
> And to knowledge temperance; and to temperance patience; and to patience godliness;
>
> And to godliness brotherly kindness; and to brotherly kindness charity.
>
> For if these things be in you, and abound, they make you that ye shall neither be barren nor unfruitful in the knowledge of our Lord Jesus Christ.
>
> But he that lacketh these things is blind, and cannot see afar off, and hath forgotten that he was purged from his old sins.
>
> Wherefore the rather, brethren, give diligence to make your calling and election sure: for if ye do these things, ye shall never fall. (2 Pet. 1:3–10)

Now that we have heard the words of the Apostle Peter, our hearts must yearn to become more godly and full of charity, which never faileth. We would do well to ask ourselves a few questions regarding the power necessary to become godly: What can we do to bring the sanctifying power of the priesthood into our lives? How will our "lists of life" take on a new dimension as a result? How can we go about doing good? How will we learn to better please God and deny ourselves of all ungodliness?

As I recently pondered these questions again, I realized that one answer to these questions is the simple phrase "Do as Jesus would do." To deny myself of all ungodliness, I must take up my cross—my trials and tribulations. I must be willing to give my all for the kingdom of God so His children may be nourished by His good word. Christ gave His all that we might live. We give our all that we might live with God and live more abundantly.

The Knowledge of God

The greater priesthood holds the key to the knowledge of God and "to administer in spiritual things" (D&C 107:8). The laws of God and highly spiritual things are administered in the temple. In the scriptures, we read, "And this is life eternal, that they might know thee the only true God, and Jesus Christ, whom thou hast sent" (John 17:3). In Greek, this verse refers to a "sure" or "absolute" knowledge of God. Life eternal is brought about as we come to truly know God and His Son.

What does it take to know God? It is more than knowing *about* God—it requires that we know Him personally. When we know God, we talk with Him and understand His merciful nature. We know Him like a father with whom we commune every day. We love Him. We can count on Him. He is our literal Father. We will come to better know our Father and our Savior as we understand and appreciate the following concepts that are taught in the temple:

- God loves us, desires our happiness, and seeks to guide us to eternal life (see Moses 1:39).
- God's motives are based on a perfect love (see John 3:16).
- We must come to recognize the perfection of God—His omniscience, omnipotence, and omnipresence—through His Spirit, and as we recognize His perfection, we worship Him and follow all of His commandments. By doing so, we experience joy.

Knowing the character of God and Christ, we can then exercise faith in Them (see 2 Ne. 9:20; Mosiah 3:5).

- When we keep the commandments, we begin to take upon ourselves the divine nature of Christ; we come to know Him and become like Him (see 2 Pet. 1:3–10).
- When we know God, we want to be like Him (see 3 Ne. 12:48).
- We must totally trust in God and "lean not unto [our] own understanding (see Prov. 3:5–6).
- We should pray and commune with God; through prayer, our relationship deepens, and we come to know Him (see Jer. 29:13; Matt. 6:6; 2 Ne. 26:15; Moro. 7:48).
- As we become humble, we are better able to see God: "The veil shall be rent and you shall see me and know that I am" (D&C 67:10; see also Moro. 7:48). Then we will recognize our deep and total dependence on Him. The grace and mercy of God are evidenced in every turn of our lives if we but take the time to look.
- Above all, we will come to know that we are the literal children of God the Father, with the divine capacity to receive all of His blessings and enjoy a life like that of the Father and the Son: "The Spirit itself beareth witness with our spirit, that we are the children of God; And if children, then heirs, heirs of God and joint-heirs with Christ" (Rom. 8:16–17).

So what can we do to gain this knowledge and light? We should commune through prayer. We should seek to please God by listening to His counsel given us through the power of the Holy Ghost. We should offer thanks and the sacrifice of our broken hearts and contrite spirits. We can begin to do these things at home, as well as in the temple, where we more fully see and feel the glory and presence of the Lord. We will begin to see and understand the doctrines, the sacred ordinances, and the covenants—the mysteries—inside His holy house.

The knowledge and light we gain in the temple will empower us. It will give us a true perspective of life. It will give us hope when we feel discouraged. It will bring into focus what matters most in life. It will bind us by drawing us into sacred covenants. It will teach us the importance of prayer and of calling on the name of the Lord. It will teach us the importance of receiving the Lord's servants, for in so doing, we receive Him. We will come to see the Atonement as the empowering doctrine of all things pertaining to the great plan of our Father. We will be filled with gratitude, the catalyst for all change and spiritual growth. We will truly want to become and progress. We will want to please God. We will go about doing good because we have been anointed with power through the ordinances and the Holy Ghost. And all of this can be done as we worship in the house of the Lord.

The Temple as a House of Grace and Godliness

The Lord, in His infinite goodness, has continually sought to gather His people so they can build a house of God where the Father and the Son can dwell, that the Saints may feel the glory and presence of God and there become endowed with power. Only in temples can we be fully secure: "I must gather together my people . . . that the wheat may be secured in the garners [the temples] to possess eternal life, and be crowned with celestial glory" (D&C 101:65). The mountain of the Lord is indeed the house of the Lord, where we gather to be taught in His ways and "walk in his paths" (Isa. 2:3). The power of godliness is manifest in every ordinance, covenant, principle, and law administered and taught in the temple.

The Prophet Joseph taught concerning the gathering of Israel and its relationship to the temple: "The object of gathering the Jews, or the people of God in any age of the world . . . was to build unto the Lord a house whereby He could reveal unto His people the ordinances of His house and the glories of His kingdom, and teach the people the way of salvation" (*HC*, 5:423). This is what Moses also sought to do for the children of Israel: "Now this Moses plainly taught to the children of Israel in the wilderness, and sought diligently to sanctify his people that they might behold the face of God; But they hardened their hearts and could not endure his presence; therefore, the Lord in his wrath, for his anger was kindled against them, swore that they should not enter into his rest while in the wilderness, which rest is the fulness of his glory. Therefore, he took Moses out of their midst, and the Holy Priesthood also" (D&C 84:23–25). Our Father can bless His children only if they prove themselves worthy to receive His blessings. This is His work and His glory—our immortality and eternal life—and this eternal life can come to pass only through the blessings of His holy house.

The knowledge of God gives us confidence. We know that He has power to do all things and that all things are done in His wisdom and for our benefit. "Behold, all things have been done in the wisdom of him who knoweth all things" (2 Ne. 2:24). With this knowledge, we can exercise faith in Him and in our Beloved Savior, Jesus Christ—and then act accordingly because faith is the foundation of all righteousness. This knowledge, like all knowledge, empowers us as we act on it. This knowledge has been strength to my life because it has strengthened my faith in Christ. "And Christ truly said unto our fathers: If ye have faith ye can do all things which are expedient unto me" (Moro. 10:23).

I pray that we will not be discouraged or overwhelmed by the knowledge and information before us. Gaining the knowledge of God will empower us as we come to understand and appreciate eternal truths. While it may seem daunting at first, I promise you this is an exciting journey. The process will fill you with gratitude and joy for the mercy and goodness of our Heavenly Father and our Savior Jesus Christ. I testify that we can joyously receive all that the Father has as we are faithfully obedient to our covenants and commandments.

Further Study

Let us seek to understand and feel the grace of God in our lives by preparing ourselves to receive the mysteries of God and His godliness in the holy temple.

From the scriptures:

- Study the Bible Dictionary on topics such as covenants, God the Father, Godhead, grace, ordinances, temple, testimony, and worship.

From the prophets, General Authorities, and officers of the Church:

- Octaviano Tenorio, "The Power of Godliness Is Manifested in the Temples of God," *Ensign*, Oct. 2007.
- At Lds.org; select Teachings—Gospel Topics; study the material under topics such as covenants, God the Father, Godhead, grace, ordinances, temple, testimony, and worship.
- Study lesson 25—"Priesthood: The Power of Godliness"—in the Doctrine and Covenants and Church History Gospel Doctrine Teacher's Manual (available online at https://www.lds.org/manual/doctrine-and-covenants-and-church-history-gospel-doctrine-teachers-manual/lesson-25-priesthood-the-power-of-godliness?lang=eng).

CHAPTER 8

The Temple—A House of Learning and Revelation

ONE OF THE CROWNING PURPOSES of the temple is to serve as a house of learning and revelation. We are the learners; we learn by the Spirit according to our prayers, faith, diligence, and heed we give to the words and actions that take place in temples.

Principles of learning fill the scriptures, reminding us that we live and learn "by every word that proceedeth forth from the mouth of God" (D&C 84:44). Symbolic of this process, the word of God came to the Nephites through the Liahona, which worked "according to the faith and diligence and heed" the Nephites demonstrated (1 Ne. 16:28). Alma later compared the word of God to the Liahona:

> For behold, it is as easy to give heed to the word of Christ, which will point to you a straight course to eternal bliss, as it was for our fathers to give heed to this compass, which would point unto them a straight course to the promised land.
>
> And now I say, is there not a type [symbol] in this thing? For just as surely as this director did bring our fathers, by following its course, to the promised land, shall the words of Christ, if we follow their course, carry us beyond this vale of sorrow into a far better land of promise.
>
> O my son, do not let us be slothful because of the easiness of the way; for so was it with our fathers; for so was it prepared for them, that if they would look they might live; even so it is with us. The way is prepared, and if we will look we may live forever. (Alma 37:44–46)

There is an important type—symbol—in Alma's reminder to the Nephites about how the Lord's people learn and grow. *We must first look.*

What does it mean to "look to God and live"? As Nephi looked for answers to his questions and pondered, the Spirit of the Lord carried him away "into an exceedingly high mountain" (1 Ne. 11:1). Nephi expressed a desire that he also behold the things his father had seen. His father's vision was unfolded to him, and the Spirit repeatedly invited Nephi to "look." Nine times Nephi was asked to *look*, and ultimately, he received further light and knowledge concerning the vision of Christ and the tree of life (see 1 Ne. 11–14).

How do we follow Nephi's example and look?

The first step in looking to God is to humbly seek Him in prayer. The prophet Nephi counseled, "Ye must pray always, and not faint. . . . Ye must not perform any thing unto the Lord save in the first place ye shall pray unto the Father in the name of Christ" (2 Ne. 32:9). When we look to God, we listen to His appointed messengers. We place our trust in Him and not in the arm of flesh, "for we know that it is by grace that we are saved, after all we can do" (2 Ne. 25:23). When we look to God with faith and a contrite spirit—as the people of Moses looked to the brazen serpent (a symbol of Christ)—we will find eternal life (see Hel. 8:15).

However, the opposite is also true. When we turn from God and love the things of the world, we become subject to the devil and begin to become "carnal, sensual, and devilish" (Moses 5:13). Our focus and our gaze must remain on God so we can be filled with His love and become like the Nephites did after the Lord appeared to them (see 4 Ne. 1:15–16). Let us follow Nephi's example. Let us follow Alma's charge to his son Helaman and "look to God and live" (Alma 37:47).

One of the best ways we can look to the Lord is by coming to the house of the Lord and learning the things of God. How can we help facilitate the process of learning? As the scriptures proclaim, the Holy Ghost is the teacher: "But the Comforter, which is the Holy Ghost, whom the Father will send in my name, he shall teach you all things, and bring all things to your remembrance, whatsoever I have said unto you" (John 14:26). When we come to worship in the temple, we come to be taught and to receive the fulness of the Holy Ghost. This is the same Spirit the early Christian Saints enjoyed when, after receiving the Holy Ghost on the Day of Pentecost, they "continued daily with one accord in the temple" (Acts 2:46).

What is it we go to the temple to learn? We want to learn the principles of intelligence, light, and truth. We want to better understand the ordinances, covenants, metaphors, and other symbolism presented in the temple. We want to learn the doctrines of the gospel. We want to learn the mysteries of God—the eternal verities and supernal truths that, when applied, help us become true sons and daughters of God. Learning these things is about becoming more like our Savior and more like our Father.

Learning in the house of the Lord completely depends on the attitude and spirit we bring with us. Part of that is to humbly offer the sacrifice of a broken heart and a contrite spirit. Sacrifice sets in motion the process of learning. Sacrifice also brings about godly sorrow and makes possible true and lasting repentance, enabling us be clean and worthy to enter the Lord's house. In a continuation of the divine process, cleanliness then enables us to receive the Spirit, which teaches us to understand the mysteries of godliness.

In our efforts to learn, we must ask the following questions: Am I humble, submissive, gentle, easily entreated, patient, temperate, full of faith, and diligent in keeping the commandments? Do I *ask* for whatsoever I stand in need of? Do I look and listen? Do I meditate and ponder? Do I seek?

There is a process prescribed for learning in the temple. Humility is the starting point of all spiritual growth, of learning to become Christlike. Humble asking is imperative to learning. Seeking and knocking—always in the name of Christ—are identified in the scriptures as models of inquiry to our Heavenly Father. When Laman and Lemuel could not understand the words of their father, Lehi, Nephi asked them, "Have ye inquired of the Lord?" Their response was, "We have not; for the Lord maketh no such thing known unto us" (1 Ne. 15:8–9). Understanding the things of God and receiving answers to our questions demands that we initiate the process of learning.

Once we have asked, we must ponder and pray fervently to show the Lord how much we want to know all that He can teach us. We must also study—something that makes us responsible and accountable for our growth and learning. Study is one of the ways we prove ourselves in mortality and is a major part of the test. We cannot simply say, "No one told us the answers." God has given us the plan. He has told us what to do in order to return to His presence. We now must daily act and not just be acted upon (see 2 Ne. 2:26) in order to prepare to meet God.

Do we truly hunger and thirst after righteousness that we may be filled with the Holy Ghost? When our mind is right—when our seeking and desires are firm—the next step becomes listening. We must listen to the voice of the Lord through His Spirit, through His word (the scriptures), and through the counsel of His living prophets. Hearkening to the voice and word of the Lord and His prophets is not only our obligation but is an act of reverence.

In order to learn in the temple, we must be alert, observant, perceptive, eager, resolute, watchful, and attentive. The temple is the Lord's school, as it were, and we as His children have been invited into His classroom, where He teaches us and endows us with power. We need to be awake so we can listen carefully to His lessons.

As learners, we will do well to become engrossed in that which we seek to learn. The enemy of learning is a resentful spirit or even just a casual attitude. Sadly, this kind of attitude is found in classrooms and institutions of learning throughout the world. If we do not become devoted to what we are learning, it may become but a passing fancy, inevitably leading us to return to our old way of doing things along the path of least resistance. There is a price to pay for genuine learning, and that price is greater than fifteen minutes in the scriptures or an occasional visit to the temple or an hour here and there doing family history research. True learning requires time and the commitment to do something with what we have learned. Like everything in life, the process of learning is a matter of priority: What matters most? What do we find joy in doing? What brings the greatest fulfillment in our lives? These are important questions we should all address in our desire to learn, grow, and become.

The learning that takes place in the house of the Lord focuses on the knowledge of eternal life—of being empowered by the Holy Spirit. It is about understanding the ordinances and covenants the Lord Himself ordained so we can be happy and find joy both here and in the hereafter. That joy is something that occurs over time as we strive to learn and attain knowledge; we must be patient with ourselves as we repeatedly and faithfully attend and worship in the temple.

With time, we will be given different opportunities to learn. As I was once participating in a live endowment session, I learned a most transcending truth when one of the officiators emphasized a certain word. Just the way he said it made all the difference, and I knew what I hadn't known before, as if by revelation. I had heard those words hundreds and hundreds of times before, but this time the truth of the doctrine was made manifest. My own preparation helped; I wanted to know more, and I was ready to learn. The Spirit then assisted the presenter and made the difference.

The experience of Adam and Eve gives us insight into the process of learning in the temple. After being shut out of the Lord's presence, Adam and Eve called upon the name of the Lord, and the voice of the Lord spoke to them:

> And he gave unto them commandments, that they should worship the Lord their God, and should offer the firstlings of their flocks, for an offering unto the Lord. And Adam was obedient unto the commandments of the Lord.
>
> And after many days an angel of the Lord appeared unto Adam, saying: Why dost thou offer sacrifices unto the Lord? And Adam said unto him: I know not, save the Lord commanded me.
>
> And then the angel spake, saying: This thing is a similitude of the sacrifice of the Only Begotten of the Father, which is full of grace and truth.
>
> Wherefore, thou shalt do all that thou doest in the name of the Son, and thou shalt repent and call upon God in the name of the Son forevermore. (Moses 5:5–8)

Although Adam and Eve had been worshipping the Lord by offering sacrifices on an altar, Adam did not know why the Lord had so commanded him. After "many days"—we do not know how long—an angelic visitor came and revealed to Adam that the sacrifice was in similitude of the Only Begotten of the Father. Further light and knowledge came to Adam with the injunction, "Thou shalt repent and call upon God in the name of His Son forevermore."

Like Adam, we are to be patient and steadfast in our temple worship if we want learn the supernal truths in the house of the Lord. If we listen well and ask the right questions, we prepare ourselves to learn by the Spirit through diligent study and by increasing our faith. "Seek ye diligently," the Lord counseled, "and teach one another words of wisdom" (D&C 109:7). In the end, we must recognize that true learning always applies to day-to-day living and should help us direct tenderness and love toward others.

Learning by Study

The Lord's words in D&C 109:7 include an important injunction: "Yea, seek ye out of the best books words of wisdom, seek learning even by study and also by faith." We should *especially* study the gospel. Look at what the Lord taught us about that through the prophet Nephi: "Angels speak by the power of the Holy Ghost; wherefore, they speak the words of Christ. Wherefore, I said unto you, feast upon the words of Christ; for behold, the words of Christ will tell you all things what ye should do" (2 Ne. 32:3).

Here we learn we are not just to study but to *feast. Feasting* is more than reading and searching; it connotes taking the word of God into our very being. We digest it and make it part of our very soul. The word lives within us. But it cannot be just an occasional feast; like vitamins, it must be continually ingested to be effective in our lives. As we treasure up the word of God, we must continually *live by* the word of God.

Nephi goes on to say that if we don't understand something, it is because *we don't ask*. And when we don't ask to know, we remain in darkness: "Wherefore, now after I have spoken these words, if ye cannot understand them it will be because ye ask not, neither do ye knock; wherefore, ye are not brought into the light, but must perish in the dark" (2 Ne. 32:4). In our study, we must always be searching, seeking, and asking to understand, else our study will be in vain—"ever learning, and never able to come to the knowledge of the truth" (2 Tim. 3:7).

Study cannot be a passive or casual experience. True study requires deep concentration and the application of all our faculties. Think back to a time when you studied to do well on a major exam, to pass the national boards, to recertify yourself in your trade or profession, or to get into graduate or professional school. I remember most vividly taking the national dental boards. I studied intently for weeks—for hundreds of hours—all the while praying constantly for the gift of remembrance. Maybe you've had a similar experience. Now the searching question: have we ever studied that hard or that long of our own free will to understand the scriptures, the mysteries of God, and the doctrines of the temple? We understand the importance of such study by the sheer number of times the Lord and His prophets remind us to look to the scriptures that we "might be remembered and nourished by the good word of God, to keep [us] in the right way" (Moro. 6:4), but we must actually do it.

While I confess that I have not always studied the gospel with such focus, I now understand the blessings of studying it intensely. From this type of study, I have come to know the things of God. It is with deliberate intent, with a meditating and pondering heart, and with reverence for the word of God that I find joy in the journey of coming to a greater knowledge of the truth. I feel a rejuvenating, joyful excitement about my greater understanding of the word of God!

Learning by Faith

We must partner the learning that takes place in the house of the Lord and within the pages of the scriptures with the power of faith. With faith, we gain knowledge in the Spirit of truth, which is of God, to come to know "things as they are, and as they were, and as they are to come," that we may receive "a fulness of truth"; as we keep the commandments, we receive "truth and light until [we are] glorified in truth and [know] . . . all things" (D&C 93:24–28). Such a promise makes learning these truths exciting and fulfilling.

When we as Saints learn by faith and the Spirit, we become truly wise. Those who suffer from pride miss out on the blessings of learning by faith because they think they already know it all. Remember the counsel of Jacob: "O that cunning plan of the evil one! O the vainness, and the frailties, and the foolishness of men! When they are learned they think they are wise, and they hearken not unto the counsel of God, for they set it aside, supposing they know of themselves, wherefore, their wisdom is foolishness and it profiteth them not. And they shall perish. But to be learned is good if they hearken unto the counsels of God" (2 Ne. 9:28–29).

We have examples of those who learned by faith. Father Adam learned by faithful obedience (see Moses 5:5–9). The Prophet Joseph learned by faithful searching about God the Father and our Savior Jesus Christ. In fact, it is through the Prophet Joseph that we know there are several degrees of exercising faith, as he taught in the School of the Prophets. I would describe those degrees as follows:

Faith begins to grow when it is embodied in hope and belief: "If ye have faith ye hope for things which are not seen, which are true" (Alma 32:21). Hope and belief bring true perspective to life.

Faith is the moving cause of all action. It motivates us to act. James described faith in these words: "Even so faith, if it hath not works, is dead being alone. . . . I will shew thee my faith by my works" (James

2:17–18). Works, stimulated by faith and by the grace of God, lead to exaltation after all we can do.

Within faith lies the power to do a multiplicity of things, as Moroni recounts in his enlightening review of the potential of faith (see Ether 12). Jesus's Apostles asked Him, "Lord, Increase our faith" (Luke 17:5), which prompted the Lord to liken faith to the grain of a mustard seed. Nephi taught that it was faith in Jesus Christ that enabled his father, Lehi, to speak by the power of the Holy Ghost (see 1 Ne. 10:17). Faith in Jesus Christ leads us to perfection in Him (see Moro. 10:32–33). Faith surely is the power of the priesthood and the foundation of all righteousness (see D&C 121:36).

In sum, we learn by acting in faith upon a truth and then by coming to know that something is true because we have lived the doctrine: "If any man will do his [the Lord's] will, he shall know of the doctrine, whether it be of God, or whether I speak of myself" (John 7:17). As we bring hearts filled with faith to the house of the Lord, we will learn by symbols and by repetition of spoken words. The meaning of the symbols and words will be revealed to us because our minds and hearts will be ready to be taught by the power of the Holy Ghost.

Revelation in the House of the Lord

Revelation comes by the power of the Holy Ghost, enabling us to understand the mysteries of godliness. We read of this process, "If thou shalt ask, thou shalt receive revelation upon revelation, knowledge upon knowledge, that thou mayest know the mysteries and peaceable things—that which bringeth joy, that which bringeth life eternal" (D&C 42:61). This blessing, like all blessings, is a gift from God. So is the personal revelation for our individual needs and concerns, which we also receive in the Lord's holy house. Elder John A. Widtsoe reminds us, "The temple is a place of revelation. The Lord may here give revelation, and every person may receive revelation to assist him in life. All knowledge, all help come from the Lord, directly or indirectly" ("Looking Toward the Temple," *Ensign*, Jan. 1972, 56).

Think about the experiences you have previously had in the temple or in studying the doctrines of the temple. Have you sincerely sought to understand and appreciate the symbolism and doctrines being taught? Have you fervently desired to know the truths available in the temple, or have you merely *attended* the temple? Have you sought revelation? Have you felt God's love as it is expressed in the temple? Revelation is the key to that kind of understanding.

We are the literal, divine children of God, and everything He does is for our happiness. God wants us to receive light and truth by the power of the Holy Ghost—revelation that endows us with gratitude, the very catalyst that draws us to our Savior. Have we felt that power and that testimony? Have we understood that concept? Have we applied that magnificent knowledge? As we continue to worship in the temple—and worship with those questions in mind—knowledge and testimony will come.

As we seek revelation, we will begin to understand the symbols as they relate to us and as the endowment portrays them. We will begin to discern which things in the endowment ceremony are figurative and which are literal. We will begin to draw more of the endowment into our individual beings. We will begin to truly receive the Savior and His doctrines. We will gain pure knowledge and power.

These concepts and questions will help us prepare our minds and senses so we will have temple eyes, ears, hearts, and souls—all necessary if we are to understand and appreciate the sacred experience of the endowment. Remember that we are not expected to grasp everything at once. The learning process takes time. It takes returning again and again to understand the knowledge that begins to distill in our hearts and souls.

When I first began attending the temple, it was difficult for me to understand; I was young, and without the benefit of a temple preparation course, I brought very limited understanding with me. It seemed there was so much to grasp! But I learned what we all must learn: time is our ally. Each time we attend the temple—especially as we witness sealing ceremonies—we learn a little more; each time we study the scriptures, we comprehend a little better. The key is to press forward, diligently seeking to know the things of God.

As I reflect on my earlier temple experiences, I realize I could have learned so much more that would have enriched my life. I have now redoubled my efforts—make that *quadrupled* my efforts!—knowing that "if a person gains more knowledge and intelligence in this life through his diligence and obedience than another, he will have so much the advantage in the world to come" (D&C 130:19). Indeed, this life is about life eternal.

Some basic truths will help prepare us for learning in the temple. All phases of the temple experience—from baptism to the initiatory to the endowment ceremony and to sealings—are portrayed in rich symbolic language that encourages deep thought and evokes corresponding questions. Through those corresponding questions, the eternal truths of the temple may be revealed to us. The process is not easy, but it is necessary, and all who diligently seek to know and understand will receive the richness of the temple experience.

Elder Widtsoe described this rich, symbolic drama as follows:

> The endowment given to members of the Church in the temples falls into several divisions. First, there is a course of instruction relative to man's eternal journey from the dim beginning towards his possible glorious destiny. Then, conditions are set up by which that endless journey may be upward in direction. Those who receive this information covenant to obey the laws of eternal progress, and thereby give life to the knowledge received. Finally, it is made clear that a man must sometime give an account of his deeds, and prove the possession of divine knowledge and religious works. It is a very beautiful, logical and inspiring series of ceremonies.
>
> . . . To make the vast elements of the endowment clear and impressive to all who partake of it, every educational device is employed. Appeal is made to every faculty of man, to eye and ear, so that the meaning of the Gospel may be clear from beginning to end. The essence of fundamental truth is not known to man, nor indeed can be. Things are known only so far as our senses permit. All knowledge is in reality known through symbols. Letters on a printed page are but symbols of mighty thoughts, easily transferred from mind to mind by these symbols. Clearly, the eternal truths encompassing all that man is or may be, cannot be expressed literally, nor does the temple ritual do this. On the contrary, the beautiful temple service is one of mighty symbolism. By the use of symbols of speech, action, color and form, the great truths connected with the story of man are made evident to the mind. (*A Rational Theology*, 125–126)

Understanding the Endowment

The endowment is a pattern that helps us better understand the plan of exaltation and those things we need to do to return to our Father's presence, which is our purpose on Earth: "For behold, this life is the time for men to prepare to meet God; yea, behold the day of this life is the day for men to perform their labors" (Alma 34:32). We are the ones who individually receive the ordinances and enter into the covenants in the temple. And in receiving, we accept and hopefully internalize the ordinances and covenants so they can become part of our very souls.

We learn many things in the temple endowment. Elder James E. Faust taught, "In the temples of the Lord, we learn obedience. We learn sacrifice. We make the vows of chastity and have our lives consecrated to holy purposes. It is possible for us to be purged and purified and to have our sins washed away so that we may come before the Lord as clean, white, and spotless as the newly fallen snow" ("'Who Shall Ascend into the Hill of the Lord?'" *Ensign*, Aug. 2001, 3).

The endowment ceremony will likely be a unique experience for each who attends the temple for the first time—largely because we don't give a lot of detail about the ceremony beforehand. What happens within the temple should be discussed reverently and with care; we covenant never to reveal certain aspects of the temple ceremony itself or to speak of them anywhere except inside the temple.

As explained, "Out of respect for its sacredness, members of the Church who have attended the temple are asked not to talk outside the temple about the details of the temple ceremony. However, the promises you as a member are asked to make will not surprise you. They are consistent with teachings you have already received, including obedience, sacrifice, order, love, chastity, and consecration" ("Questions and Answers," *New Era*, Jan. 1994, 17).

The central features of the endowment are the laws, ordinances, and covenants we make, which we honor by obedience. According to the Lord, learning obedience is the principal test of life (see Abr. 3:25). It is through obedience that we become the sons and daughters of a merciful God. In this regard, President James E. Faust counseled, "The price of discipleship is obedience" ("The Price of Discipleship," *Ensign*, April 1999). In fact, obedience is the first law of heaven; all blessings are predicated on this law (see D&C 130:20–21). One of the great blessings of keeping the commandments is that the Spirit attends us when we are obedient, as we learn in the sacramental prayers. On the other hand, when we disobey, we lose the blessing of the Spirit in our lives, as the Lamanites and Nephites did in the final battles in the Book of Mormon (see Morm. 1:13–14). When we gain mastery over our conduct through obedience, our spiritual nature desires that which is good, and we align ourselves in a Christlike manner.

Covenants enhance our learning and growth through the principle of commitment, which leads to further obedience. Covenants empower the learning process, as the scriptures abundantly attest. The sons of Helaman, for example, were full of faith and were exactly obedient, something that was a shield to them (see Alma 53–57).

We will all have moments when we are not at our best—when we fall short of exact, immediate, and courageous obedience. After all we are able to do, the Atonement makes up for our weakness (see 2 Ne. 25:23). Adam and Eve taught their children the plan of redemption, but then Satan came among them, commanding them "to believe it not," and some of them "believed it not, and they loved Satan more than God." The result was that they became carnal, sensual, and devilish (see Moses 5:11–13). They became by choice—and hence by nature—willfully disobedient, and they suffered the consequences. How deeply do we love God? Deeply enough that we will forsake mammon and be obedient to the laws of God? The blessing of obedience is righteousness, which leads us to a state of happiness, the ultimate desire of our hearts.

Prior to the Atonement of our Savior, the children of God offered blood sacrifices as a symbol of their obedience to covenants made with God. Such sacrifices served as both a similitude of the Savior's Atonement and an offering of thanksgiving (see Moses 5:5–7). Following the Atonement, the Savior gave a new commandment; as a result, we now offer a different kind of sacrifice: a broken heart and a contrite spirit (see 3 Ne. 9:20), which means we offer our very self—our will and our choices—to the will of God.

Through the spirit of sacrifice, we enter a condition of profound change. We are now in a state of humility: we depend on God; we are easily entreated; we have no pride or ego to uphold; we are willing to learn and to change. In short, we fully accept the Lord's magnificent, infinite, and eternal Atonement. The law of sacrifice requires that we, as disciples of Jesus Christ, give all that we have—our time, our talents, and all that we possess—in order to build up the kingdom of God and to gain exaltation: "For if ye will not abide in my covenant, ye are not worthy of me" (D&C 98:15).

Elder Bruce R. McConkie taught,

> That law by obedience to which men gain an inheritance in the kingdom of God in eternity is called celestial law. It is the law of the gospel, the law of Christ, and it qualifies men for admission to the celestial kingdom because in and through it men are "sanctified by the reception of the Holy Ghost," thus becoming clean, pure, and spotless. (3 Nephi 27:19–21.)
>
> "And they who are not sanctified through the law which I have given unto you, even the law of Christ," the Lord says, "must inherit another kingdom, even that of a terrestrial kingdom, or that of a telestial kingdom. For he who is not able to abide the law of a celestial kingdom cannot abide a celestial glory." (D&C 88:21–22)
>
> Those who have the companionship of the Holy Ghost and are guided thereby in their lives are "able to abide the law of a celestial kingdom," including the law of consecration or anything else the Lord might ask of them. They are the ones who—"united according to the union required by the law of the celestial kingdom" (D&C 105:1–5)—will build up Zion in the last days. (*Mormon Doctrine,* 117)

It is critical to recognize that if we break these covenants or fail to live up to the law of sacrifice, we become subject to the devil. In a pure, chaste, and virtuous life, on the other hand, we are protected by the Lord. The Prophet Joseph reminded us, "The devil has no power over us only as we permit him. The moment we revolt at anything which comes from God, the devil takes power" (*TPJS*, 181).

The Lord has asked His people to consecrate their lives to learning and to building up the kingdom of God. When we so consecrate our lives, we dedicate and set apart our time, talents, and material goods. Consecration is closely related to the depth of our conversion to the Savior and our willingness to gain knowledge to further our effectiveness in carrying out the Lord's plan. Through consecration, we truly sacrifice all things for the Lord. We begin the process of purification in our own lives, and in turn, we become better able to bless our brothers and sisters so they too can enjoy eternal life. Consecration is an attitude as well as an observable act of goodness. It is truly the building up of the kingdom of God.

President Ezra Taft Benson taught the importance of exactness in keeping these covenants and laws:

> We covenant to live the law of consecration. This law is that we consecrate our time, talents, strength, property, and money for the upbuilding of the kingdom of God on this earth and the establishment of Zion.
>
> Until one abides by the laws of obedience, sacrifice, the gospel, and chastity, he cannot abide the law of consecration, which is the law pertaining to the celestial kingdom. (*TETB*, 121)

In the end, it does not matter how much time, money, and other possessions we give—it matters *how* we give them. If our hearts are truly set on building up the kingdom of God, even our widow's mite can be a great offering.

The Price of Discipleship—Living a Christlike Life

We can learn much from all that is taught and covenanted in the temple. The meaning and purpose of those ordinances and covenants will teach us everything we need to know to walk back into the presence of God. Our covenants are given to help us see the goodness of God and the presence of our Savior in and through all things; we are able to gain an endless amount of knowledge from Them. Do we understand the things we should do because of the promises we have made? Do we have a plan to maintain a level of holiness by keeping the covenants when we return to our homes? Do we recognize the power of gratitude?

All of us as children of God are trying to be better, to become more holy and sanctified. Our learning curve is a long and often steep one. Let us study the scriptures with temple eyes and hearts, an experience that will enhance our temple worship and help us keep our covenants. Let us make a time and find a place and a way that will enable us to prepare diligently to learn and understand the things we need to know as we worship our God in His holy house. As we do, we will begin to see His glory and feel His presence there.

CHAPTER 9

Understanding Symbolism in the House of the Lord

IT IS IN TEMPLES THAT GOD most fully manifests Himself to mortals on Earth; we go there to interact with Him in a special way. The holiest places on Earth, temples are where the Lord comes to dwell upon the Earth (see D&C 97:15; 124:27). And it is in the temples that the Lord uniquely blesses us. He said, "I gave unto you a commandment that you should build a house, in the which house I design to endow those whom I have chosen with power from on high" (D&C 95:8).

Our special communication with God in the temple is marked by the extensive use of *symbols*. Symbols can be words, objects, gestures, positions, dramatic presentations, or other material resources—such as water, oil, clothing, altars, and veils—that have meanings in addition to or other than their literal meaning. In the temple, these symbolic meanings represent different manifestations of the presence and mission of the Lord. That is why the temple is known as "the house of the Lord."

The scriptures teach us that symbols in the temple represent the teachings and mission of our Lord and Savior Jesus Christ; they stand for or suggest His doctrines, principles, ordinances, covenants, and commandments. To begin to understand the symbolism of the temple, then, we must first seek to understand the doctrines of the temple. And as we begin to understand the symbols in the temple, we need to remember that each symbol in the temple may have a number of meanings or levels. For example, if we consider all of the Savior's titles throughout scripture (look under "Christ, names of" in the Bible Dictionary), we see an example of the great power and depth of symbolism. Each title represents some aspect of His mission of redemption.

Why are there so many symbols in the temple? Because symbols have a special ability to teach deep and often hidden meanings that arouse our thoughts and motivate our actions. According to Hugh Nibley, who dedicated much of his lifelong scholarship to the study of the temple, "[Symbols] direct, concentrate, discipline, and inform . . . thought. To be effective, thought must be so motivated and directed" (*Temple and Cosmos*, 14). Symbolism brings rich meaning and a greater depth of understanding to the doctrines we are taught and the covenants we enter into in the temple. When we more fully understand the symbols of the temple, gratitude fills our hearts and souls, and the love of God begins to consume our very beings, leading to an overwhelming desire to do good.

The scriptures themselves are full of symbolic words and other figurative representations, and there is symbolism in all of the ordinances of the gospel. For example, every Sunday we partake of the sacrament, bread and water that are symbolic emblems of the Lord's broken flesh and spilt blood that are part of His infinite Atonement. When we are buried in the waters of baptism, we are symbolically buried in death; when we rise out of the water, we are symbolically resurrected, as the Apostle Paul taught: "Therefore we are buried with him by baptism into death: that like as Christ was raised up from the dead by the glory of the Father, even so we should also walk in newness of life" (Rom. 6:4).

Consider these additional meanings in the ordinance of baptism, which introduces us into the Lord's Church:

In baptism, we symbolically take upon us the name and mission of Christ (see Gal. 3:27).

Because we are immersed in water, baptism symbolizes the washing away and the remission of sins (see Acts 22:16; D&C 19:31).

Through taking Christ's name upon us, we symbolize through baptism that we have become sons and daughters of Christ (see Mosiah 5:7).

Our obedience to submit to the ordinance of baptism symbolizes our willingness to be humbly obedient to the commands of God (see Matt 3:15–16; 3 Ne. 11:34–35).

Jesus explained to His chosen disciples that He used *parables*—short symbolic stories—"because it is given unto you to know the mysteries of the kingdom of heaven, but to them [the multitudes] it is not given" (Matt 13:11). In other words, the Savior often cloaked His meaning in such stories so only a certain number of His followers or even some of His enemies would grasp their symbolic meaning. This is another reason symbolism is used in so much of the temple and the scriptures; the Lord wants only those who are prepared to unlock His truths.

In gathering his people and urging them to renew their covenants, King Benjamin used the key words of symbolism: "And many *signs*, and *wonders*, and *types*, and *shadows* showed he unto [the Israelites], concerning [the Lord's] coming" (Mosiah 3:15). From the scriptures, we learn that the essence of the law of Moses and *all* things from the beginning *typify*—that is, symbolize or foreshadow—and bear record of the advent of the Lord and Savior Jesus Christ. Not only was this the way the Lord taught ancient Israel and the Nephites, but it is also the way He teaches us today, since the Book of Mormon was directed specifically at us, the latter-day house of Israel.

Indeed, as the Book of Mormon prophet Jacob taught, "All things which have been given of God from the beginning of the world, unto man, are the typifying of him" (2 Ne. 11:4)—that is, all things *prefigure* or *represent* Jesus Christ and His atoning sacrifice.

A list of symbolic language in the gospel and in the temple could almost be endless. My purpose here is not to list or explain every symbol—not even the ones in the temple. Part of the knowledge and power that comes from searching out meanings and understanding symbols comes from the process of personally learning by oneself. Rather, my purpose here is only to show that the gospel is rich in symbolism and that we need to embrace it rather than shy away from it—especially as it pertains to worship in the temple.

Like many, I once shied away from the symbolism of the gospel and the temple; I did not study the symbols as I should have, and I didn't understand their significance and potential power. In my later years, especially as a temple worker, I am finding great joy in the study of gospel symbolism and its application to my life. I've found that it's not just a matter of simply asking for the meaning of a symbol; we are to follow the counsel of the Lord when He said, "Behold, you have not understood; you have supposed that I would give it unto you, when you took no thought save it was to ask me. But, behold, I say unto you, that you must study it out in your mind; then you must ask me if it be right, and if it is right I will cause that your bosom shall burn within you; therefore, you shall feel that it is right" (D&C 9:7–8). In addition to asking, we must study, ponder, and allow the Spirit to accompany us.

My friend and former colleague Joseph Fielding McConkie commented further on the challenge of symbolic language: "The difficulties of interpretation and the barriers posed by scriptural language have discouraged some Saints from feasting upon the inspired word [or participating in the ordinances of the temple]. But those hungering for this greater substance have turned to the scriptures and commenced the struggle to learn the language of revelation. They have discovered that to be fluent in the language of the Spirit one must be fluent in the language of symbolism" (*Gospel Symbolism*, ix).

Maybe you've been counseled not to worry about symbolism. That might be wise counsel for someone in the early stages—someone newly converted or reconverted to basic gospel principles. But that can't be a permanent state of mind. We are urged to learn line upon line; as we make progress in the gospel, we recognize that an understanding of even common and basic symbols can lead to a greater desire—a deeper commitment—to keep the commandments. There is symbolism in every aspect of the gospel, and the Holy Ghost is ever ready to reveal the truth of all things as we prepare ourselves diligently to understand symbolism. As Moroni wrote, "And by the power of the Holy Ghost ye may know the truth of all things" (Moro. 10:5).

A prayerful study of symbolism in the gospel enables us to understand and better appreciate the doctrines, principles, commandments, ordinances, and covenants of the gospel more completely. When we do, we are filled with gratitude, which is the ultimate catalyst for personal change. As our understanding of the gospel and the ordinances of the temple matures, we want to know even more. We become more like the Savior, and we desire more strongly to please God. That has been for me a delicious and deeply satisfying spiritual experience. My hope is that you will have the same kind of experience.

For example, there are two words that, when understood, will give us greater understanding of our lives and the endowment. Those words are *garment* or *garments* and *naked* or *nakedness.*

Adam and Eve, having transgressed by partaking of the forbidden fruit, knew they were now "naked" (see Moses 4:13, 16–17), so the Lord made a covering for them: "Unto Adam, and also unto his wife, did I, the Lord God, make coats of skins, and clothed them" (Moses 4:27). Thus "nakedness," as used figuratively in the scriptures, often seems to indicate a fallen, sinful, or guilt-ridden state away from the presence of God: "For behold, when ye [those who have transgressed and not repented] shall be brought to see your nakedness before God, and also the glory of God, and the holiness of Jesus Christ, it will kindle a flame of unquenchable fire upon you" (Morm. 9:5).

The prophet Jacob indicates that two groups are involved in this concept: the "naked" and the "clothed." At the day of judgment, not only will we "have a perfect knowledge of all our guilt, and our uncleanness, and our nakedness," but the righteous shall have a perfect knowledge of their enjoyment, and their righteousness, "*being clothed with purity*, yea, even *with the robe of righteousness*" (2 Ne. 9:14).

The Apostle John also wrote of clothes covering our nakedness: "I counsel thee to buy of me gold tried in the fire, that thou mayest be rich; and white raiment, that thou mayest be clothed, and that the shame of thy nakedness do not appear; and anoint thine eyes with eyesalve, that thou mayest see" (Rev. 3:18). What does it mean to wear rich raiment or be clothed in the robes of righteousness? Isaiah teaches us, "I will greatly rejoice in the Lord, my soul shall be joyful in my God; for he hath clothed me with the garments of salvation, he hath covered me with the robe of righteousness, as a bridegroom decketh himself with ornaments, and as a bride adorneth herself with her jewels" (Isa. 61:10).

Isaiah rejoiced, for he had been clothed in "the garments of salvation," a symbol of eternal life. The "robes of righteousness" are a direct reference to the holy garment. Nephi also speaks of being encircled by the Lord's robe of righteousness: "O Lord, wilt thou encircle me around in the robe of thy righteousness! O Lord, wilt thou make a way for mine escape before mine enemies! Wilt thou make my path straight before me! Wilt thou not place a stumbling block in my way—but that thou wouldst clear my way before me, and hedge not up my way, but the ways of mine enemy" (2 Ne. 4:33).

We read that Nephi, encircled within the robe of the Lord's righteousness, may now escape from his enemies (and anything associated with evil). Elder Carlos E. Asay associated the robe of righteousness with the armor of God: "We must put on the armor of God spoken of by the Apostle Paul and reiterated in a modern revelation (see D&C 27:15–18). We must also 'put on the armor of righteousness' (2 Ne. 1:23) symbolized by the temple garment. Otherwise, we may lose the war and perish." Elder Asay continued:

> And in a letter to priesthood leaders dated 10 October 1988, the First Presidency made the following important statements regarding how the garment should be worn: "Church members who have been clothed with the garment in

> the temple have made a covenant to wear it throughout their lives. This has been interpreted to mean that it is worn as underclothing both day and night. This sacred covenant is between the member and the Lord. Members should seek the guidance of the Holy Spirit to answer for themselves any personal questions about the wearing of the garment. . . . The promise of protection and blessings is conditioned upon worthiness and faithfulness in keeping the covenant." ("The Temple Garment: An Outward Expression of an Inward Commitment," *Ensign*, Aug. 1997, 19)

Elder J. Richard Clark spoke of the garment as a protection against temptation and evil: "Sacred temple clothing is a shield and protection against Satan. As you receive your endowments in the temple, you receive the privilege of wearing the sacred temple clothing and the garments of the holy priesthood. The garments are a tangible reminder of your covenants with God. . . . The temple garment reminds us that virtue sets us apart from the world and, in a special way, makes us one with God" ("The Temple—What It Means to You," *New Era*, Apr. 1993, 4).

The garments are also associated with being prepared to greet the Bridegroom. In the parable of the bridegroom, some invited guests were rejected because they were not wearing the wedding garment (see Matt. 22:11–13). Others were welcomed: "Let us be glad and rejoice, and give honour to him: for the marriage of the Lamb is come, and his wife hath made herself ready. And to her was granted that she should be arrayed in fine linen, clean and white: for the fine linen is the righteousness of saints" (Rev. 19:7–8).

We understand from scripture that the garment must be made clean through the blood of the Lamb—that is to say, it symbolizes our need to repent and apply the enabling power of the Atonement to our lives. As we know, it is only by grace—after all we can do—that we may enter into the presence of the Father (see Rev. 7:14; 1 Ne. 12:11; Alma 13:11; 34:36; Morm. 9:6; Ether 13:10–11).

Speaking to the Saints, the Prophet Joseph Smith prayed at the dedication of the Kirtland Temple "that our garments may be pure, that we may be clothed upon with robes of righteousness, with palms in our hands, and crowns of glory upon our heads, and reap eternal joy for all our sufferings" (D&C 109:76.)

Through studying the symbolism and scriptures related to the garment, we come to see that the garment of the holy priesthood symbolizes both coats of skin and robes of righteousness. They are a protection against temptation and evil and a reminder of the covenants we make in the temple. Our garments may be cleansed in the Lord's blood, even the blood of the Lamb, through the enabling power of the Atonement, and we are to wear them when we meet the Lord. They cover our nakedness—our sins and our guilt—and they are an armor or righteousness that protects us in our hour of need, as they did Nephi. Above and beyond these things, there is yet more to understand and appreciate concerning *naked* and *garments* that personal study and revelation can reveal to us.

Seeking to Understand the Temple Symbols

How can we come to an understanding of the symbols of the temple that are so central to our salvation? Consider the following suggestions:

Always be worthy to worship in the house of the Lord.

Pay close attention to the symbolism of all of the words and actions that take place in the temple, as well as the context in which they are being presented. Seek with temple eyes, ears, and hearts to grasp what is being taught.

Pose questions in your mind and heart that may help you understand what you are being taught in the temple. The Holy Spirit teaches and confirms the sacred meanings of symbols. Light and truth burst into our beings, and by the witness of the Spirit, we see more clearly and fully.

Ponder prayerfully what you see and hear in the temple, for prayer will lead to the revelation that will help you more fully understand the symbols of the gospel ordinances, especially the symbols of the temple. We not only contemplate the meaning of symbols, but we also experience visual impressions that further deepen our understanding. As we learn in the Doctrine and Covenants, "In the *ordinances* [of the greater priesthood] the power of godliness is manifest" (D&C 84:20).

Feast diligently on the scriptures and the words of living prophets that relate to the temple.

Exercise faith in the great doctrine of the redemption of the dead and in the enabling power of the Atonement to redeem all humankind.

Read what General Authorities and other faithful Church writers have said about the temple. (See the Appendix for a list of several books on temples and temple symbolism.)

It can also be helpful to read what scholars of symbolism have learned about the meaning of symbols. In his landmark work on symbolism, *The Lost Language of Symbolism*, Alonzo Gaskill suggests the following to enhance our learning as we study the scriptures. (The italicized portions are used with permission of the author.)

"*Rightly determine which elements of the verse under consideration are meant to be interpreted as symbols.*"

Do the words or the object make common sense? If so, it can be taken literally and be applied to life. If the meaning seems obscured or beyond what we now know, it is more likely highly symbolic—such is what is found throughout the book of Revelation—and will require diligent effort and study over time (see Rev. 12:1–4; 13:1–2). Remember that you can always find additional meanings or explanations from other scriptures (see John 2:19, 21).

"*Look beyond the symbol.*"

Symbols have *denotations* (their literal meaning) and *connotations* (those things our mind associates with the symbol and the meaning the symbol stirs within us). This is exemplified repeatedly in the temple ceremonies. If we are watchful, attentive, and prayerful, we can come to understand the doctrines of the temple.

"*Consider what the scriptures or modern prophets teach regarding the symbol.*"

The symbol may be explained in the same verse or in verses that follow. For example, consider the account of Nephi's brothers: "And they said unto me: What meaneth the rod of iron which our father saw, that led to the tree? And I said unto them that it was the word of God; and whoso would hearken unto the word of God, and would hold fast unto it, they would never perish; neither could the temptations and the fiery darts of the adversary overpower them unto blindness, to lead them away to destruction" (1 Ne. 15:23–24). Likewise, when the Prophet Joseph inquired concerning several scriptures in the book of Revelation, the Lord revealed to him the symbolic meanings (see D&C 77).

"*Let the nature of the symbol help clarify its meaning.*"

As noted earlier, the temple garment covers our nakedness. We can discern more about the meaning of that symbolism by considering the nature of the garment. How does it cover us? What does it represent? As we answer these questions, we come to realize that when we understand a doctrine, we can better understand the symbol that represents it. For example, we understand that the degrees of glory are symbolized by the glories of the sun, the moon, and the stars; the nature of each of these bodies and the degree of light each emits helps us understand more about each degree of glory.

"*Watch for consistency in use of particular symbols.*"

Words and symbols are generally used in consistent ways, though they often represent quite different things. Words like *water*, *serpent*, and *lion* connote different meanings, both good and bad, depending on the context in which those words occur.

"*Study the meaning and origin of the idioms employed.*"

Symbols that are not to be taken literally are called idioms. Exodus 3:8 refers to a land "flowing with milk and honey," which means that the land is fertile. Ezekiel 3:7 speaks of a hard "forehead," which means someone is stubborn.

"*Balance the interpretation of symbols with an overall knowledge of gospel teachings.*"

All interpretations should be in harmony with the doctrines of the gospel and the teachings of the prophets.

"*Use the footnotes, chapter headings, dictionary, and other study aids provided in the standard works of the Church.*"

Throughout the scriptures, footnotes help us understand certain words or phrases. The "Explanation Concerning Abbreviations" on the page facing Genesis 1 in the Bible is also helpful. Footnotes, cross-references, and abbreviations are study aids to searching the scriptures. Chapter headings provide a concise summary for a chapter. Section headings in the Doctrine and Covenants provide background information on the setting for each revelation.

"*Be attentive to linguistic issues.*"

Our scriptures are translations from Hebrew, Greek, and—in the case of the Book of Mormon—"reformed Egyptian" text. As we understand the root meaning of words, we may better understand the English translation. As an example of how important this is, recall that many words used in the Book of Mormon reflect meanings common in the early nineteenth century, when that book of scripture was translated. Dictionaries and lexicons (the vocabulary for a language or branch of knowledge) are of great assistance.

Finally, if you just don't get something, I encourage you to study, ponder, and pray for a better understanding. I would offer one word of caution: In learning to understand symbols, it is wise to stay close to what the Spirit reveals and confirms; what the prophets, ancient and modern, have said; and what careful and reliable students of the scriptures have written. It is unwise to make "private interpretation" of the scriptures (2 Pet. 1:20) or any gospel or temple symbolism.

I relate to what Sister Camilla Kimball said about learning the gospel; her counsel especially applies to learning to interpret symbols: "I've always had an inquiring mind. I'm not satisfied just to accept things. I like to follow through and study things out. I learned early to put aside those gospel questions that I couldn't answer. I had a shelf of things I didn't understand, but as I've grown older and studied and prayed and thought about each problem, one by one I've been able to better understand them."

She then added, "I still have some questions on that shelf, but I've come to understand so many other things in my life that I'm willing to bide my time for the rest of the answers" ("Lady of Constant Learning," *Ensign*, Oct. 1975, 61).

This is good advice. Let us learn what we can, line upon line. In the meantime, let us go about doing good. Those things that are necessary or helpful to our understanding will be revealed to us according to the will of God and our diligence in seeking to understand. Let us always stay on the safe side rather than the extreme. Because symbols can have a multiplicity of meanings, our goal should be neither to limit nor to overstate the meaning of a symbol but simply to better understand it. Then we will have a greater understanding of the gospel and a greater desire to do good.

Chapter 10

Worshipping in the Lord's Holy House—Calling on the Name of the Lord

As we worship in the house of the Lord, we literally *call upon the name of the Lord,* an act that has deep and eternal significance: we come to Him through sacrificial worship. At one time in history, individuals expressed gratitude through animal sacrifice for this opportunity. Today we offer a living sacrifice, as Paul explained: "I beseech you therefore, brethren, by the mercies of a living God, that ye present your bodies a living sacrifice, holy, acceptable unto God, which is your reasonable service" (Rom. 12:1). In receiving the ordinances and covenants that prepare us to enter our Father's presence, we offer the sacrifice of a broken heart and contrite spirit, and we perform the labor of vicarious service to redeem the dead.

In urging us to attend the temple, our latter-day prophets have sought to do the same thing Moses tried to do: "Now this Moses plainly taught to the children of Israel in the wilderness, and sought diligently to sanctify his people that they might behold the face of God" (D&C 84:23). We also understand, through the words of modern prophets, that in our day we are also a "gathered" people, according to the parable of the wheat and the tares, "that the wheat may be secured in the garners [the temples] to possess eternal life, and be crowned with celestial glory, when I shall come in the kingdom of my Father to reward every man according as his work shall be" (D&C 101:65). This is the exhortation given to the priesthood leaders of the Church to ensure that all might be taught and blessed according to the greater priesthood: "*Emphasize the place of the higher priesthood in helping individuals and families qualify for exaltation* (see D&C 84:19–22)" (*Handbook 2: Administering the Church,* 3.4).

Worshipping in the house of the Lord is an honor and privilege. That's something we need to fully understand if we want to fully harness the blessings of the temple for ourselves and others—to reccive sacred ordinances and covenants and to serve as saviors on Mount Zion by redeeming the dead. This is no small matter but, rather, is one of the most supernal, with eternal significance.

Calling upon the Name of the Lord as a Sacrifice of Thanksgiving

A series of scriptures beautifully captures the sacrifice and worship related to the temple and to calling upon the name of the Lord. As we feast on those scriptures, we'll see that gratitude is key to expressing and receiving the blessings of God: "What shall I render unto the Lord for all his benefits toward me? I will take the cup of salvation, and call upon the name of the Lord. . . . I will offer to thee the sacrifice of thanksgiving, and will call upon the name of the Lord" (Ps. 116:12–13, 17).

The Psalmist poses the question of how to thank the Lord for all of His blessings. The words *cup of salvation* and *call upon the name of the Lord* refer to the infinite sacrifice and Atonement and the offering of a sacrifice on an altar, all of which point to the Lord Jesus Christ. We offer a broken heart and contrite spirit when we receive our own temple blessings; we also offer ourselves as vicarious servants for those who have passed to the other side of the veil. This offering of sacrifice is an expression of thanksgiving. "Calling upon the name of the Lord" connotes an offering at an altar with thanksgiving to the Lord through sacrificial worship. This form of symbolic worship in Old Testament times is now performed through consecrated service and worship in the temple.

Failure to Call upon the Name of the Lord

In contrast, the idea of *not* calling upon the name of the Lord means much more than simply failing to say our prayers. It reflects not offering our true worship of calling upon the name of the Lord in thanksgiving by offering an acceptable sacrifice. Consider what happened to the brother of Jared:

> And it came to pass at the end of four years that the Lord came again unto the brother of Jared, and stood in a cloud and talked with him. And for the space of three hours did the Lord talk with the brother of Jared, and chastened him because *he remembered not to call upon the name of the Lord.*
>
> And the brother of Jared repented of the evil which he had done, and did call upon the name of the Lord for his brethren who were with him. And the Lord said unto him: I will forgive thee and thy brethren of their sins; but thou

> shalt not sin any more, for ye shall remember that my Spirit will not always strive with man; wherefore, if ye will sin until ye are fully ripe ye shall be cut off from the presence of the Lord. And these are my thoughts upon the land which I shall give you for your inheritance; for it shall be a land choice above all other lands. (Ether 2:14–15)

As we have discussed, before the coming of Christ, the Israelites built altars and called upon the name of Lord, offering thanksgiving through animal sacrifice (see 1 Ne. 2:7; Moses 5:4–8; Abr. 2:17). This form of worship and covenant-making was done at an altar constructed in tabernacles or on mountaintops, both sites being considered holy ground. When we call upon the name of the Lord, we accept the invitation of the Lord to come to His holy house, where we make sacred covenants and receive sacred ordinances at the altar of God. It is in the presence of the Lord and in temples where we are endowed with power and the fulness of the Holy Spirit, being "prepared to obtain every needful thing" (D&C 109:15).

It is difficult to truly comprehend the depth and meaning of the simple phrase *call upon the name of the Lord.* Its sublime importance leads us to the conclusion that the sin of ingratitude could have been the reason the Lord chastised the brother of Jared for not worshipping Him by offering sacrifice. After all, ingratitude is one of the greatest sins we can commit.

If we do not receive the gift God has offered us, we refuse Christ the Lord and His holy priesthood: "Therefore, all those who receive the priesthood, receive this oath and covenant of my Father, which he cannot break, neither can it be moved. But whoso breaketh this covenant after he hath received it, and altogether turneth therefrom, shall not have forgiveness of sins in this world nor in the world to come" (D&C 84:40–41). The Lord has said, "For what doth it profit a man if a gift is bestowed upon him, and he receive not the gift? Behold, he rejoices not in that which is given unto him, neither rejoices in him who is the giver of the gift" (D&C 88:33).

One of the more severe chastisements we read of in the Book of Mormon, as shown above, was given to the brother of Jared. He received it because he did not show gratitude and thanksgiving to the Lord by offering an acceptable sacrifice. The Lord repeatedly admonishes us to confess His hand in all things and to express thanksgiving (see Rom. 1:21; Col. 3:15; D&C 8; 59:21; 78:19).

So what constitutes an expression of gratitude? It involves more than prayer, although prayer is always a part of worship. Here's the key: there can be no true worship or expression of gratitude without sacrifice.

They Began to Call on the Name of the Lord

It is taught in the temple that the doctrine and covenant of sacrifice are part of what enables us to return to the presence of Heavenly Father. In Old Testament times, an animal was brought forth daily as an offering in similitude of the atoning sacrifice of the Messiah.

At one point, Adam's sons were in great need of repentance. When Enos was born to Seth, God revealed Himself to Seth, who offered an acceptable sacrifice. The phrase indicates that men then "began" to call on the name of the Lord (see Gen. 4:26; Moses 6:4), and they were blessed for their efforts.

Calling on the name of the Lord is more than simply offering prayer, though prayer is always a part of worship. There can be no true worship save it involves sacrifice. It is in the temple that the covenant of sacrifice is made part of enabling us to return to the presence of Heavenly Father.

The Lord at a Temple Altar

"And he [Abraham] removed from thence unto a mountain on the east of Beth-el, and pitched his tent, having Beth-el on the west, and Hai on the east: and there he builded an altar unto the Lord, and *called upon the name of the Lord*" (Gen. 12:8). Abraham built an altar and then called *again* upon the name of the Lord (see Abr. 2:20).

An altar has always been closely associated with worshipping God. It is a place where sacred ordinances are performed and covenants are made. Expressed throughout scripture are the acts of building an altar, calling on the name of the Lord, and offering thanksgiving, sin, peace, and other offerings. The first thing the patriarch Isaac did on arriving in Beer-sheba was to follow this pattern: "And he builded an altar there, and *called upon the name of the Lord*, and pitched his tent there: and there Isaac's servants digged a well" (Gen. 26:25).

Call on the Name of the Lord, and They Shall Be Delivered

In our dispensation, as soon as the Saints have gathered, they have begun to build a temple, as exemplified by the Kirtland, Nauvoo, and Salt Lake temples.

"And it shall come to pass, that whosoever shall *call on the name of the Lord* shall be delivered: for in mount Zion and in Jerusalem shall be deliverance, as the Lord hath said, and in the remnant whom the Lord shall call" (Joel 2:32). This verse, quoted to the Prophet Joseph by the angel Moroni, speaks of the last days and the millennial reign. Who will be delivered? Where is deliverance? "For then will I turn to the people a pure language, that *they may all call upon the name of the Lord,* to serve him with one consent" (Zeph. 3:9).

During the millennial reign, endowment and sealing work will bind together the entire family of God, that we might be *one.* For if we are to be God's people, we must knit our hearts together as one: "And if ye are not one ye are not mine" (D&C 38:27).

They Shall Be Saved

We read in Romans, "For whosoever *shall call upon the name of the Lord* shall be saved" (Rom. 10:13). Surely there is more to this verse than an admonition to pray in order to be saved. Total rebirth and cleansing are required to enter the presence of the Lord. Those who receive all the priesthood ordinances and are true and faithful can and will be saved and exalted. Again, this verse connotes the temple and sacrifice. The same words also occur in Acts 2:21.

We also read, "Verily, thus saith the Lord: It shall come to pass that every soul who forsaketh his sins and cometh unto me, *and calleth on my name,* and obeyeth my voice, and keepeth my commandments, shall see my face and know that I am" (D&C 93:1). This all-encompassing verse rings of the total plan of exaltation, the culmination of which is being in the presence of the Lord and knowing Him. These words clearly refer to the temple and its exalting covenants and ordinances as dramatized and symbolized in the endowment (see D&C 84:19–21).

The Lord in Holy Places

When we call on the name of the Lord, we worship in holy places according to the principles of the everlasting gospel: "Behold, it is my will, that *all they who call on my name,* and worship me according to mine everlasting gospel, should gather together, and stand in holy places; And prepare for the revelation which is to come, when the veil of the covering of my temple, in my tabernacle . . . shall be taken off, and all flesh shall see it together" (D&C 101:22–23). These verses speak of going to the temple.

As we read the following verse, we might be led to think of daily prayers, but at the time these words were given, the Nephites were living the law of Moses, a law that *required daily sacrifices*: "And again I say unto you as I have said before, that as ye have come to the knowledge of the glory of God, or if ye have known of his goodness and have tasted of his love, and have received a remission of your sins, which causeth such exceedingly great joy in your souls, even so I would that ye should remember, and always retain in remembrance, the greatness of God, and your own nothingness, and his goodness and long-suffering towards you, unworthy creatures, and humble yourselves even in the depths of humility, *calling on the name of the Lord daily*, and standing steadfastly in the faith of that which is to come, which was spoken by the mouth of the angel" (Mosiah 4:11).

Receiving the Full Mercy of the Atonement

The full mercy of the Atonement is expressed in the covenants and ordinances of the temple, not merely in prayer. It is in the temple that we are cleansed and anointed to become like Christ, endowed with power from on high and sealed for time and eternity, with the promised blessings of eternal lives. "And at some period of time they will be brought to believe in his word, and to know of the incorrectness of the traditions of their fathers; and many of them will be saved, for the Lord will be *merciful unto all who call on his name*" (Alma 9:17).

Note that we humble ourselves by coming to His holy house, where we receive an endowment and are clothed so we can be protected against temptation and evil and so we can receive a fulness of the Spirit, which will help us be "submissive, meek, humble, patient, full of love" (Mosiah 3:19). The Spirit also leads us to always do good, to do justly, and to judge righteously, our minds being enlightened and our souls filled with joy: "But that ye would humble yourselves before the Lord, and *call on his holy name*, and watch and pray continually, that ye may not be tempted above that which ye can bear, and thus be led by the Holy Spirit, becoming humble, meek, submissive, patient, full of love and all long-suffering" (Alma 13:28).

Standing in Holy Places

We read of standing in holy places—or in the temple: "When you, therefore, shall see the abomination of desolation, spoken of by Daniel the prophet, concerning the destruction of Jerusalem, then you shall stand in the holy place; whoso readeth let him understand" (JS—Matt.

1:12–13). "Standing in holy places" refers to the temple, as we likewise read in D&C 101:22: "Behold, it is my will, that all they who call on my name, and worship me according to mine everlasting gospel, should gather together, and stand in holy places." That reference to the temple becomes clear in the verse that follows: "And prepare for the revelation which is to come, when the veil of the covering of my temple, in my tabernacle, which hideth the earth, shall be taken off, and all flesh shall see me together" (D&C 101:23).

In the temple, we learn that "the Lord is merciful unto all who will, in the sincerity of their hearts, *call upon his holy name*. Yea, thus we see that the gate of heaven is open unto all, even to those who will believe on the name of Jesus Christ, who is the Son of God" (Hel. 3:27–28). Verse 28 speaks of the gate of heaven, and the connotation is the house of the Lord (see also Gen. 28:17).

We will "sit at the right hand of God" and "with Abraham, and Isaac, and with Jacob, and with all our holy fathers, to go out no more" (Hel. 3:30). The significance of that is stunning: those who inherit such glory are no longer angels but are gods, "because they have no end" (D&C 132:20), having received the blessing of exaltations and eternal lives.

As we read these scriptures, we truly see why the Lord severely chastised the brother of Jared for failure to offer up his sacrifices, which displeased and offended the Lord. We also better understand why this ritual of calling on the name of the Lord is symbolized in the temple today. We begin to see the sacredness of temple worship and the importance of offering up our sacrifice, thereby receiving our own endowment and giving vicarious service to those who are dead. Implicit in all this is an expression of gratitude, which pleases our Heavenly Father. It is gratitude that draws us to Christ and His infinite Atonement.

Once we understand the significance of temple worship as the Lord explained it to the brother of Jared, we begin to see that temple worship is not a passive activity in the Church. It is a matter of truly worshipping the Lord by calling on His name and assisting in bringing about the immortality and eternal lives of our Father's children.

Chapter 11

A Premise with a Promise—Asking and the Blessings of the Atonement

As we begin the journey to better understand and appreciate the Lord's holy house, we must rely on the Spirit and the word of God to see how the doctrines, covenants, and ordinances of the gospel are connected to the infinite and eternal Atonement of our Savior Jesus Christ. We gain understanding through personal revelation, which we are promised if we will only ask for it. Just as the Prophet Joseph Smith prayed and received a revelation after reading James 1:5, so must we ask! Asking, seeking, and knocking are the gateways to inspiration and revelation. It is not only our responsibility but also our *right* to receive this further light and knowledge—it is a premise with a promise.

As I have studied and prayed over the years, the Lord's promise that I would be given knowledge and light if I simply asked has been fulfilled; I have come to see, feel, and understand that the Lord's holy house is indeed where we receive the saving ordinances that allow us back into the Father's presence. That joyous journey has enabled me to see the true meaning of the oft-quoted scripture, "All things which have been given of God from the beginning of the world, unto man, are the typifying of him [Jesus Christ]" (2 Ne. 11:4). Everything in the great plan of happiness speaks of Christ, the Anointed One, the Redeemer and Savior, for it is only through Him that we can come back into the presence of the Father.

Learning from the endowment is one way we seek knowledge because the endowment prepares us—first symbolically and then literally—to enter into the presence of the Father. If we keep our covenants, the endowment fulfills the Atonement in our lives. The two are inseparably linked: The endowment also expresses and is enabled by the Atonement—both through its symbolism and because it enables us to fully lay hold of the blessings of the Atonement.

President Brigham Young gave an excellent definition of the endowment: "Your endowment is to receive all those ordinances in the House of the Lord, which are necessary for you, after you have departed this life, to enable you to walk back to the presence of the Father" (*DBY*, 416). Brigham Young's definition applies to all the ordinances of the temple, including the initiatory ordinances, the endowment ceremony, and the sealing ordinance.

The Lord's Intercessory Prayer has greater significance when we consider it in light of the Atonement because Christ prayed that God's children might be one with the Father and the Son (see John 17:20–23). As we come to understand the *at-one-ment*, which allows us to become one with God and return to His presence, we come to see why all aspects of the gospel center in our Savior and His Atonement. And as we ask and knock, the promised blessings of the Atonement will flow into our lives. I have often gone to the temple with a prayerful heart, seeking to understand and appreciate some of the doctrines, and to my joy, my prayers were answered. I was immediately filled with gratitude for the goodness of God in making these things known to me. What followed was an overwhelming desire to do good—evidence of the truth that an understanding and appreciation of doctrine results in change.

The more we learn, the more we find that everything in the gospel is an appendage to the Atonement of the Lord Jesus Christ, and knowledge leads to action, which builds on itself until we are changed. The Savior draws us to Him through His infinite and eternal sacrifice: "Even that he layeth down his own life, that he may draw all men unto him" (2 Ne. 26:24). We may not be able to comprehend all aspects of the Atonement, but we can start to grasp the act of sacrifice it entails, and as a result, our souls fill with gratitude. Gratitude then becomes the catalyst that begins a mighty change in our hearts and lives. We desire to please Heavenly Father and begin with diligence to become as the Savior is. We start to acquire His divine nature, as the Apostle Peter explained: "Whereby are given unto us exceeding great and precious promises: that by these ye might be partakers of the divine nature" (2 Pet. 1:4). And we inevitably draw closer to Christ.

Our temple worship teaches that the endowment and entering into covenants with God is the symbolic presentation of how we receive and access the Savior's Atonement in order to return to God's presence. We make sacred covenants through sacred ordinances, which bring the

Atonement more deeply into our lives. We become perfected in and through Jesus Christ and thus become worthy to return to the presence of the Father.

Promised Blessings through the Atonement

The premise to the promise of eternal life occurs in the temple, where we pass through the veil in a symbolic return to the presence of the Father and the Son. Through the covenants and ordinances of the temple, we accept Christ as our Savior and Redeemer and are blessed to be reconciled to one-ness with God the Father and Christ. The Atonement is the enabling power, and the ordinances and covenants of the temple are how we symbolically implement that power. The temple ordinances prepare us to receive the promised blessings of eternal life—God's life, living in a state of never-ending happiness—by honoring our temple covenants.

Oh, the joy of it all! Though I have attended the temple countless times and served within the temple walls for many years, I am still excited to continue learning in the temple as I try to live according to the covenants I have made there. Each day is an adventure, an opportunity to bless someone's life. Each day is a chance to please my Heavenly Father and be more like my Savior when He said, "And he that sent me is with me: the Father hath not left me alone; for I do always those things that please him" (John 8:29).

Let us go forward together on this journey of joy to truly understand the things of God, to serve Him, and to follow our Savior Jesus Christ. Let us remember the premise of asking, seeking, and learning, as well as the promise of blessings, knowledge, and joy. Remember that as you search the scriptures and study the words of the living prophets, you will come to see that the Atonement and endowment are inseparably connected, welded in bringing us back into the presence of God.

Further Study

To better understand the premise of the empowering nature of the Atonement and the endowment given to us in the temple, consider some of the following:

From the scriptures:

- Topical Guide—Jesus Christ, Atonement through
- Topical Guide—Reconciliation, Reconcile
- Topical Guide—Redemption
- Topical Guide—Endowment, Endow
- 2 Ne. 9; Alma 34

From the prophets, General Authorities, and officers of the Church:

- Elder Russell M. Nelson, "The Atonement," *Ensign*, Nov. 1996.
- Elder Jeffrey R. Holland, "The Atonement of Jesus Christ," *Ensign*, March 2008.
- Wolfgang H. Paul, "Gratitude for the Atonement," *Ensign*, June 2007.
- President Boyd K. Packer, "Atonement, Agency, Accountability," *Ensign*, May 1988.
- Elder M. Russell Ballard, "The Atonement and the Value of One Soul," *Ensign*, May 2004.
- Elder Lynn A. Mickelsen, "The Atonement, Repentance, and Dirty Linen," *Ensign*, Nov. 2003.
- President James E. Faust, "The Supernal Gift of the Atonement," *Ensign*, Nov. 1988.
- Hugh W. Nibley, "The Atonement of Jesus Christ," Parts 1, 2, 3 and 4, *Ensign*, July, Aug., Sept., Oct., 1990.
- Linda K. Burton, "Is Faith in the Atonement of Jesus Christ Written in our Hearts?" *Ensign*, Nov. 2012.
- "The Atoning Sacrifice: Modern Prophets Testify," *Ensign*, 1974.
- Lds.org, Gospel Topics: The Atonement (and other related topics you choose to explore)

Chapter 12

The Atonement and the Endowment—Inseparably Connected

I was always taught that Jesus Christ was in and through everything in the gospel, including the temple and the endowment. While I could see that most of the time, sometimes I just didn't make the connection. But as time passed, I came to see Christ, the Atonement, and the endowment as integrally connected in every aspect of the gospel. Even though it was an "aha" experience, it resulted from time, great effort, and serious study. Now it is so empowering—and so fills my soul with gratitude—that I want to share the core doctrines so you can experience the same kind of joy they bring me.

The word *atonement* means "to cover, to become at one"—that is, to be reconciled to God, to be in harmony with God, to return to the presence of the Father. The endowment is a symbolic representation of the process by which we return to our Father's presence. Amulek explains the great enabling power of the Atonement that makes the journey back possible: "For it is expedient that there should be a great and last sacrifice; yea, not a sacrifice of man, neither of beast, neither of any manner of fowl; for it shall not be a human sacrifice; but it must be an infinite and eternal sacrifice" (Alma 34:10).

The words *infinite* and *eternal* do not occur by chance or coincidence in that verse. *Infinite* refers to something immeasurable, unlimited, boundless, endless, and exceedingly great. *Eternal* means without beginning or end—timeless. Christ's sacrifice has no bounds and fulfills *all* aspects of God the Father's plan. How grateful we should be! Through faithful commitment to the covenants and ordinances of the temple, we accept the Atonement and thus become fully reconciled to God the Father. We symbolically participate in the Atonement, and our participation, combined with obedience, enables us to return to the presence of the Father.

When terms of Deity are used in the endowment (and throughout the scriptures), it is important to realize that references to the Son and the Father—as well as Lord, Lord God, God, and Father—are the same. They are *one*. And They seek that *we* might be one with Them in purpose, cause, and action (see John 17:11, 22). Whether it be the Father or the Son, the meaning is the same because the Son always follows and obeys the Father and because of divine investiture. The Father almost always speaks through and defers to His Son. We can learn much from this example of such complete oneness.

However, there are times when we should also understand who is speaking—the Father or the Son—so that we better understand doctrines more clearly. That especially applies to the doctrines of the temple.

The term *father* is a name, a title, and a role. God the Son is the Father's Only Begotten Son in the flesh. He also acts as the Father and in behalf of the Father. Jehovah, the promised Messiah, even Christ the Lord, has been given many descriptions, titles, and roles. Three specific examples explain His Fatherhood.

First, Christ is the Father of heaven and Earth. God the Father's first-born Son in the spirit is called Jehovah. Jehovah, who is Jesus Christ, is "*the Father of heaven and earth, the Creator of all things* from the beginning; and his mother shall be called Mary" (Mosiah 3:8; see also Ether 4:7; Alma 11:39).

Second, Christ becomes our Father as we covenant with Him. When we covenant with Him, we are spiritually begotten of Him; we become His sons and daughters, and we are reborn: "And now, because of the covenant which ye have made ye shall be called the children of Christ, his sons, and his daughters; for behold, this day he hath spiritually begotten you; for ye say that your hearts are changed through faith on his name; therefore, ye are born of him and have become his sons and his daughters" (Mosiah 5:7). Speaking to the brother of Jared, the premortal Christ—Jehovah—said, "Behold, I am Jesus Christ. *I am the Father and the Son.* In me shall all mankind have life, and that eternally, even they who shall believe on my name; and they shall become my sons and my daughters" (Ether 3:14–15; see also Mosiah 15:1–4).

Finally, Christ becomes the Father as He acts for God the Father through a principle we call divine investiture. Through divine investiture, Jesus Christ speaks and acts for and in behalf of God the Father, with all the Father's power and authority. God the Father and

Jesus Christ truly are *one* in all things. And the Lord Jesus Christ said, "I and my Father are one" (John 10:30; see also 3 Ne. 20:35; D&C 50:43).

The Lord spoke of Himself as being the "Great I Am" when He said, "Listen to the voice of Jesus Christ, your Redeemer, the Great I Am, whose arm of mercy hath atoned for your sins" (D&C 29:1). On another occasion, He said, "Thus saith the Lord your God, even Jesus Christ, the Great I Am, Alpha and Omega, the beginning and the end, the same which looked upon the wide expanse of eternity, and all the seraphic hosts of heaven, before the world was made" (D&C 38:1; see also D&C 39:1).

Who is this Great I Am? "And God said unto Moses, I AM THAT I AM: and he said, Thus shalt thou say unto the children of Israel, I AM hath sent me unto you" (Ex. 3:14). We see that Christ the Lord is indeed Jehovah, the Great I Am of the Old Testament, acting for His Father with divine investiture. The Lord made mention of this in John when He said, "Verily, verily, I say unto you, Before Abraham was, I am" (John 8:58).

The endowment ceremony is a dramatic portrayal of the Father's plan, the plan of exaltation that is centered in His Son, Jesus Christ. It is in the temple where this great manifestation of Christ is portrayed, where we experience and appreciate the great role of our beloved Savior in all things. He was the great Creator of heaven and Earth, under the direction of the Father (see Mosiah 3:8). Through the endowment ceremony, we learn that the Father and the Son formed man in Their own likeness and image (see Moses 2:26). We know, too, that Christ came to Earth to do the will of the Father (see 3 Ne. 27:13–14). He reveals the will of God to mankind and speaks for the Father, for the Father always defers to Him (see JS—H 1:17)—again, whether the Father or the Son, it is the same.

The temple endowment symbolically follows the Father's plan through His Son. They create the Earth and form man and woman. They prepare a garden for Adam and Eve eastward in Eden and command them not to eat of the fruit of the tree of knowledge of good and evil or to even touch it (see Moses 4:9). Yet Adam and Eve, being agents unto themselves, are told that they are free to choose (see Moses 4:3). Eve, being beguiled by Satan (see Moses 4:19), partakes of the fruit and then gives it to Adam (see Moses 4:12), who also partakes.

Realizing they are naked (symbolically lost and fallen), they fashion aprons for themselves out of fig leaves (see Moses 4:13); ashamed of their nakedness, they hide themselves when they hear the voice of the Lord (see Moses 4:14). Jehovah—the Lord God—makes coats of skins for Adam and Eve to cover their nakedness (see Moses 4:27), and they are driven out of the garden (see Moses 4:29–31).

Adam and Eve begin to have children. They call upon the Lord, who responds by commanding Adam to worship Him and offer sacrifices. An angel appears and asks Adam why he is offering sacrifices (see Moses 5:6). Adam has been faithfully obedient to the commandments even though he has not fully understood them, and he tells the angel he doesn't know why he is offering sacrifices, only that the Lord commanded him to do so (see Moses 5:6). The angel then explains that sacrifice is "a similitude of the sacrifice of the Only Begotten of the Father, which is full of grace and truth" (Moses 5:7).

James E. Talmage dutifully reviews the modern endowment as relating to the beginnings of mankind:

> The Temple Endowment, as administered in modern temples, comprises instruction relating to the significance and sequence of past dispensations, and the importance of the present as the greatest and grandest era in human history. This course of instruction includes a recital of the most prominent events of the creative period, the condition of our first parents in the Garden of Eden, their disobedience and consequent expulsion from that blissful abode, their condition in the lone and dreary world when doomed to live by labor and sweat, the plan of redemption by which the great transgression may be atoned, the period of the great apostasy, the restoration of the Gospel with all its ancient powers and privileges, the absolute and indispensable condition of personal purity and devotion to the right in present life, and a strict compliance with Gospel requirements. (*The House of the Lord*, 83–84)

These statements help us understand our responsibility in receiving power through the endowment. As we receive the ordinances and covenants, we know what is expected of us in order to qualify to return to our Father's presence.

The prophet Brigham Young made abundantly clear the purpose of the endowment—"to receive all those ordinances in the House of the

Lord, which are necessary for you, after you have departed this life, *to enable you to walk back to the presence of the Father*" (*DBY*, 416).

As we read in D&C 105:10–12, the purpose of the endowment is "that my people may be taught more perfectly, and have experience, and know more perfectly concerning their duty, and the things which I require at their hands. And this cannot be brought to pass until mine elders are endowed with power from on high. For behold, I have prepared a great endowment and blessing to be poured out upon them, inasmuch as they are faithful and continue in humility before me."

In 1903, President John R. Winder of the First Presidency spoke of the daily effect of the endowment on our lives: "I wish to say to you all, and you can bear testimony of the same, that every ordinance, every ceremony that is performed therein [in the holy temple] is of a sacred and holy character. Every ordinance performed there makes better fathers, better mothers, better children, better husbands and wives, better citizens of the state, and better citizens of the United States. Nothing occurs in that house that we need be ashamed of; but everything that takes place there is for the betterment of all who attend" (*CR*, Apr. 1903, 97). Our leaders have repeatedly echoed this statement.

As we are faithfully obedient, offer ourselves as living sacrifices, and live by every word that proceeds from the mouth of God, we will keep all the covenants and consecrate ourselves for the kingdom of God.

The endowment is also a source of personal rejoicing:

> Let the hearts of your brethren rejoice, and let the hearts of all my people rejoice, who have, with their might, built this house to my name.
>
> For behold, I have accepted this house, and my name shall be here; and I will manifest myself to my people in mercy in this house.
>
> Yea, I will appear unto my servants, and speak unto them with mine own voice, if my people will keep my commandments, and do not pollute this holy house.
>
> Yea the hearts of thousands and tens of thousands shall greatly rejoice in consequence of the blessings which shall be poured out, and the endowment with which my servants have been endowed in this house. (D&C 110:6–9)

All power and gifts of God operate according to His laws (see D&C 130:20–21), which in turn are predicated on the great commandment of love. Likewise, all laws are predicated and hang upon the great commandment of love (see Matt. 22:37–40). God loved us so much that He gave us His Only Begotten Son, that we might have everlasting life (see John 3:16). This simple scripture chain shows that our beloved Savior, through the grace of His Father, is truly in everything. If we open our eyes, we will see Christ in every covenant and ordinance within the walls of the holy temples.

To fully receive the endowment, we must be sanctified, which is a process of becoming. Elder Bruce R. McConkie defines *sanctification* very plainly: "To be sanctified is to become clean, pure, and spotless; to be free from the blood and sins of the world; to become a new creature of the Holy Ghost, one whose body has been renewed by the rebirth of the Spirit. *Sanctification* is a state of saintliness, a state attained only by conformity to the laws and ordinances of the gospel. The plan of salvation is the system and means provided whereby men may sanctify their souls and thereby become worthy of a celestial inheritance" (*Mormon Doctrine*, 675). Indeed, sanctification should be our goal, and regular temple worship is the ultimate path to that end.

Receiving the gifts from God that are part of the endowment is not always done within a ritual ceremony in a temple. Evidence of the Lord's own endowment from His Father is apparent in several events in the Savior's life. We read,

> Then Jesus was led up of the Spirit, into the wilderness, *to be with God.*
>
> *And when he had fasted forty days and forty nights, and had communed with God*, he was afterwards an hungered, and was left to be tempted of the devil,
>
> And when the tempter came to him, he said, If thou be the Son of God, command that these stones be made bread.
>
> But Jesus answered and said, It is written, *Man shall not live by bread alone, but by every word that proceedeth out of the mouth of God.*
>
> Then Jesus was taken up into the holy city, and the Spirit setteth him on the pinnacle of the temple.
>
> Then the devil came unto him and said, If thou be the Son of God, cast thyself down, for it is written, He shall

> give his angels charge concerning thee, and in their hands they shall bear thee up, lest at any time thou dash thy foot against a stone.
>
> Jesus said unto him, It is written again, *Thou shalt not tempt the Lord thy God.*
>
> And again, Jesus was in the Spirit, and it taketh him up into an exceeding high mountain, and showeth him all the kingdoms of the world and the glory of them.
>
> And the devil came unto him again, and said, All these things will I give unto thee, if thou wilt fall down and worship me.
>
> Then said Jesus unto him, Get thee hence, Satan; for it is written, *Thou shalt worship the Lord thy God, and him only shalt thou serve.* Then the devil leaveth him. (JST—Matt. 4:1–10)

It is interesting that in every temptation the Lord answers with the word of God. Surely the word has power to help us overcome our temptations. Later—along with Peter, James, and John—Jesus was empowered by His Father on a high mountain and was transfigured before His Apostles:

> And after six days Jesus taketh Peter, James, and John his brother, and bringeth them up into an high mountain apart,
>
> And was transfigured before them: and his face did shine as the sun, and his raiment was white as the light.
>
> And, behold, there appeared unto them Moses and Elias talking with him.
>
> Then answered Peter, and said unto Jesus, Lord, it is good for us to be here: if thou wilt, let us make here three tabernacles; one for thee, and one for Moses, and one for Elias.
>
> While he yet spake, behold, a bright cloud overshadowed them: and behold a voice out of the cloud, which said, This is my beloved Son, in whom I am well pleased; hear ye him.
>
> And when the disciples heard it, they fell on their face, and were sore afraid.
>
> And Jesus came and touched them, and said, Arise, and be not afraid.

> And when they had lifted up their eyes, they saw no man, save Jesus only.
>
> And as they came down from the mountain, Jesus charged them, saying, Tell the vision to no man, until the Son of man be risen again from the dead. (Matt. 17:1–9)

As recorded in Acts 10:38: "How God anointed Jesus of Nazareth with the Holy Ghost and with power: who went about doing good, and healing all that were oppressed of the devil; for God was with him." The endowment is about receiving the power from on high to do good. Service to others is the essence of life and happiness. How happy we become when we think of and serve others, but how hard life becomes when we think only about ourselves and our own problems. It is the love of God and the Spirit, available in its fulness in the temple, that holds the keys to happiness.

When we are busy with the responsibilities and cares of the world, we often miss the better part of life. With everything and everyone clamoring for our attention, we are tempted to neglect our responsibilities and our spirit. But let us not become so overwhelmed that we miss that which matters most in regard to preparing to meet God and having an eternal family.

I am not implying that we cannot love life and enjoy the journey. Happiness is the object of our efforts here, despite life's many challenges. Our Heavenly Father desires that we enjoy a variety of things in life—our families, our employment, wholesome activities and diversions of various kinds. But we need to learn to focus on and do those things that please God. As we do, the demands on our time and attention take on a new perspective; we no longer compartmentalize our lives—we prioritize them. The temple is one of the best places to discern those things that will bring ultimate balance and joy into our lives.

Further discernment comes through the endowment ceremony, which teaches us to call upon the Father in the name of the Son, listen to the prophets of God, and search the scriptures, which teach of Christ and how redemption comes through Him. They teach us the laws that we must understand, the significance of the ordinances we have received, and the covenants we have made with the Lord.

As I already mentioned, everything in the temple centers on the Savior. When we understand this, we will realize "that all [our] incomings . . . into this house, may be in the name of the Lord; that all [our] outgoings from this house may be in the name of the Lord; that all [our] salutations may be in the name of the Lord, with holy hands, uplifted unto the Most High" (D&C 109:17–19). Let us meditate on each covenant, each promise we have made as part of receiving our endowment. We will see and feel the goodness of Christ and be filled with gratitude—which is indeed a life-changing experience.

Speaking of Christ, Donald Parry has written,

> Years ago, Susan Easton Black tabulated all of the occurrences of the names and titles of Jesus in the Book of Mormon. . . . According to Black, 101 names or titles of Christ are presented in the Book of Mormon. These include the names/titles Lord God Omnipotent, Redeemer of Israel, Shepherd, and Son of the Living God, each of which is found once in the work. The names/titles Stone, True Messiah, Mighty One of Jacob, and Great Creator are each found twice; the names/titles Holy One of Israel, Lamb of God, Lord Jesus Christ, Redeemer, and Messiah each appear 10 or more times; and the names/titles Christ, God, Jesus, Lord, and Lord God are each found at least 100 times in the book. In all, the 101 names/titles of Christ are collectively presented 3,925 times in 6,607 Book of Mormon verses. Black's tabulation of the names and titles shows that on average, one name or title of Christ appears once every 1.7 verses.
>
> The names and titles are used by the various Book of Mormon prophets to teach of Jesus' prebirth affiliations with the world, his earthly ministry, his atoning sacrifice (including his sufferings in Gethsemane, his death on the cross, and his resurrection from the garden tomb), his workings among American civilizations, his ministry to other peoples, his future mission with the latter-day church, his judgments upon the world, and his Second Coming to the inhabitants of the earth. By way of example, a number of names/titles of Jesus deal especially with the Atonement. These include Christ, Christ Jesus, Christ the Son, Creator, Eternal Father, Everlasting Father, Father of Heaven, Holy Messiah, Jesus, Jesus Christ, Lamb, Lamb of God, Lord Jesus Christ, Mediator, Messiah, Only Begotten of the Father,

> Only Begotten Son, Redeemer, Redeemer of Israel, Savior, Savior of the World, Shepherd, and True Redeemer. Note also that Jesus serves in the capacity of an advocate, a fact that is explicitly mentioned in the Doctrine and Covenants (D&C 29:5; 32:3; 45:3; 62:1). Several statements imply this idea: the Holy Messiah "shall make intercession for all . . . men" (2 Nephi 2:9), "the Lord and thy God pleadeth the cause of his people" (2 Nephi 8:22), "the Lord standeth up to plead, and standeth to judge the people" (2 Nephi 13:13), God "will plead your cause" (Jacob 3:1), and Christ "advocateth the cause of the children of men" (Moroni 7:28). (*Expressions of Faith*, 216–217)

The Doctrine and Covenants indeed has many more references; I would particularly encourage a careful reading and deep pondering of D&C 88. As we notice such things and begin to see Christ in every aspect of the gospel, we will feel gratitude for Him and see that He is truly in all things.

Chapter 13

The Endowment—A Review and Summary

To better understand the endowment, sometimes it's helpful to review it using different words or a different point of view. I have found that understanding is key—and simply put, some people struggle to understand. Some find it difficult to understand the doctrine and what is expected of them. Some misunderstand the commandments of God. Understanding is where it all begins. And where there is no understanding, there can be no gratitude. When there is no gratitude, nothing is received or acted on.

A simple experience with one of my sons teaches this point clearly. His math score in elementary school was exceedingly low—something like 25 percent. The teacher wrote me a lovely note imploring me as his father to sit down with him and help him understand subtraction. We began with seven *minus* three. He seemed flustered and blurted out, "Ten." I mentioned that that was addition. He smiled and said, "Oh yeah." So I tried another number, a little harder, and asked, "What is twenty-two *subtract* ten?" He seemed unsure, so I explained the answer.

I stopped, went to the very beginning, and asked, "What is nine *take away* six?" Without hesitation, he answered, "That's easy—three." Ecstatic, I said, "You got it. You subtracted six from nine." Then his voice broke, his chin quivered, and he said, "Why didn't she tell me we were doing take-aways?"

My son experienced success because he finally understood. Then together we appreciated subtraction and all of the synonyms that went along with it. Everyone was grateful. Math became easier for him because he understood the assignments as well as the principles. His actions and behavior changed, his scores were always high, and he was happy.

You don't have to be a child to feel confused or uncertain. As adults, we don't understand everything at once; we grow, and God gives us understanding a little at a time as we are ready to receive it—line upon line, precept upon precept, grace upon grace. To understand is to comprehend, to discern, to be enlightened, to perceive, to grasp, to accept, to have knowledge of, and to bring meaning to a subject. That's what we want when it comes to understanding the doctrines of the temple.

The endowment represents the mortal path we take to return to the presence of our Heavenly Father. It leads us through knowledge, actions, and covenants, and we are blessed with God's grace. Then we are able to draw upon the powers of heaven through the Holy Ghost, as activated by our faith in Jesus Christ, and according to our obedience and righteousness, we, like the Savior, are endowed with power and become worthy to enter into our Father's presence.

The *Encyclopedia of Mormonism* defines the endowment as follows:

> An Endowment generally is a gift, but in a specialized sense it is a course of instruction, ordinances, and covenants given only in dedicated temples of The Church of Jesus Christ of Latter-day Saints. The words "to endow" (from the Greek *enduein*), as used in the New Testament, mean to dress, clothe, put on garments, put on attributes, or receive virtue. . . .
>
> The prophet Joseph Smith taught that these were "of things spiritual, and to be received only by the spiritual minded" (*TPJS*, p. 237). The Endowment was necessary, he said, to organize the Church fully, that the Saints might be organized according to the laws of God, and, as the dedicatory prayer of the Kirtland Temple petitioned, that they would "be prepared to obtain every needful thing" (D&C 109:15). The Endowment was designed to give "a comprehensive view of our condition and true relation to God" (*TPJS*, p. 324), "to prepare the disciples for their missions in the world" (p. 274), to prevent being "overcome by evils" (p. 259), to enable them to "secure the fulness of those blessings which have been prepared for the Church of the Firstborn" (p. 237). (454)

We can see why the Lord wants to gather His people—He wants to endow them with power and righteousness by clothing them in the garments of the holy priesthood. He wants to help us put on the virtues and attributes of the Lord so we can be organized in every needful way. Through temple worship and the endowment, our relationship to and dependence on the Lord are established. We are enabled to go forth on our missions, being able to overcome temptation and secure our eternal blessings from God. This is the purpose of the endowment.

Again from the *Encyclopedia of Mormonism*:

> The Endowment of "power from on high" in modern temples has four main aspects. First is the preparatory ordinance, a ceremonial washing and anointing, after which the temple patron dons the sacred clothing of the temple.
>
> Second is a course of instruction by lectures and representations. These include a recital of the most prominent events of the Creation, a figurative depiction of the advent of Adam and Eve and of every man and every woman, the entry of Adam and Eve into the Garden of Eden, their consequent expulsion from the garden, their condition in the world, and their receiving of the Plan of Salvation leading to the return to the presence of God (Talmage, [*The House of the Lord*], 84). The Endowment instructions utilize every human faculty so that the meaning of the gospel may be clarified through art, drama, and symbols. All participants wear white temple robes symbolizing purity and the equality of all persons before God the Father and his Son Jesus Christ. The temple becomes a house of revelation whereby one is instructed more perfectly "in theory, in principle, and in doctrine" (D&C 97:14). "This completeness of survey and expounding of the gospel plan makes temple worship one of the most effective methods of refreshing the memory concerning the entire structure of the gospel" (Widtsoe, 1986, p. 5).
>
> Third is making covenants. The temple Endowment is seen as the unfolding or culmination of the covenants made at baptism. Temple covenants give "tests by which one's willingness and fitness for righteousness may be known" (Widtsoe, p. 335). They include the "covenant and promise to observe the law of strict virtue and chastity, to be charitable, benevolent, tolerant and pure; to devote both talent and material means to the spread of truth and the uplifting of the [human] race; to maintain devotion to the cause of

> truth; and to seek in every way to contribute to the great preparation that the earth may be made ready to receive Jesus Christ" (Talmage, 84). One also promises to keep these covenants sacred and to "trifle not with sacred things" (D&C 6:12).
>
> Fourth is a sense of divine presence. In the dedicatory prayer of the temple at Kirtland, Ohio, the Prophet Joseph Smith pleaded "that all people who shall enter upon the threshold of the Lord's house may feel thy power, and feel constrained to acknowledge that thou hast sanctified it, and that it is thy house, a place of thy holiness" (D&C 109:13). Of temples built by sacrifice to the name of the Lord Jesus Christ, dedicated by his authority, and reverenced in his Spirit, the promise is given, "My name shall be here; and I will manifest myself to my people in mercy in this holy house" (D&C 110:8). In the temples there is an "aura of deity" manifest to the worthy (Kimball, pp. 534–35). Through the temple Endowment, one may seek "a fulness of the Holy Ghost" (D&C 109:15). Temple ordinances are seen as a means for receiving inspiration and instruction through the Holy Spirit, and for preparing to return to the presence of God. (454–456)

This quote teaches us what we actually do in the temple and what to expect, including a sense of the divine presence of God and a fulness of the Holy Ghost, which enables us to receive inspiration and instruction.

The Gift of the Endowment

The endowment is, above all else, a gift—an endowment of power from on high. As a presentation, it shows how we, through ordinances and covenants, can return to the presence of our Heavenly Father. Because the endowment is a gift, it is given freely to the worthy and must be received and accepted by covenant. The essential requirement is to prepare ourselves to receive that gift, and we do that through holiness of heart and obedience to the Lord's commandments.

I've often asked myself how we know we have received that gift. The answers I have found come in the form of more questions: Have I sought to change and become holy and obedient? Do my prayers reflect my commitment to my covenants? Do I understand what it means to be endowed by being clothed? Do I prayerfully and diligently return to the house of the Lord to remind myself of the covenants I have made? Have I set aside time to teach my family the plan of redemption? Do I express gratitude to my Father for His goodness in providing the endowment? Oh, how I wish I had integrated these questions into my life as a young husband and father. I encourage you to ask them of yourselves.

The Endowment Is Received by the Spiritually Minded

As we read in 2 Nephi 9:39, "To be spiritually-minded is life eternal." *Spirituality* refers to the nature and condition of one's heart. That is why Alma queried, "Have ye spiritually been born of God? Have ye received his image in your countenances? Have ye experienced this mighty change in your hearts?" (Alma 5:14). It has been said that humility is the beginning of spiritual growth.

So to be spiritually minded could embrace the following qualities, attributes, or capacities: We would be sensitive to the promptings of the Spirit. We would seek the comfort and power of the Spirit through prayer. Our hearts would be "soft" and not "past feeling" (1 Ne. 17:45). We would yield to the enticings of the Holy Spirit (see Mosiah 3:19). Our nature would become like that of our Savior (see Moro. 7:48), full of the love of God and thus able to radiate that love (see 4 Ne. 1:15–16). We would be like King Benjamin's people when they felt only to "do good continually" (see Mosiah 5:2).

The Endowment as Part of the Complete Restoration of All Things

It was part of the plan that the Lord would provide a way for us to return to our Father's presence. The endowment is that way. Let's increase our understanding by discussing each of the ordinances.

Preparatory or Initiatory Ordinances

Regarding the washing and anointing aspect of the initiatory, we learn the following from the *Encyclopedia of Mormonism*:

> Washings and anointings are preparatory or initiatory ordinances in the temple. They signify the cleansing and sanctifying power of Jesus Christ applied to the attributes of the person and to the hallowing of all life. They have biblical precedents. . . . Latter-day Saints look forward to receiving these inspired and inspiring promises with the same fervent

> anticipation they bring to baptism. They come in the spirit of a scriptural command: "Cleanse your hands and your feet before me (D&C 88:74; cf. 1 John 2:27)." (1444)

Later in the *Encyclopedia of Mormonism*, Donald Parry goes on to explain,

> The washings and anointings of the biblical period have a parallel today in The Church of Jesus Christ of Latter-day Saints. In response to a commandment to gather the saints and to build a house "to prepare them for the ordinances and endowments, washings, and anointings" (*TPJS*, p. 308), these ordinances were introduced in the Kirtland Temple on January 21, 1836 (*HC* 2:379–83). In many respects similar in purpose to ancient Israelite practice and to the washing of feet by Jesus among his disciples, these modern LDS rites are performed only in temples set apart and dedicated for sacred purposes (see D&C 124:37–38; *HC* 6:318–319).
>
> Many symbolic meanings of washings and anointings are traceable in the scriptures. Ritual washings (Heb. 9:10: D&C 124:37) symbolize the cleansing of the soul from sins and iniquities. They signify the washing-away of the pollutions of the Lord's people (Isa. 4:4). Psalm 51:2 expresses the human longing and divine promise: "Wash me thoroughly from mine iniquity, and cleanse me from my sin" (cf. Ps. 73:13; Isa. 1:16). The anointing of a person or object with sacred ointment represents sanctification (Lev. 8:10–12) and consecration (Ex. 28:41), so that both become "most holy" (Ex. 30:29) unto the Lord. In this manner, profane persons and things are sanctified in similitude of the messiah (Hebrew "anointed one"), who is Christ (Greek "anointed one")." (1551)

A second significant aspect of the initiatory is clothing. Being clothed in sacred temple clothing is an integral part of the endowment ceremony, as Elder J. Richard Clark explains: "Sacred temple clothing is a shield and protection against Satan. As you receive your endowments in the temple, you receive the privilege of wearing the sacred temple clothing and the garments of the holy priesthood. The garments are a tangible reminder of your covenants with God. It has been said that modesty is the hallmark of a true Latter-day Saint. The temple garment reminds us that virtue sets us apart from the world and, in a special way, makes us one with God" ("The Temple—What It Means to You," *New Era*, Apr. 1993, 4).

The garment truly is like armor, even the armor of God mentioned by the Apostle Paul (see Eph. 6:13–17). Isaiah also reminds us, "I will greatly rejoice in the Lord, my soul shall be joyful in my God; for he hath clothed me with the garments of salvation, he hath covered me with the robe of righteousness" (Isa. 61:10).

In the temple ceremony, we covenant that we will not defile our garments, something that would prevent us from enjoying the blessings of exaltation. In this regard, we learn from President Joseph Fielding Smith:

> "Save yourselves from this untoward generation, and come forth out of the fire, hating even the garments spotted with the flesh" [D&C 36:6]. This expression is found in Jude (3), and the Lord said to John (Rev. 3:1), "Thou hast a few names even in Sardis which have not defiled their garments; and they shall walk with me in white; for they are worthy." This is symbolic language, yet is plain to understand. This is an untoward generation, walking in spiritual darkness, and the punishment for sin is spoken of as punishment in fire. Garments spotted with flesh are garments defiled by the practices of carnal desires and disobedience to the commandments of the Lord. We are commanded to keep our garments unspotted from all sin, from every practice that defiles. We are therefore commanded to come out of the world of wickedness and forsake the things of this world. (*Church History and Modern Revelation*, 1:50)

Our garments are made clean as we take the gospel to the world, as President Wilford Woodruff counseled: "Can we fold our arms in peace and cry 'all is peace in Zion,' when, so far as we have the power of the priesthood resting upon us, we can see the condition of the world? Can we imagine that our garments will be clean without lifting our voices before our fellow men and warning them of the things that are at their doors? No, we cannot. . . . This is our calling. It is our duty" (*JD*, 21:124).

What can we do to better remember and receive the blessings and power of the garment of the holy priesthood? We can pause and remember our covenants as we dress and prepare for each day. As we go throughout the day, we can remember the sacred garment we are wearing—and that remembering will help us keep in mind the things we need to do. This has been a blessing in my life.

Naming

Another significant aspect of temple ordinances is the use of names. Susan Easton Black explained it this way:

> I have found it interesting that in the scriptures a new name is often involved when a covenant relationship is formed. When Adam and Eve were given dominion over the earth (see Gen. 1:28), Adam was given the responsibility of naming the animals (see Gen. 2:19–20). Likewise, in receiving Eve as his wife, Adam named her. (See Gen. 3:20.) God himself, after creating bodies for our first parents, "blessed them, and called their name Adam" (Gen. 5:2.). Later, when Jehovah entered into a covenant relationship with Abram, he changed Abram's name to Abraham (see Gen. 17:5). The Lord did the same thing with Jacob when He extended to Jacob the same covenant He had made with Abraham (see Gen. 35:10). We follow a similar pattern when entering into covenants with Christ in the waters of baptism. At that time, we take upon ourselves the name of Christ, and that becomes the name by which we are called. (See Mosiah 5:7–12.) *The higher covenants of the temple also involve the giving and receiving of names.* ("I Have a Question," *Ensign*, Dec. 1988, 53–54)

A Course of Instruction by Lectures and Representations

A dramatic ritual presentation, the endowment ceremony consists of intimate, individual instruction that is linked to making covenants. It is the intimacy of this instruction that enables us to see more clearly and apply the teachings of the endowment to our lives. The presentation is about us and for us. It is in the presentation of the dialogues that we are taught the doctrines of the temple by the word of God.

Making Covenants and Receiving Ordinances

The blessings of God are always given to mankind through ordinances, which are associated with the covenants we make and receive in the temple. Covenants become our commitments to promise to keep the laws of God. Our Father, being true, binds Himself: "I, the Lord, am bound when ye do what I say; but when ye do not what I say, ye have no promise" (D&C 82:10). When we are faithful in keeping the covenants and commandments, we have a promise. The ordinances and covenants received in the holy temple qualify us for exaltation if we are faithful and true to our promises.

The Presence of the Lord

We can feel the glory, power, and presence of the Lord in His holy house. We are also promised that through the grace of God and through the infinite and eternal Atonement, we—after all we can do—can gain eternal life and enter into the presence of the Lord (see Hel. 14:17; Morm. 9:13; D&C 14:7).

Have you ever wondered if what you are feeling is the presence of the Lord? The feelings we experience in the presence of the Lord are much like those we experience in the presence of the Holy Ghost. They are personal and deep. They are life changing and live giving because they lead us to be good and to do good. All ordinances and covenants are made in the presence of God in His holy house. The law of witnesses is always in force: "In the mouth of two or three witnesses shall every word be established" (2 Cor. 13:1). Life-saving and exalting ordinances are pronounced "in the name of the Father, and of the Son, and of the Holy Ghost" (Matt. 28:19).

Oh, that we might understand and appreciate the endowment, that our hearts may swell with thanksgiving and gratitude. Surely the Lord will help us as we diligently seek to understand. Then we will appreciate that which we have received, and our hearts will be full of gratitude. That gratitude will change our souls as we begin to become—that is, to have a new heart and to have His image in our countenance. Then we will truly be spiritually born again, and we will go about doing good.

We can experience the "mighty change" Alma admonished his people to seek. We can symbolically receive "[Christ's] image in [our] countenances." We can be "spiritually . . . born of God" (Alma 5:14). We have within us the capacity and power to realize Alma's admonitions. President Ezra Taft Benson taught, "Men and women who turn their lives over to God will discover that He can make a lot more out of their lives than they can. He will deepen their joys, expand their vision, quicken their minds, strengthen their muscles, lift their spirits, multiply their blessings, increase their opportunities, comfort their souls, raise up friends, and pour out peace. Whoever will lose his life in the service of God will find eternal life (see Matthew 10:39)" (*TETB*, 361).

The blessing of making these choices is that we come to enjoy the fruits of the Spirit: "Love, joy, peace, longsuffering, gentleness, goodness, faith, Meekness, temperance" (Gal. 5:22–23). It is through worship in God's holy house that we are empowered to make those choices.

Let us remember and ponder these things each time we think of our own endowment or hear the words *endow*, *temple worship*, or *gift from God*.

We must keep our covenants to make all of these blessings efficacious in our lives. It is by our faithfulness in keeping them that we are able to walk back to our Heavenly Parents. There is no other way. The temple is the only way, through Christ the Lord.

CHAPTER 14

The Oath and Covenant of the Priesthood and the Temple

Revelation on the Priesthood, Including the Oath and Covenant of the Priesthood

The Prophet Joseph Smith recorded these words prior to receiving the revelation on the priesthood contained in D&C 84: "The Elders during the month of September began to return from their missions to the Eastern States, and present the histories of their several stewardships in the Lord's vineyard; and while together in these seasons of joy, I inquired of the Lord, and received on the 22nd and 23rd of September, *the following revelation on Priesthood*" (*HC*, 1:286–287).

Because the ordinances and covenants of the priesthood are highly symbolic, let us look with temple eyes, hear with temple ears, and feel with temple hearts and souls to better understand and appreciate the supernal truths contained within this glorious section on the priesthood and its oath and covenant.

The greater priesthood, or Melchizedek Priesthood, administers the gospel and the oath and covenant of the priesthood, which entails all of the ordinances and covenants associated with the priesthood. It is in the fulfillment of this oath and covenant that our Father will give us eternal life and exaltation—all that He has. This gift is centered in and culminates in the house of the Lord, where His children are endowed with power from on high and receive all the sealings and blessings pertaining to eternal lives and exaltation.

It is likewise the greater priesthood that holds the key to the doctrines and blessings of the temple: "And this greater priesthood administereth the gospel and holdeth the key of the mysteries of the kingdom, even the key of the knowledge of God. Therefore, in the ordinances thereof, the power of godliness is manifest. And without the ordinances thereof, and the authority of the priesthood, the power of godliness is not manifest unto men in the flesh; For without this no man can see the face of God, even the Father, and live" (D&C 84:19–22).

Oh, the goodness of God in allowing His children to officiate in His holy house, that all His children may be partakers of the heavenly gifts available there. The Prophet Joseph taught, "All men who become heirs of God and joint-heirs with Jesus Christ will have to receive the fulness of the ordinances of his kingdom; and those who will not receive all the ordinances will come short of the fulness of that glory, if they do not lose the whole" (*HC*, 5:424). The temple is the only way back to our Heavenly Parents. The ordinances and covenants received in the house of the Lord ultimately enable us, if we are faithful, to literally enter into the presence of our Father. Without these ordinances and the authority of the priesthood, no one can see the face of God. (Little children are alive in Christ; therefore, they have no need for any ordinances; see Moro. 8:9–22.)

God made the same promises to the ancient Israelites, who rejected them: "Now this Moses plainly taught to the children of Israel in the wilderness, and sought diligently to sanctify his people that they might behold the face of God; But they hardened their hearts and could not endure his presence; therefore, the Lord in his wrath, for his anger was kindled against them, swore that they should not enter into his rest while in the wilderness, which rest is the fulness of his glory. Therefore, he took Moses out of their midst, and the Holy Priesthood also" (D&C 84:23–25). The resulting lot of the Israelites was the lesser priesthood and the law of Moses.

However, through the higher priesthood, God has made available the promises in their fulness to the Saints in these latter days. Let's go verse by verse in section 84, starting with verse 31 and going through verse 44, to gain a more complete understanding of the importance of the priesthood and its restoration in these latter days.

31. "Therefore, as I said concerning the sons of Moses—for the sons of Moses and also the sons of Aaron shall offer an acceptable offering and sacrifice in the house of the Lord, which house shall be built unto the Lord in this generation, upon the consecrated spot as I have appointed."

Verse 31 sets the stage: all of these things are associated with the temple. The temple is where the sons of God offer an acceptable offering and sacrifice to the Lord, whose house is to be built so that He, the Lord, can come to it: "And inasmuch as my people build a house unto me in the name of the Lord, and do not suffer any unclean thing to come into it, that it be not defiled, my glory shall rest upon it; Yea, and my presence shall be there, for I will come into it, and all the pure in heart that shall come into it shall see God" (D&C 97:15–16).

32. "And the sons of Moses and of Aaron shall be filled with the glory of the Lord, upon Mount Zion in the Lord's house, whose sons are ye; and also many whom I have called and sent forth to build up my church."

The sons of God are filled with the glory of the Lord because they have made an acceptable offering and sacrifice in the temple. This glory of the Lord is part of His power and represents the fulness and majesty of the Lord.

33. "For whoso is faithful unto the obtaining these two priesthoods of which I have spoken, and the magnifying their calling, are sanctified by the Spirit unto the renewing of their bodies."

34. "They become the sons of Moses and of Aaron and the seed of Abraham, and the church and kingdom, and the elect of God."

Verses 33 and 34 refer to obtaining the two priesthoods. By magnifying our calling, we are sanctified (made holy) by the Spirit (the fulness of the Holy Spirit, which is received in the temple) and become the sons of Moses and Aaron and the elect of God. The word *sanctify* in Hebrew comes from *kdsh*, the same root word as *temple*. When the word *sanctification* is completed, the word becomes *kodash* or *kadesh*, which means "to be made holy," a state that comes through the Holy Ghost and through the grace of the Lord (see D&C 20:31) as a result of the Atonement (see Heb. 10:10; 13:12). Our part in becoming sanctified comes in "yielding [our] hearts unto God" (Hel. 3:35), that "his people . . . might behold the face of God" (D&C 84:23). This is the intent of the law of Christ, given so that we can be sanctified and enter the celestial kingdom (see D&C 88:21) with others who abide this celestial law (see D&C 88:22). This process is often referred to as the temple text of the Lord's ministry as given in the Sermon on the Mount; it was also given at the temple at Bountiful in the Book of Mormon.

35. "And also all they who receive this priesthood receive me, saith the Lord." *All* who receive this priesthood receive me. Is not this what Moses sought to do? We read further, "Now this Moses plainly taught to

the children of Israel in the wilderness, *and sought diligently to sanctify his people that they might behold the face of God*" (D&C 84:23). This is the essence of the endowment in the temple—that all of God's children may receive Christ the Lord and through Him come back to the Father, for He is the only way: "Jesus saith unto him [Thomas], I am the way, the truth, and the life: no man cometh unto the Father, but by me" (John 14:6).

The endowment—the receiving of all of the priesthood ordinances and covenants—symbolizes the enabling power of the Atonement, which brings us back into the presence of God our Father. It makes us one with Him, and being *at one*, we become worthy to be in His presence.

An endowment is a gift. John W. Welch explains:

> What is the meaning of the word endued or endowed? In Luke 24:49, shortly after his resurrection, Jesus told his Apostles, "I send the promise of my Father upon you," but they were to remain in Jerusalem, "until ye be endued with power from on high." (Emphasis added; see also Acts 1:4–5, 8). The Greek word in the text is *enduo.*
>
> Webster's *American Dictionary of the English Language* (published in 1829) noted that the English word *endue* (or *indue*) "coincides nearly in signification with *endow*, that is, to put on, to furnish, . . . to put on something; to invest; to clothe." The *Compact Edition of the Oxford English Dictionary* notes that *endue* means "to put on as a garment; to clothe or cover": Indeed, Joseph Smith's diary uses the spellings *endument* and *endowment* interchangeably, as he prayed in December 1835 that all the elders might "receive an endument, in thy house."
>
> The Greek word *enduo* has two main meanings. The first is "to dress, to clothe someone," or "to clothe oneself in, to put on." Second, the word can be used figuratively, meaning to take on "characteristics, virtues, intentions."
>
> Thus, the endowment is a dressing, not in ordinary clothes but "with power from on high" (Luke 24:49) and in the virtues and intentions of God. It involves the opportunity to "put on [*enedus as the*] Christ" (Gal. 3:27), so that "this mortal [can] put on [*endusasthai*] immortality" (1 Cor. 15:53). It is possible to see both literal and figurative

> significance in the word *enduo* in connection with the desire of the pure in heart to be encircled in the robes of God's righteousness." ("New Testament Word Studies," *Ensign*, Apr. 1993, 28–30)

From further study, we learn that "*enduo* means 'to draw on' or 'to put on something.' It means 'to clothe oneself with something' or 'to draw on something.' It 'relates to the putting on of clothes.' 'Quite common is the application to investing with ethical and religious qualities.' . . . It can mean 'to be invested with power' or 'with incorruptibility' or 'with immortality'" (*Theological Dictionary*, 2:319–20).

Likewise, the Lord instructed the Brethren in this dispensation to tarry so they could be endowed with power from on high (see D&C 95:8–9).

The Lord's endowment of power is described in the book of Acts as "how God anointed Jesus of Nazareth with the Holy Ghost and with power: who went about doing good, and healing all that were oppressed of the devil; for God was with him" (10:38). The purpose of the endowment is to receive the fulness of the Holy Ghost and the power to go about doing good. That is the essence of life. As noted earlier, the endowment refers to *virtue*, which word connotes "righteousness, purity, and power." When the Lord healed the woman with the issue of blood, He described it as "virtue . . . gone out of me" (Luke 8:46; see also Mark 5:30). Virtue in this sense is described as power, or strength, which is, in fact, the literal meaning of *virtue* in Greek. This blessing can be ours to draw on the powers of heaven to bless others.

36. "For he that receiveth my servants receiveth me."

The Lord continues in this same vein: we must receive His servants in order to receive Him. In what is often referred to as the "temple text" of 3 Nephi, we read, "Blessed are ye if ye shall give heed unto the words of these twelve whom I have chosen from among you to minister unto you, and to be your servants" (12:1). Again, the Lord said, "And wo be unto him that will not hearken unto the words of Jesus, and also to them whom he hath chosen and sent among them; for whoso receiveth not the words of Jesus and the words of those whom he hath sent receiveth not him; and therefore he will not receive them at the last day" (3 Ne. 28:34). To receive Christ, we must receive His prophets and servants.

If we fail to receive them, the Lord reminds us, "And it would be better for them if they had not been born. For do ye suppose that ye can get rid of the justice of an offended God, who hath been trampled under feet of men, that thereby salvation might come?" (3 Ne. 28:35) Receiving Christ brings wonderful blessings; failure to receive Him has devastating consequences.

We receive the Savior completely thorough His priesthood ordinances. We begin at baptism when we put on Christ (see Gal. 3:27); because we believe in Christ, the Father gives us the transcendent gift of the Holy Ghost (see 3 Ne. 19:22). It is then in the temple that all the blessings and ordinances of the priesthood are fulfilled and completed. We are clothed symbolically in the robes of righteousness, the garment of the holy priesthood, which becomes our protection from temptation and evil. We receive a fulness of the Holy Ghost: "And do thou grant, Holy Father, that all those who shall worship in this house may be taught words of wisdom. . . . And that they may grow up in thee, and receive a fulness of the Holy Ghost, and be organized according to thy laws, and be prepared to obtain every needful thing" (D&C 109:14–15).

37. "And he that receiveth me receiveth my Father."

Everything points to the goodness of God the Father and His perfect plan. He so ordained that through His beloved Son, all mankind will be redeemed and be given exaltation if they are faithful—so it is only through Christ the Lord that we receive the Father. He is the keeper of the gate: "And the keeper of the gate is the Holy One of Israel; and he employeth no servant there; and there is none other way save it be by the gate; for he cannot be deceived, for the Lord God is his name" (2 Ne. 9:41).

The gate through which we enter into the kingdom of God on the Earth is baptism: "For the gate by which ye should enter is repentance and baptism by water; and then cometh a remission of your sins by fire and by the Holy Ghost" (2 Ne. 31:17). There is also the gate of heaven: "Yea, thus we see that the gate of heaven is open unto all, even to those who will believe on the name of Jesus Christ, who is the Son of God" (Hel. 3:28). In Genesis, we read, "And he [Jacob] was afraid, and said, How dreadful is this place! this is none other but the house of God, and this is the gate of heaven" (28:17). The gate of heaven is the temple of our God, and Jesus Christ is the one who symbolically allows us through that gate into the presence of our Father (see Heb. 10:19–20).

Once we have passed through the gate, we "have eternal life through Christ, who has broken the bands of death" (Mosiah 15:23), and "redemption cometh through Christ the Lord" (Mosiah 16:15). This plan of redemption was "prepared from the foundation of the world, through Christ, for all whosoever would believe on his name" (Alma 22:13). God the Father "may bring about, through his most Beloved, his great and eternal purpose" (Morm. 5:14). Alma's counsel to his son Shiblon expands on this principle: "My son, I have told you this that ye may learn wisdom, that ye may learn of me that there is no other way or means whereby man can be saved, only in and through Christ. Behold, he is the life and the light of the world. Behold, he is the word of truth and righteousness" (Alma 38:9).

Christ the Lord, the Son of the Living God the Father, became one with His Father because He did all that the Father commanded Him to do. In the process of Christ's ultimate sacrifice and infinite Atonement, He prayed the great Intercessory Prayer that we might be one with Him through the *at-one-ment* (see John 17). God's children who truly receive Christ can be made one, even as Christ prayed to the Father. This transcendent doctrine pertaining to eternal life and exaltation becomes clear when we carefully read in its entirety the sacred Intercessory Prayer:

> These words spake Jesus, and lifted up his eyes to heaven, and said, Father, the hour is come; glorify thy Son, that thy Son also may glorify thee:
>
> As thou hast given him power over all flesh, that he should give eternal life to as many as thou hast given him.
>
> And this is life eternal, that they might know thee the only true God, and Jesus Christ, whom thou hast sent. [This is part of receiving the ordinances of the greater priesthood when we received the key to the knowledge of God in the temple.]
>
> I have glorified thee on the earth: I have finished the work [see 3 Ne. 27:13–14; John 8:28–29] which thou gavest me to do.
>
> And now, O Father, glorify thou me with thine own self with the glory, which I had with thee before the world was.
>
> I have manifested thy name unto the men which thou gavest me out of the world: thine they were, and thou gavest them me; and they have kept thy word.
>
> Now they have known that all things whatsoever thou hast given me are of thee.

For I have given unto them the words which thou gavest me; and they have received them, and have known surely that I came out from thee, and they have believed that thou didst send me.

I pray for them: I pray not for the world, but for them which thou hast given me; for they are thine.

And all mine are thine, and thine are mine; and I am glorified in them.

And now I am no more in the world, but these are in the world, and I come to thee. Holy Father, keep through thine own name those whom thou hast given me, that they may be one, as we are.

While I was with them in the world, I kept them in thy name: those that thou gavest me I have kept, and none of them is lost, but the son of perdition; that the scripture might be fulfilled.

And now come I to thee; and these things I speak in the world, that they might have my joy fulfilled in themselves.

I have given them thy word [to live by every word which proceedeth forth from the mouth of God [see D&C 84:43–46]; and the world hath hated them, because they are not of the world, even as I am not of the world.

I pray not that thou shouldest take them out of the world, but that thou shouldest keep them from the evil.

They are not of the world, even as I am not of the world.

Sanctify them through thy truth: thy word is truth. [We are made holy and sanctified through the sacred temple ordinances and through being faithful to the covenants we have made.]

As thou hast sent me into the world, even so have I also sent them into the world.

And for their sakes I sanctify myself, that they also might be sanctified through the truth.

Neither pray I for these alone, but for them also which shall believe on me through their word;

That they all may be one; as thou, Father, art in me, and I in thee, that they also may be one in us: that the world may believe that thou hast sent me.

And the glory which thou gavest me I have given them; that they may be one, even as we are one:

> I in them, and thou in me, that they may be made perfect in one; and that the world may know that thou hast sent me, and hast loved them, as thou hast loved me. (John 17:1–23)

The Atonement's perfection and completion come together through the oneness for which Christ prayed. Without becoming one with the Savior and Heavenly Father, we are not Theirs: "Behold, this I have given unto you as a parable, and it is even as I am. I say unto you, be one; and if ye are not one ye are not mine" (D&C 38:27).

As Christ's brothers and sisters, the following scripture—a pleading portion of the great Intercessory Prayer—is very personal to us. He wants for us what He has with the Father. I feel a closeness to our Savior because of His great concern and love for us:

> Father, I will that they also, whom thou hast given me, be with me where I am; that they may behold my glory, which thou hast given me: for thou lovedst me before the foundation of the world.
>
> O righteous Father, the world hath not known thee: but I have known thee, and these have known that thou hast sent me.
>
> And I have declared unto them thy name, and will declare it: that the love wherewith thou hast loved me may be in them, and I in them. (John 17:24–26)

The Intercessory Prayer also helps us better understand our potential to be perfected through Christ, as Moroni's benedictory address in the Book of Mormon reminds us:

> Yea, come unto Christ, and be perfected in him, and deny yourselves of all ungodliness; and if ye shall deny yourselves of all ungodliness, and love God with all your might, mind and strength, then is his grace sufficient for you, that by his grace ye may be perfect in Christ; and if by the grace of God ye are perfect in Christ, ye can in nowise deny the power of God.
>
> And again, if ye by the grace of God are perfect in Christ, and deny not his power, then are ye sanctified in

> Christ by the grace of God, through the shedding of the blood of Christ, which is in the covenant of the Father unto the remission of your sins, that ye become holy, without spot. (Moro. 10:32–33)

It is interesting that the prophets in the Book of Mormon use the word *yea* 1,047 times. *Yea* is used to precede something that is considered very important or is to be emphasized. Moroni surely knew that the purpose of coming unto Christ and being perfected in Him is of vital importance in our lives. It is through Christ the Lord that perfection, or completeness, takes place. We are made complete through Christ, the Anointed One, who not only saves but exalts. If we receive Christ, then and only then can we receive the Father and all that He has, which is perfection and completeness, to become even as He is with all the blessings of exaltation and eternal lives. It is only through Christ that all of the greater priesthood ordinances, including the sealing ordinance, make it possible to have the power of the Gods—that is, to have eternal increase.

We know that the blessings of justification and sanctification—being made holy and pure—come from Jesus Christ and His Atonement. As the Lord states in the Doctrine and Covenants, "Justification through the grace of our Lord and Savior Jesus Christ is just and true; And we know also, that sanctification through the grace of our Lord and Savior Jesus Christ is just and true, to all those who love and serve God with all their might, mind, and strength" (D&C 20:30–31). At this point, in a state of sanctification and holiness, we are better able to understand and appreciate how to take Christ's name upon ourselves and seek to typify Him in all things.

The word *through* as a preposition in the phrase "Justification *through* the grace of our Lord" brings to mind such concepts as "instrumentality" and "dependence on." Therefore we pray to our Heavenly Father *in the name of Jesus Christ as we have been commanded* (see 3 Ne. 18:19, 23). We are redeemed, reconciled, made clean, purified, and sanctified *through* Jesus Christ. We are ultimately perfected *through* Him. The scriptures in this chapter explain the transcendent truth of how on Earth, and especially in the temple, we symbolically and then literally in the Resurrection return to the presence of the Father and receive the blessings of exaltation. All of this is possible only *through* our

Savior Jesus Christ: "Jesus saith unto him, I am the way, the truth, and the life: no man cometh unto the Father, but by me" (John 14:6).

38. "And he that receiveth my Father receiveth my Father's kingdom; therefore all that my Father hath shall be given unto him."

The scriptures refer to a multiplicity of blessings the Father waits anxiously to give to us. The Lord has said concerning these blessings, "To their exaltation and glory in all things, as hath been sealed upon their heads, which glory shall be a fulness and a continuation of the seeds forever and ever. Then shall they be gods, because they have no end; therefore shall they be from everlasting to everlasting, because they continue; then shall they be above all, because all things are subject unto them. Then shall they be gods, because they have all power, and the angels are subject unto them. Verily, verily, I say unto you, except ye abide my law ye cannot attain to this glory" (D&C 132:19–21).

The temple is the only way back to the presence of our Father. It provides symbolic reminders of the path we must follow here in mortality and the ordinances and covenants of the greater priesthood that, when kept, enable us to return to our Father's presence. For the brethren, receiving only the Melchizedek Priesthood and being ordained to an office in that priesthood does not qualify them for exaltation. They need all of the ordinances and covenants of the greater priesthood in order to return to the presence of our Father.

39. "And this is according to the oath and covenant which belongeth to the priesthood."

This verse plainly points out that the doctrines taught in the endowment and regarding the temple refer to the oath and covenant of the priesthood, for they belong to it. This wonderful greater priesthood—which administers all of the priesthood ordinances pertaining to exaltation with an oath and a covenant made with God—blesses all of our Heavenly Father's children who partake of the ordinances of the greater priesthood, as mentioned in D&C 84:19–22. It is the ultimate transcending blessing in my life that allows me to partake of heavenly blessings from my Father through His Son. And I know He will never break His promise. That is a foundational truth that empowers my life.

40. "Therefore, all those who receive the priesthood, receive this oath and covenant of my Father, which he cannot break, neither can it be moved."

Verse 40 elaborates on verse 39. The oath and covenant of the priesthood belongs to and defines the priesthood. All they who receive the priesthood can receive the priesthood ordinances and covenants in the temple, and they are the ones who will receive all that the Father has. This refers to all of God's children, male and female alike. Again, receiving the priesthood and being ordained to a priesthood office is not enough; one must magnify the priesthood by receiving all the priesthood ordinances of the temple.

41. "But whoso breaketh this covenant after he hath received it, and altogether turneth therefrom, shall not have forgiveness of sins in this world nor in the world to come."

Receiving the ordinances and covenants of the temple should not be taken lightly; they are sacred and holy. As we have discussed previously, we must each be accountable for the degree of light and knowledge we have attained in this life while at the same time refraining from judging others who seem to have lost their way. We must also bear in mind that while the Lord is perfectly just, He is also perfectly merciful.

Why is it, then, that there is an unpardonable sin that does not qualify for the Atonement? How can that be? What sin is it, and why is it so unforgiveable and inexcusable?

Alma taught his son Coriantumr, "For behold, if ye *deny the Holy Ghost when it once has had place in you, and ye know that ye deny it*, behold, this is a sin which is unpardonable; yea, and whosoever murdereth against the light and knowledge of God, it is not easy for him to obtain forgiveness; yea, I say unto you, my son, that it is not easy for him to obtain a forgiveness" (Alma 39:6).

Paul reminds us, "For it is impossible for those who were once enlightened, and *have tasted of the heavenly gift*, and were made partakers of the Holy Ghost, And have tasted *the good word of God, and the powers of the world to come, If they shall fall away*, to renew them again unto repentance; seeing *they crucify to themselves the Son of God afresh, and put him to an open shame*" (Heb. 6:4–6).

Matthew records, "But the blasphemy against the Holy Ghost shall not be forgiven unto men. And whosoever speaketh a word against the Son of man, it shall be forgiven him: but *whosoever speaketh against the Holy Ghost, it shall not be forgiven him*, neither in this world, neither in the world to come" (Matt. 12:31–32). Again, Paul states, "For if we *sin wilfully* after that *we have received the knowledge of the truth*, there remaineth no more sacrifice for sins" (Heb. 10:26).

In the revelation on the degrees of glory, the Lord Himself made it clear: "Thus saith the Lord concerning all those who know my power, and have been made partakers thereof, and suffered themselves through the power of the devil to be overcome, and to deny the truth and defy my power—They are they who are the sons of perdition, of whom I say that it had been better for them never to have been born; For they are vessels of wrath, doomed to suffer the wrath of God, with the devil and his angels in eternity; Concerning whom I have said there is no forgiveness in this world nor in the world to come—Having denied the Holy Spirit after having received it, and having denied the Only Begotten Son of the Father, having crucified him unto themselves and put him to an open shame" (D&C 76:31–35).

Those who have committed the unpardonable sin have:

- Lied to God.
- Denied the Christ.
- Knowingly denied the Holy Ghost.
- Denied the heavenly gift (the Holy Ghost). Having tasted the word of God and the powers of the worlds to come, they have broken the covenants after they have received them and have altogether turned away (see D&C 84:41), for they crucify the Lord and put Him to open shame.
- Willfully blasphemed and spoken against the Holy Ghost.

As we look at all these scriptures and their salient points, we come to understand why denying the Holy Ghost is an unpardonable sin. Those who participate in this sin choose willfully to *not accept or receive* the infinite sacrifice of Christ's Atonement *after* having actually received the knowledge that it is true by the power of the Holy Ghost. They openly deny Christ by refusing to receive His infinite Atonement. And this is exactly what Lucifer did. He willfully rebelled against the truth after having been taught the truth by the Father. Therefore, he was denied a body. The word of God speaks likewise to the sons of perdition, "of whom [He] say[s] that it had been better for them never to have been born" (D&C 76:32). Surely in sorrow we weep, "for the heavens wept over him—he was Lucifer, a son of the morning" (D&C 76:26). And we weep for all who deny our Beloved Savior, He who gave His all for the children of God.

42. "And wo unto all those who come not unto this priesthood which ye have received, which I now confirm upon you who are present

this day, by mine own voice out of the heavens; and even I have given the heavenly hosts and mine angels charge concerning you."

A warning is given in this verse to all those who refuse to "come unto" this priesthood (the ordinances and covenants in the temple, which are part of the oath and covenant of the priesthood) and all the blessings associated with it. The Lord speaks in subsequent verses about why He gathers His people to "come unto" the priesthood in the temple: "I must gather together my people, according to the parable of the wheat and the tares, *that the wheat may be secured in the garners to possess eternal life, and be crowned with celestial glory, when I shall come in the kingdom of my Father to reward every man according as his work shall be*" (D&C 101:65). The garners are the temples, safe and secured places. This is why the Lord commands His people to build temples—so He can provide a way for His people to return to His Father. This is what Moses was trying to do. This is why we as Latter-day Saints are a temple-building and temple-worshipping people.

43. "And I now give unto you a commandment to beware concerning yourselves, to give diligent heed to the words of eternal life.

44. "For you shall live by every word that proceedeth forth from the mouth of God."

Another warning tells us to give heed to the words of eternal life (the directions and admonitions we have received from the Lord, including the priesthood and its oath and covenant). Where do we find those words? Where do we make the covenants with God that can give us the opportunity to gain eternal life? Where are we taught the law? We find the answers in His holy house and in His word. We read: "Wherefore, for this cause I gave unto you the commandment that ye should go to the Ohio; and there I will give unto you my law; and there you shall be endowed with power from on high" (D&C 38:32).

We are to live by every word that proceeds forth from the mouth of God. The word of God is given in His temples, as well as in the scriptures; the prophets also speak the word of God, which is Christ the Lord (see John 1:14; Rev. 19:13) and all of His teachings, ordinances, covenants, and commandments. It is the iron rod—the word of God—that leads to the tree of life (which is the love of God, as expressed in all things, especially through His beloved Son's infinite and atoning sacrifice), eternal life, and the source of all happiness. As Elder Neal A. Maxwell noted, "The love of God for His children is most profoundly expressed in His gift of Jesus as our Redeemer: 'God so loved the world, that he gave his only begotten Son' (John 3:16). To partake of the love of God is to partake of Jesus' Atonement and the emancipations and joys which it can bring" ("Lessons Learned from Laman and Lemuel," *Ensign*, Nov. 1999, 6).

Yes, if we follow our Savior Jesus Christ in all things, the blessings of eternity are ours. We read, "And moreover, I would desire that ye should consider on the blessed and happy state of those that keep the commandments of God. For behold, they are blessed in all things, both temporal and spiritual; and if they hold out faithful to the end they are received into heaven, that thereby they may dwell with God in a state of never-ending happiness" (Mosiah 2:41). This is why everything in the gospel and kingdom of God points to the temple, for it is in the temple that we are empowered to do good and carry out our duties and responsibilities as children of God. The endowment gave the Saints strength to cross the plains. The endowment is what gives strength to all of the Lord's missionaries. The temple ordinances, including the sealing ordinance, empowers our marriage through our faithfulness. All blessings are predicated on our obedience to our covenants and commandments.

In sum, the Lord teaches us the great truth about His priesthood:

> I am the Lord thy God, and will give unto thee the law of my Holy Priesthood [the law set forth in His holy house], as was ordained by me and my Father before the world was.
>
> Abraham received all things, whatsoever he received, by revelation and commandment, by my word, saith the Lord, and hath entered into his exaltation and sitteth upon his throne.
>
> Abraham received promises concerning his seed, and of the fruit of his loins—from whose loins ye are, namely, my servant Joseph—which were to continue so long as they were in the world; and as touching Abraham and his seed, out of the world they should continue; both in the world and out of the world should they continue as innumerable as the stars; or, if ye were to count the sand upon the seashore ye could not number them.
>
> This promise is yours also, because ye are of Abraham, and the promise was made unto Abraham; and by this law is the continuation of the works of my Father, wherein he glorifieth himself.

> Go ye, therefore, and do the works of Abraham; enter ye into my law and ye shall be saved.
>
> But if ye enter not into my law ye cannot receive the promise of my Father, which he made unto Abraham. (D&C 132:28–33)

We can receive all the blessings of Abraham, Isaac, and Jacob and sit down with them at the right hand of God in the kingdom of heaven if we keep our garments symbolically spotless: "And may the Lord bless you, and keep your garments spotless, that ye may at last be brought to sit down with Abraham, Isaac, and Jacob, and the holy prophets who have been ever since the world began, having your garments spotless even as their garments are spotless, in the kingdom of heaven to go no more out" (Alma 7:25). These are the blessings of those who receive the priesthood blessings in the temple and continue faithful in all things as they live by the word of God:

> Yea, we see that whosoever will may lay hold upon the word of God, which is quick and powerful, which shall divide asunder all the cunning and the snares and the wiles of the devil, and lead the man of Christ in a strait and narrow course across that everlasting gulf of misery which is prepared to engulf the wicked—
>
> And land their souls, yea, their immortal souls, at the right hand of God in the kingdom of heaven, to sit down with Abraham, and Isaac, and with Jacob, and with all our holy fathers, to go no more out. (Hel. 3:29–30)

We should live by the word of God. It will lead us to the tree of life. It will bring about change in our lives (see Alma 31:5). It will tell us all things to do (see 2 Ne. 32:3). It will nourish our spirit.

Chapter 15
The Gathering of the Lord's People to His House

"This is my work and my glory—to bring to pass the immortality and eternal life of man" (Moses 1:39). All Latter-day Saints know these oft-quoted words—but do we really understand and appreciate what this "work and glory" is all about? Do we truly appreciate that it is all about how God our Father and our Savior have blessed us and provided a way for us to enjoy lives like Theirs—even eternal lives?

From the Creation to the Resurrection, everything in the plan of salvation is about us and for us. The ultimate example of this is that our Heavenly Father gave us a Savior who would redeem us from the Fall and provide a way to receive exaltation through His grace and our obedience. He has also provided the gift of power and authority through the priesthood to bless His children and lead them back home:

> And this greater priesthood administereth the gospel and holdeth the key of the mysteries of the kingdom, even the key of the knowledge of God.
>
> Therefore, in the ordinances thereof, the power of godliness is manifest.
>
> And without the ordinances thereof, and the authority of the priesthood, the power of godliness is not manifest unto men in the flesh;
>
> For without this no man can see the face of God, even the Father, and live. (D&C 84:19–22)

These verses express the very purpose for which the house of the Lord was dedicated. It is the place where the Lord empowers His people. It is the way through which all humankind, both the living and the dead, can receive all blessings and can be empowered by God to return to His presence. No one can be exalted without the ordinances and covenants of the temple—whether that happens in this life or posthumously through vicarious work. The temple is the only way.

The Lord commands us to build a house where He may come and dwell for the sake of blessing His children. Temples now dot the Earth, and more are announced at each general conference. The building of temples in these latter days began with the Kirtland Temple, where a partial endowment was given. The next temple was built in Nauvoo, where the first full endowment was given:

> And verily I say unto you, let this house be built unto my name, that I may reveal mine ordinances therein unto my people;
>
> For I deign to reveal unto my church things which have been kept hid from before the foundation of the world, things that pertain to the dispensation of the fulness of times.
>
> And I will show unto my servant Joseph all things pertaining to this house, and the priesthood thereof, and the place whereon it shall be built.
>
> And ye shall build it on the place where you have contemplated building it, for that is the spot which I have chosen for you to build it.
>
> If ye labor with all your might, I will consecrate that spot that it shall be made holy.
>
> And if my people will hearken unto my voice, and unto the voice of my servants whom I have appointed to lead my people, behold, verily I say unto you, they shall not be moved out of their place. (D&C 124:40–45)

Look at that promise: We will not be moved "out of our place"—that is, the place where we may receive the blessings of exaltation—if we are obedient to the Lord's wishes.

It is not enough to simply build temples; we must serve and worship in them. The Church spends millions of dollars to build and maintain these holy edifices; it remains simply for us as a people to make the commitment to fulfill the dedicated purpose of the Lord's holy houses. It is up to us to ensure that the work of exaltation is done. This is why the Lord gathers His people—so that they can come as a body and receive the lifesaving ordinances and covenants for themselves and for their dead. The temple beckons all the living to gather so we can bless ourselves and the dead who wait in bondage, pleading for us to be saviors on Mount Zion (see Obadiah 1:21).

We are the instruments through which all mankind may be blessed. The Lord depends on us. He invites us to come to His holy house, where He stands waiting to bless us and the dead in all things. The Prophet Joseph Smith exhorted the Saints in his day, as well as in our day:

> Brethren, shall we not go on in so great a cause? Go forward and not backward. Courage, brethren; and on, on to the victory! Let your hearts rejoice, and be exceedingly glad. Let the earth break forth into singing. Let the dead speak forth anthems of eternal praise to the King Immanuel, who hath ordained, before the world was, that which would enable us to redeem them out of their prison; for the prisoners shall go free.
>
> Let the mountains shout for joy, and all ye valleys cry aloud; and all ye seas and dry lands tell the wonders of your Eternal King! And ye rivers, and brooks, and rills, flow down with gladness. Let the woods and all the trees of the field praise the Lord; and ye solid rocks weep for joy! And let the sun, moon, and the morning stars sing together, and let all the sons of God shout for joy! And let the eternal creations declare his name forever and ever! And again I say, how glorious is the voice we hear from heaven, proclaiming in our ears, glory, and salvation, and honor, and immortality, and eternal life; kingdoms, principalities, and powers!
>
> Behold, the great day of the Lord is at hand; and who can abide the day of his coming, and who can stand when he appeareth? For he is like a refiner's fire, and like fuller's soap; and he shall sit as a refiner and purifier of silver, and he shall purify the sons of Levi, and purge them as gold and silver, that they may offer unto the Lord an offering in righteousness. Let us, therefore, as a church and a people, and as Latter-day Saints, offer unto the Lord an offering in righteousness; and let us present in his holy temple, when it is finished, a book containing the records of our dead, which shall be worthy of all acceptation. (D&C 128:22–24)

I have read this scripture many times, and I joy in each reading. This is the very work the angel Moroni prophesied to the Prophet Joseph on September 21, 1823, seven years before the Church was organized. Section 2 reveals this telling truth about the work of redeeming the dead—if this work is not done, "the whole earth would be utterly wasted at his coming" (D&C 2:3) This doctrine and principle is repeated numerous times.

Think about it: every time we go to the temple, we see the same presentation. My purpose in repeating many of the same scriptures in this book is the same as the Lord's purpose in repeating our experience in the temple ceremony. It is through these repeated covenants and doctrines that we come to better understand that we must live by every word that proceeds from the mouth of God. It is through this repetition that we understand that we must give heed to His every word, then go forth with all diligence in order to be protected from evil. The Book of Mormon explains:

> And now Alma began to expound these things unto him [Zeezrom], saying: It is given unto many to know the mysteries of God; nevertheless they are laid under a strict command that they shall not impart only according to the portion of his word which he doth grant unto the children of men, according to the heed and diligence which they give unto him.
>
> And therefore, he that will harden his heart, the same receiveth the lesser portion of the word; and he that will not harden his heart, to him is given the greater portion of the word, until it is given unto him to know the mysteries of God until he know them in full.
>
> And they that will harden their hearts, to them is given the lesser portion of the word until they know nothing concerning his mysteries; and then they are taken captive by the devil, and led by his will down to destruction. Now this is what is meant by the chains of hell. (Alma 12:9–11)

As we read these words, it becomes clear why the Lord wants to gather His people to the temples—to enjoy as a body the blessings of exaltation. He loves us with a perfect love, as only a father can love. What gratitude should fill our souls as we realize this truth. How can we possibly repay our Heavenly Father and our Savior? Their motives are pure: "He doeth not anything save it be for the benefit of the world; for he loveth the world, even that he layeth down his own life that he may draw [gather] all men unto him" (2 Ne. 26:24).

"Learn of me," the Lord invites, "and listen to my words; walk in the meekness of my Spirit, and you shall have peace in me" (D&C 19:23). It is in the temple—a house of learning and revelation—that we learn of the Father and the Son. The temple is the place where the Father gathers His people to receive the ordinances and covenants that can lead them back into His presence as they are faithfully obedient: "Therefore, I must gather together my people, according to the parable of the wheat and the tares, that the wheat may be secured in the garners [the temples] to possess eternal life, and be crowned with celestial glory, when I shall come in the kingdom of my Father to reward every man according as his work shall be" (D&C 101:65).

This is what Moses also sought to do: "Now this Moses plainly taught to the children of Israel in the wilderness, and sought diligently to sanctify his people that they might behold the face of God" (D&C 84:23). As we attend the temple and allow temple doctrines to fill our souls, we too will "see the face of God" (D&C 84:22). And as we are gathered to the Lord's house to do His work, we will set our feet firmly on the path back to God's presence.

Chapter 16

Eternal Families and the Sealing Power of God

We are taught that the whole Earth would be wasted and cursed and the plan of God not fulfilled without the great sealing power of the priesthood as it has been restored in its fulness in these latter days (see Mal. 4:5–6; D&C 2:3; 138:48). The restoration of all things includes eternally linking the members of God's family.

The gospel itself is about families. It naturally follows that the Church is about families as well, for they are the basic unit of the Church, and we are all members of a family. This doctrine is an eternal verity. Families really are forever. "The Family: A Proclamation to the World" teaches this about members of families: "Each is a beloved spirit son or daughter of heavenly parents, and, as such, each has a divine nature and destiny."

The power to bind families together throughout the eternities lies in the keys of the priesthood, as Elder Bruce R. McConkie explains:

> Whenever the fulness of the gospel is on earth, the Lord has agents to whom he gives power to bind on earth and seal eternally in the heavens. (Matt. 16:19; 18:18; Hela. 10:3–10; D. & C. 132:46–49.) This sealing power, restored in this dispensation by Elijah the Prophet (D. & C. 2:1–3; 110:13–16), is the means whereby "All covenants, contracts, bonds, obligations, oaths, vows, performances, connections, associations, or expectations" attain "efficacy, virtue, or force in and after the resurrection from the dead" (D. & C. 132:7). (*Mormon Doctrine*, 683)

Sister Julie B. Beck, former general Relief Society president, taught clearly and succinctly the doctrine of the family:

> In The Church of Jesus Christ of Latter-day Saints, we have a theology of the family that is based on the Creation, the Fall, and the Atonement. The Creation of the earth provided a place where families could live. God created a man and a woman who were the two essential halves of a family. It was part of Heavenly Father's plan that Adam and Eve be sealed and form an eternal family. The Fall provided a way for the family to grow. Adam and Eve were family leaders who chose to have a mortal experience. The Fall made it possible for them to have sons and daughters. The Atonement allows for the family to be sealed together eternally. It allows for families to have eternal growth and perfection. The plan of happiness, also called the plan of salvation, was a plan created for families. The rising generation needs to understand that the main pillars of our theology are centered in the family.
>
> When we speak of qualifying for the blessings of eternal life, we mean qualifying for the blessings of eternal families. This was Christ's doctrine, and it was restored through the Prophet Joseph Smith." ("Teaching the Doctrine of the Family," *Ensign*, March 2011, 12–13)

The family is an eternal, intimate, multigenerational unit. Our role as a member of the family of God extends not only to our immediate families but also to the entire human race, for we are all brothers and sisters. That is why the Prophet Joseph Smith counseled, "Love is one of the chief characteristics of Deity, and ought to be manifested by those who aspire to be the sons of God. A man filled with the love of God, is not content with blessing his family alone, but ranges through the whole world, anxious to bless the whole human race" (*HC*, 174).

Sometimes when we were little, we imagined that when we grew up, we would be doctors or farmers, teachers or students; I testify that those are not the case. When we truly "grow up"—that is, in a spiritual sense, which is the truest sense of the phrase—we will become as our Father and Mother in heaven. If we believe this basic doctrine of our theology, then we must live to do the work of sealing all of God's children into the eternal family. This great work takes place first in the home and extends to the temple, because the temple is the place where members of the human race are reunited and sealed as families.

The sealing of a couple for time and all eternity is but the beginning of an eternal family. We should do all in our power to help the youth of the Church grasp the significance of their potential to begin such a family. The Lord taught us a great deal about the oneness and eternal union of a married couple sealed for time and all eternity: "But from the beginning of the creation God made them male and female. For this cause shall a man leave his father and mother, and cleave to his wife; And they twain shall be one flesh: so then they are no more twain, but one flesh. What therefore God hath joined together, let not man put asunder" (Mark 10:6–9).

Man and woman are designed to be equally yoked, with complementary roles that enhance and strengthen their marriage. We learn from Paul's letter to the Saints at Ephesus,

> Wives, submit yourselves unto your own husbands, as unto the Lord.
>
> For the husband is the head of the wife, even as Christ is the head of the church: and he is the saviour of the body.
>
> Therefore as the church is subject unto Christ, so let the wives be to their own husbands in every thing.
>
> Husbands, love your wives, even as Christ also loved the church, and gave himself for it;
>
> That he might sanctify and cleanse it with the washing of water by the word,
>
> That he might present it to himself a glorious church, not having spot, or wrinkle, or any such thing; but that it should be holy and without blemish.
>
> So ought men to love their wives as their own bodies. He that loveth his wife loveth himself.
>
> For no man ever yet hated his own flesh; but nourisheth and cherisheth it, even as the Lord the church. (Eph. 5:22–29)

We learn that the husband is to love and cherish his wife even as Christ loves the Church. The husband becomes a "servant-leader," a role the Lord clearly expressed when He said, "Thou shalt love thy wife with all thy heart, and shalt cleave unto her and none else" (D&C 42:22). I have learned from the Apostle Paul: "Husbands, love your wives, even as Christ also loved the church, and gave himself for it" (Eph. 5:25). This is the role of the husband, to be even as Christ to his family.

As we sacrifice for one another and keep our temple covenants, I am reminded of President Gordon B. Hinckley's statement: "If you will make your first concern the comfort, the well-being, and the happiness of your companion, sublimating any personal concern to that loftier goal, you will be happy, and your marriage will go on through eternity" ("Nurturing a Love That Lasts," *Ensign*, Feb. 2000). This is the magic key of selfless service for each other, and it is the key to a happy marriage.

The New and Everlasting Covenant of Marriage

With our finite understanding, it is very difficult to comprehend the great blessings of marriage and posterity. The Lord describes them in section 131 of the Doctrine and Covenants. Verses 1 and 2 read, "In the celestial glory there are three heavens or degrees; And in order to obtain the highest, a man must enter into this order of the priesthood [meaning the new and everlasting covenant of marriage]."

The keys to the sealing power that Elijah restored can bring us back into the presence of God our Father and our Savior and enable us to be in the highest degree of glory within the celestial kingdom. This blessing is conditional upon our being sealed for time and all eternity and upon our faithfulness in keeping our covenants.

We read in verses 3 and 4, "And if he does not, he cannot obtain it. He may enter into the other, but that is the end of his kingdom; he cannot have an increase."

As we discuss this new and everlasting covenant, it is also expedient that we talk about the order of the priesthood, which brings us the highest blessings, including eternal increase. Without this sealing ordinance, we are unable to have an increase in posterity. It is the end of our kingdom.

Verse 5 continues: "The more sure word of prophecy means a man's knowing that he is sealed up unto eternal life, by revelation and the spirit of prophecy, through the power of the Holy Priesthood."

We can know that this blessing is real and binding by the power of revelation.

The Lord continued the revelation concerning the new and everlasting covenant, which includes the eternity of the marriage covenant, in section 132 of the Doctrine and Covenants. The following was given to the Prophet Joseph and refers to an order of the priesthood that brings us the highest degree of glory within the celestial kingdom: "Therefore, prepare thy heart to receive and obey the instructions which I am about to give unto you; for all those who have this law revealed unto them must obey the same. For behold, I reveal unto you a new and an everlasting covenant; and if ye abide not that covenant, then are ye damned; for no one can reject this covenant and be permitted to enter into my glory" (D&C 132:3–4).

This blessing of "entering into this order of the priesthood"—meaning the new and everlasting covenant of marriage—is what allows the blessing of eternal lives and a continuation of seeds, as we have discussed. The word *damned* is troubling to some, and rightfully so; however, at its most elemental meaning, the phrase is simply descriptive. If we are not eternally married, we are stopped (or damned) from having eternal posterity because we have not entered into the covenant relationship requisite to attaining the highest degree of exaltation.

We read further, in verses 5 and 6, "For all who will have a blessing at my hands shall abide the law which was appointed for that blessing, and the conditions thereof, as were instituted from before the foundation of the world. And as pertaining to the new and everlasting covenant, it was instituted for the fulness of my glory; and he that receiveth a fulness thereof must and shall abide the law, or he shall be damned, saith the Lord God."

In verse 7, the Lord repeats the commandment and emphasizes its importance through repetition: "And verily I say unto you, that the conditions of this law are these: All covenants, contracts, bonds, obligations, oaths, vows, performances, connections, associations, or expectations, that are not made and entered into and sealed by the Holy Spirit of promise, of him who is anointed, both as well for time and for all eternity, and that too most holy, by revelation and commandment through the medium of mine anointed, whom I have appointed on the Earth to hold this power (and I have appointed unto my servant Joseph to hold this power in the last days, and there is never but one on the Earth at a time on whom this power and the keys of this priesthood are conferred), are of no efficacy, virtue, or force in and after the resurrection from the dead; for all contracts that are not made unto this end have an end when men are dead."

It is part of the Father's plan that all the ordinances and covenants be made here on the Earth. This is why we do proxy work, engaging in these earthly ordinances that reach through the eternities by the power of the holy priesthood. I testify that there is no other way.

Reading further:

> Behold, mine house is a house of order, saith the Lord God, and not a house of confusion.
>
> Will I accept of an offering, saith the Lord, that is not made in my name?
>
> Or will I receive at your hands that which I have not appointed?
>
> And will I appoint unto you, saith the Lord, except it be by law, even as I and my Father ordained unto you, before the world was?
>
> I am the Lord thy God; and I give unto you this commandment—that no man shall come unto the Father but by me or by my word, which is my law, saith the Lord.
>
> And everything that is in the world, whether it be ordained of men, by thrones, or principalities, or powers, or things of name, whatsoever they may be, that are not by me or by my word, saith the Lord, shall be thrown down, and shall not remain after men are dead, neither in nor after the resurrection, saith the Lord your God.
>
> For whatsoever things remain are by me; and whatsoever things are not by me shall be shaken and destroyed.
>
> Therefore, if a man marry him a wife in the world, and he marry her not by me nor by my word, and he covenant with her so long as he is in the world and she with him, their covenant and marriage are not of force when they are dead, and when they are out of the world; therefore, they are not bound by any law when they are out of the world. (D&C 132:8–15)

From these verses we understand that we live by the word of God and His laws. It is by His word that we are married for time and all eternity. It is by His word that all the covenants and ordinances of the temple are made possible, and there is no other way save it be through the Lord Jesus Christ. This is the way to the Father. This is the way to the highest degree in the celestial kingdom.

In verses 16 and 17 of D&C 132, we read: "Therefore, when they are out of the world they neither marry nor are given in marriage; but are appointed angels in heaven, which angels are ministering servants, to minister for those who are worthy of a far more, and an exceeding, and an eternal weight of glory. For these angels did not abide my law;

therefore, they cannot be enlarged, but remain separately and singly, without exaltation, in their saved condition, to all eternity; and from henceforth are not gods, but are angels of God forever and ever."

We begin to see that obedience is the first law of heaven: "There is a law, irrevocably decreed in heaven before the foundations of this world, upon which all blessings are predicated—And when we obtain any blessing from God, it is by obedience to that law upon which it is predicated" (D&C 130:20–21). Obedience is requisite!

The Lord goes on to explain in verse 18, "And again, verily I say unto you, if a man marry a wife, and make a covenant with her for time and for all eternity, if that covenant is not by me or by my word, which is my law, and is not sealed by the Holy Spirit of promise, through him whom I have anointed and appointed unto this power, then it is not valid neither of force when they are out of the world, because they are not joined by me, saith the Lord, neither by my word; when they are out of the world it cannot be received there, because the angels and the gods are appointed there, by whom they cannot pass; they cannot, therefore, inherit my glory; for my house is a house of order, saith the Lord God."

It is through our faithful obedience that God honors all ordinances and covenants. Then the power of the Holy Spirit of Promise ratifies that blessing.

The Lord says in verses 19 and 20:

> And again, verily I say unto you, if a man marry a wife by my word, which is my law, and by the new and everlasting covenant, and it is sealed unto them by the Holy Spirit of promise, by him who is anointed, unto whom I have appointed this power and the keys of this priesthood; and it shall be said unto them—Ye shall come forth in the first resurrection; and if it be after the first resurrection, in the next resurrection; and shall inherit thrones, kingdoms, principalities, and powers, dominions, all heights and depths—then shall it be written in the Lamb's Book of Life, that he shall commit no murder whereby to shed innocent blood, and if ye abide in my covenant, and commit no murder whereby to shed innocent blood, it shall be done unto them in all things whatsoever my servant hath put upon them, in time, and through all eternity; and shall be of full force when they are out of the world; and they shall pass by the angels, and

> the gods, which are set there, to their exaltation and glory in all things, as hath been sealed upon their heads, which glory shall be a fulness and a continuation of the seeds forever and ever.
>
> Then shall they be gods, because they have no end; therefore shall they be from everlasting to everlasting, because they continue; then shall they be above all, because all things are subject unto them. Then shall they be gods, because they have all power, and the angels are subject unto them.

The condition described in these verses—"that he shall commit no murder whereby to shed innocent blood, and if ye abide in my covenant, and commit no murder whereby to shed innocent blood, it shall be done unto them in all things whatsoever my servant hath put upon them, in time, and through all eternity; and shall be of full force when they are out of the world"—refers to shedding the innocent blood of the Lord (see Heb. 6:6), as verse 26 explains: "Verily, verily, I say unto you, if a man marry a wife according to my word, a*nd they are sealed by the Holy Spirit of promise, according to mine appointment* [calling and election being made sure] and he or she shall commit any sin or transgression of the new and everlasting covenant whatever, and all manner of blasphemies, and if they commit no murder wherein they shed innocent blood, yet they shall come forth in the first resurrection, and enter into their exaltation; but they shall be destroyed in the flesh, and shall be delivered unto the buffetings of Satan unto the day of redemption, saith the Lord God." This "murder wherein they shed innocent blood" refers to denying Christ after we have had a sure knowledge of Him. "For it is impossible for those who were once enlightened, and have tasted of the heavenly gift, and were made partakers of the Holy Ghost, And have tasted the good word of God, and the powers of the world to come, If they shall fall away, to renew them again unto repentance; seeing they crucify to themselves the Son of God afresh, and put him to an open shame" (Heb. 6:4–6).

We read further, "The blasphemy against the Holy Ghost, which shall not be forgiven in the world nor out of the world, is in that ye commit murder wherein ye shed innocent blood, and assent unto my death, after ye have received my new and everlasting covenant, saith the Lord God; and he that abideth not this law can in nowise enter into my glory, but shall be damned, saith the Lord" (D&C 132:27).

At one point in the Lord's discussion of eternal marriage, we find a transcendent blessing that is a challenge to comprehend. It is humbling to attempt to grasp the goodness of God in His making available these magnificent blessings. How can we ever pay the price to prepare for and understand the significance of such wondrous blessings? It seems too grand an endeavor at times, yet that is the end purpose of the temple covenants and ordinances. Here is the blessing: "Then shall they be gods, because they have no end; therefore shall they be from everlasting to everlasting, because they continue; then shall they be above all, because all things are subject unto them. Then shall they be gods, because they have all power, and the angels are subject unto them" (D&C 132:20).

What do the key words in this revelation mean? Elder Bruce R. McConkie explains them as he describes *thrones*:

> In the eternal sense, thrones are reserved for exalted persons who rule and reign as kings and queens in the highest heaven of the celestial world. It is in such a sphere that "God, even the Father, reigns upon his throne forever and ever" (D. & C. 76:92; Rev. 20:11).
>
> Then shall all those who are joint-heirs with him—who have been "crowned with the glory of his might," and "made equal with him" (D. & C. 88:107)—then shall they also sit upon their thrones and even sit down with our Lord on his throne. "To him that overcometh will I grant to sit with me in my throne, even as I also overcame, and am set down with my Father in his throne" (Rev. 3:21). Enoch foresaw this state of exaltation and said: "Thou art God, thou hast made me, and given unto me a right to thy throne" (Moses 7:59).
>
> In token of their kingship, sovereignty, and dominion, exalted beings shall sit on thrones in eternity. "All thrones and dominions, principalities and power, shall be revealed and set forth upon all who have endured valiantly for the gospel of Jesus Christ." (D. & C. 121:29.) "Abraham hath entered into his exaltation and sitteth upon his throne, as also have other righteous saints of former ages" (D. & C. 132:29, 37). (*Mormon Doctrine*, 794)

Kingdoms are those dominions where the righteous will rule and reign in righteousness. *Principalities* refer to places—that is, jurisdictions—where one would rule in relation to a larger sphere or dominion. *Power* is authority given by God to act within our sphere and to do all things necessary to accomplish the immortality and eternal life of our eternal increase (see D&C 131). *Dominions* refer to the power or right of self-government. All the promised blessings can be ours individually if we keep our covenants, for then and only then can the Holy Spirit of Promise seal our eternal marriage.

The Holy Spirit of Promise

The blessings of marriage in the new and everlasting covenant are contingent on our being sealed by the Holy Spirit of Promise, which is the ratifying power of the Holy Ghost. This power confirms the promises of God to all those who are faithful to their covenants: "And who overcome by faith, and are sealed by the Holy Spirit of promise, which the Father sheds forth upon all those who are just and true" (D&C 76:53).

Marriage for time and all eternity in the new and everlasting covenant of marriage is much more than a social event or just something special. It is sacred. It is the highest ordinance of the greater priesthood that bestows all the blessings to become like our Heavenly Father: "Then shall they be gods, because they have all power, and the angels are subject unto them" (D&C 132:20). I have the honor and joy of serving as a sealer, and I have witnessed in those who are well prepared a sacred and wonderful moment during the sealing ceremony when they are promised that they shall be gods. I feel their hearts at this tender moment as they are joined with love, covenants, and commitment. It is a transcendent feeling that words cannot describe—it is a truth only the heart comprehends.

The Lord reaffirms to us the great blessings that come from remaining faithful to the binding covenants of eternal marriage: "But if ye receive me in the world, then shall ye know me, and shall receive your exaltation; that where I am ye shall be also. This is eternal lives—to know the only wise and true God, and Jesus Christ, whom he hath sent. I am he. Receive ye, therefore, my law" (D&C 132:23–24).

And so the Lord has written and decreed. We qualify for the blessings of God through obedience to covenants and participation in the ordinances of the temple. Then we will become gods.

Our Father is a loving and caring Father who seeks to have His children enjoy a life like His. We must follow His Beloved Son and live as the Holy Spirit directs. Then we too will enjoy the blessings of exaltation as explained in the scriptures and dramatized in the temple. That is the only way. The everlasting covenant of marriage, the way to eternal lives, happens only in the temple and makes possible these eternal blessings.

Chapter 17

Redemption of the Dead—Elijah—Turning Our Hearts

One of our greatest responsibilities in this dispensation is to redeem the dead by serving as saviors on Mount Zion. The prophet Joseph reminds us, "The greatest responsibility in this world that God has laid upon us is to seek after our dead. The Apostle Paul says, 'They without us cannot be made perfect' (Hebrews 11:40), for it is necessary that the sealing power should be in our hands to seal our children and our dead for the fulness of the dispensation of times—a dispensation to meet the promises made by Jesus Christ before the foundation of the world for the salvation of man" (*TPJS*, 356).

As Abinadi taught, the great Redeemer Himself, even Jesus Christ, made this work possible: "The bands of death shall be broken, and the Son reigneth, and hath power over the dead; therefore, he bringeth to pass the resurrection of the dead" (Mosiah 15:20). The dead spoken of include those in the spirit world.

Not until my older years did I understand the significant doctrine of the redemption of the dead. For years, I merely attended the temple, glad to offer a service but failing to see how temple worship works in concert with redeeming the dead. Now, better appreciating the work that goes on in the Lord's house, I am truly grateful for our Father's perfect plan and the role of our beloved Savior in bringing about the redemption of the dead. This gratitude has become the catalyst for my change of heart, attitude, and actions regarding this magnificent work and the blessings associated with it. Through vicarious temple work, we are the ones to bring this part of the plan of redemption to pass. *We are the ones.* And the time is now. Those in the spirit world wait on us. That is why the temple and what goes on there is our greatest responsibility.

Great blessings are available to us when we serve and worship in the house of the Lord (in fact, at the end of this book, I devote an entire chapter to those blessings). We can grow spiritually every time we go to the Lord's house to refresh our covenants and be edified and uplifted by the Spirit. The doctrines of the temple empower us with knowledge. More importantly, the blessings extend to those on the other side as they are redeemed from prison—and as vicarious servants, we are perfected along with those we serve. As we are taught in the Doctrine and Covenants, "And now, my dearly beloved brethren and sisters, let me assure you that these are principles in relation to the dead and the living that cannot be lightly passed over, as pertaining to our salvation. For their salvation is necessary and essential to our salvation, as Paul says concerning the fathers—*that they without us cannot be made perfect—neither can we without our dead be made perfect*" (D&C 128:15). The work and glory of the Father and the Son (see Moses 1:39) literally become our work.

Though we often refer to those on the other side of the veil as *dead*, they are very much alive. They are eager to receive their long-awaited blessings—"For the dead had looked upon the long absence of their spirits from their bodies as a bondage" (D&C 138:50)—and they receive them through the gospel of repentance that has been and is being preached to them, as made clear in both the Bible and the Doctrine and Covenants (see 1 Pet. 4:6; D&C 138:18–19, 31–37, 57–60).

The question we must ask ourselves is this: Do we have a clear vision of the redemption of the dead and our role in bringing this great work to fruition?

The Vision

I encourage you to carefully reread Doctrine and Covenants 138. If we follow the same process President Joseph F. Smith—who received this magnificent revelation—did, it is easy to understand and catch the glorious vision of the importance of work for the dead. We must study the Atonement, search the scriptures, and prayerfully ponder in order to come to know and understand the doctrine of the redemption of the dead. As we come to better understand and appreciate this doctrine and work, there will follow a vision of its scope; our eyes and hearts will be opened. Our attitudes and behavior will change.

Nearly seven years before the Church was organized, Moroni came to the boy Joseph Smith three times during the same night and once again the next day, each time rehearsing the *same* message. Among other things, Moroni related the great prophecy of Malachi (see Mal. 4:5–6) regarding Elijah's coming to "plant in the hearts of the children the promises made to the fathers" (JS—H 1:39). Moroni also described the consequences of our not responding to Elijah's mission: "If it were not so [if Elijah did not come], the whole Earth would be utterly wasted at his [Christ's] coming" (JS—H 1:39).

Let us speak of two critical truths we know regarding this work:

1. The prophet Elijah *did* come (see D&C 110:13–16). President Joseph Fielding Smith explained:

> But what was the nature of his [Elijah's] mission to the earth in these latter days? It was to restore power and authority which once was given to men on the earth and which is essential to the complete salvation and exaltation of man in the kingdom of God. In other words, Elijah came to restore to the earth, by conferring on mortal prophets duly commissioned of the Lord, the fulness of the power of the priesthood. This priesthood holds the keys of binding and sealing on earth and in heaven of all the ordinances and principles pertaining to the salvation of man, that they may thus become valid in the celestial kingdom of God. . . .
>
> These keys of the binding, or sealing power, which were given to Peter, James, and John in their dispensation, are keys which make valid all the ordinances of the gospel. They pertain more especially to the work in the temples, both for the living and for the dead. They are the authorities, which prepare men to enter the celestial kingdom and to be crowned as sons and heirs of God.
>
> These keys hold the power to seal husbands and wives for eternity as well as for time. They hold the power to seal children to parents, the key of adoption, by which the family organization is made intact forever. This is the power, which will save the obedient from the curse in the coming of the great and dreadful day of the Lord. Through these keys the hearts of the children have turned to their fathers (*Doctrines of Salvation*, 2:118–119).

2. The Lord gave great promises regarding the work of redeeming the dead.

The prophet Isaiah recorded, "I the Lord have called thee in righteousness, and will hold thine hand, and will keep thee, and give thee for a covenant of the people, for a light of the Gentiles; To open the blind eyes, to bring out the prisoners from the prison, and them that sit in darkness out of the prison house" (Isa. 42:6–7). The great covenant of the seed of Abraham—us!—is to bless the entire world, including those in bondage in spirit prison.

Isaiah wrote further and in greater clarity, "The Spirit of the Lord God is upon me; because the Lord hath anointed me to preach good tidings unto the meek; he hath sent me to bind up the brokenhearted, to proclaim liberty to the captives, and the opening of the prison to them that are bound" (Isa. 61:1).

While there are great blessings for doing the work, we must also remember that there are serious consequences if we do *not* do the work. The dead will lie in bondage, and we as a people will fail to redeem them.

An Expansive Mission

Many hearts have already been turned as a great genealogical surge rolls throughout the Earth. In a master's thesis written a decade ago, Pamela J. Drakes noted that according to some sources, genealogy and family history work is the number-one hobby in the United States. Sixty percent of people surveyed in 2000 were interested in family history.

The Lord truly wants us to know the importance of this work—and as we recognize the importance, we realize we must take care in recording what is done. In fact, we are told in the scriptures that we must present a record of the work done for the dead that is "worthy of all acceptation" (D&C 128:24).

President Howard W. Hunter reminded us,

> We are obligated to do the work for our dead. Through the means of revelation in the beginning of the re-establishment of the Church, there was clarified to all future members what Joseph Smith the Prophet later declared was our most important responsibility while in this world (see Joseph Smith—H 1:36–39). He further emphasized this truth by saying: "It is necessary that those who are going before and

> those who come after us should have salvation in common with us; and thus hath God made it obligatory upon man" (History of the Church 6:313). (*THWH*, 238)

The great work of redeeming the dead centers in the family. The great millennial reign is all about putting together the family of God—each family in its place, sealed together for eternity. President Hunter further said,

> The great work of this dispensation is to seal family units. Not only may baptisms be performed for the dead, but endowments; also sealings, by which wives become eternal companions to husbands and their children are sealed to them as a family. The sealing of family units can be continued until the family of God is made perfect. This is the great work of the dispensation of the fullness of times, by which the hearts of the fathers are turned to the children and the hearts of the children to the fathers (see D&C 110:13–15). The uniting and redemption of the family of God was the divine plan before the foundations of the earth were laid. (*THWH*, 233)

The work of our Father and our Savior is focused on the immortality and eternal life of every man, woman, and child who has ever lived or will live. That now becomes *our* work and *our* glory, so we must step up our efforts, as President Hunter concluded in his plea: "Temple work must expand. We know that our responsibility is for every son and daughter of God even though they have left mortality. No one really dies. The great work of the temples, and all that supports it, must expand. It is imperative!" (*THWH*, 234).

Saviors on Mount Zion

Through serving in the house of the Lord, we become saviors on Mount Zion, as the prophet Obadiah expressed it (see Obad. 1:21). We do for departed souls what they cannot do for themselves. Vicarious service is one of the noblest and most Christlike ways we can serve, and participating in temple work is a transforming enterprise of the highest spiritual order. We first prepare ourselves to return in righteousness to the presence of our Heavenly Father and His Son by receiving the blessings of the temple—then, in turn, we become fully committed to ensuring that all forebears as well as all posterity have the same privilege and opportunity for salvation and exaltation in the courts on high. It is an extraordinary partnership with God to bring to pass the program of eternal life for all mankind.

The Prophet Joseph Smith explained this office and calling in a discourse given on the Nauvoo Temple grounds in January 1844:

> The Bible says, "I will send you Elijah the Prophet before the coming of the great and dreadful day of the Lord; and he shall turn the hearts of the fathers to the children, and the hearts of the children to the fathers, lest I come and smite the earth with a curse."
>
> Now, the word *turn* here should be translated *bind*, or seal. But what is the object of this important mission? or how is it to be fulfilled? The keys are to be delivered, the spirit of Elijah is to come, the Gospel to be established, the Saints of God gathered, Zion built up, and the Saints to come up as saviors on Mount Zion.
>
> But how are they to become saviors on Mount Zion? By building their temples, erecting their baptismal fonts, and going forth and receiving all the ordinances, baptisms, confirmations, washings, anointings, ordinations and sealing powers upon their heads, in behalf of all their progenitors who are dead, and redeem them that they may come forth in the first resurrection and be exalted to thrones of glory with them; and herein is the chain that binds the hearts of the fathers to the children, and the children to the fathers, which fulfills the mission of Elijah. And I would to God that this temple [in Nauvoo] was now done, that we might go into it, and go to work and improve our time, and make use of the seals while they are on earth.
>
> The Saints have not too much time to save and redeem their dead, and gather together their living relatives, that they may be saved also, before the earth will be smitten, and the consumption decreed falls upon the world.
>
> I would advise all the Saints to go to with their might and gather together all their living relatives to this place, that they may be sealed and saved, that they may be prepared against

> the day that the destroying angel goes forth; and if the whole Church should go to with all their might to save their dead, seal their posterity, and gather their living friends, and spend none of their time in behalf of the world, they would hardly get through before night would come, when no man can work; and my only trouble at the present time is concerning ourselves, that the Saints *will be divided, broken up, and scattered*, before we get our salvation secure; for there are so many fools in the world for the devil to operate upon, it gives him the advantage oftentimes. (*HC*, 6:184)

Brigham Young confirmed this doctrine a few years later:

> We are called, as it has been told you, to redeem the nations of the earth. The fathers cannot be made perfect without us; we cannot be made perfect without the fathers. There must be this chain in the holy Priesthood; it must be welded together from the latest generation that lives on the earth back to Father Adam, to bring back all that can be saved and placed where they can receive salvation and a glory in some kingdom. This Priesthood has to do it; this Priesthood is for this purpose.
>
> Can the fathers be saved without us? No. Can we be saved without them? No, and if we do not wake up and cease to long after the things of this earth, we will find that we as individuals will go down to hell, although the Lord will preserve a people unto himself. Now, we are ready to give endowments, do you have any feelings for those who have died without having the Gospel? (*DBY*, 407)

Every prophet since then has testified of the responsibility placed on the Saints to fulfill the purpose of God's temples in extending the blessings of eternity to all of mankind. In this same spirit, President Harold B. Lee proclaimed:

> *We can be saviors for the dead.* This work for the dead, performed in holy temples by members of the Church, does in reality make of them who do this work "saviors" to those who have died without a knowledge of the gospel, for thereby

> they may claim the complete gift of the Savior promised to all mankind through His atonement.
>
> It might be said of all who engage in this great work of salvation that they are "saviors on mount Zion" (see Obadiah 1:21)—building temples, erecting baptismal fonts, and receiving all the ordinances in behalf of their progenitors who are dead, redeeming them that they might come forth in the morning of the first resurrection. May we all, by engaging in this work, be as saviors on Mount Zion. (*THBL*, 584)

Preparing to be Saviors on Mount Zion

If we are to serve faithfully as saviors on mount Zion and return as families to the presence of God, we must follow the guidelines in the scriptures and the counsel of our prophets. We are to be servants of the Most High in carrying out the provisions of the Abrahamic covenant: to convey the saving truths of the gospel—including the blessings of temple work—to all quarters of the world (see Abr. 2:10–11). As President Hunter confirmed: "The temple is at the center of the mission of the Church. All of our efforts in proclaiming the gospel, perfecting the Saints, and redeeming the dead lead to the holy temple. This is because the temple ordinances are absolutely crucial; we cannot return to God's presence without them" (*THWH*, 44).

Fundamental to our preparation is to seek to become more like the Savior day by day, allowing Him to lift us, bless us, and transform us through the "mighty change in [our] hearts" (Alma 5:14; compare Mosiah 5:2)—thus imparting to us a measure of His divine nature that operates on the power of vicarious service. We do those things for others that they are not able to do for themselves, just as the Savior did for us what was not in our power to transact on our own behalf.

The venue of dynamic vicarious charity is the temple, where we serve as proxy in ordinances on behalf of those who have gone before us into the world of spirits. We receive our own endowment and the sealing blessings to ensure that our families are of an eternal character, and then, as saviors on mount Zion, we repeat the process of providing saving ordinances for our departed:

> For we without them cannot be made perfect; neither can they without us be made perfect. Neither can they nor we be made perfect without those who have died in the gospel also;

> for it is necessary in the ushering in of the dispensation of the fulness of times, which dispensation is now beginning to usher in, that a whole and complete and perfect union, and welding together of dispensations, and keys, and powers, and glories should take place, and be revealed from the days of Adam even to the present time. And not only this, but those things which never have been revealed from the foundation of the world, but have been kept hid from the wise and prudent, shall be revealed unto babes and sucklings in this, the dispensation of the fulness of times. (D&C 128:18)

How great our opportunity to prepare ourselves for the unique and divine service that transpires in the temples of the Lord! Whether we are going for the first time or are on the Lord's errand continually, let us remember that the exaltation of the dead and our exaltation are intertwined and dependent on each other.

Our beloved Savior gave us a new birth into His kingdom and to eternal life. We likewise become instruments in the hands of the Lord to open the doors of bondage to those who have gone before.

Elijah and the Priesthood Keys—Turning Our Hearts

The prophet Malachi prophesied Elijah's message and bestowal of priesthood power and keys approximately 450 years before the coming of Christ. All the standard works reference it or give it in whole or in part (see Mal. 4:5–6; Luke 1:17; D&C 2:2 ; JS—H 1:39): "And he shall plant in the hearts of the children the promises made to the fathers, and the hearts of the children shall turn to their fathers" (D&C 2:2).

This great promise, given again in our dispensation to the Prophet Joseph, has been quoted repeatedly to remind us of the promises made to the fathers so our hearts will turn to them. We are to seek after them, which means having a desire to assist in their redemption. If we don't do this, we are warned, "the whole earth would be utterly wasted at his [Christ's] coming" (D&C 2:3).

The Prophet Joseph Smith explained how Malachi's great prophecy would come about:

> But what is the object of this important mission? or how is it to be fulfilled? The keys are to be delivered, the spirit of Elijah is to come, the Gospel to be established, the

> Saints of God gathered, Zion built up, and the Saints to come up as saviors on Mount Zion. But how are they to become saviors on Mount Zion? By building their temples, erecting their baptismal fonts, and going forth and receiving all the ordinances, baptisms, confirmations, washings, anointings, ordinations and sealing powers upon their heads, in behalf of all their progenitors who are dead, and redeem them that they may come forth in the first resurrection and be exalted to thrones of glory with them; and herein is the chain that binds the hearts of the fathers to the children, and the children to the fathers, which fulfills the mission of Elijah. (*HC*, 6:184)

Elijah restored the sealing power spoken of to the Prophet Joseph on April 3, 1836:

> After this vision had closed, another great and glorious vision burst upon us; for Elijah the prophet, who was taken to heaven without tasting death, stood before us, and said:
>
> Behold, the time has fully come, which was spoken of by the mouth of Malachi—testifying that he [Elijah] should be sent, before the great and dreadful day of the Lord come—
>
> To turn the hearts of the fathers to the children, and the children to the fathers, lest the whole earth be smitten with a curse—
>
> Therefore, the keys of this dispensation are committed into your hands; and by this ye may know that the great and dreadful day of the Lord is near, even at the doors. (D&C 110:13–16)

We as a Church and people are to engage in this critical work of redeeming the dead in the temples of the Lord: "Let us, therefore, as a church and a people, and as Latter-day Saints, offer unto the Lord an offering in righteousness; and let us present in his holy temple, when it is finished, a book containing the records of our dead, which shall be worthy of all acceptation" (D&C 128:24).

Without Elijah restoring the keys, "the whole earth would be utterly wasted at his [the Lord's] coming" (D&C 2:3) and the "whole earth be smitten with a curse" (D&C 110:15). Without Elijah and the restoration of the keys, God's family would not be sealed together, and

His purpose would not be fulfilled in bringing to pass the immortality and eternal life of man. Hence, the purpose of the Creation would be wasted and the Earth would be cursed.

I have read all of these scriptures many times, and the truth touches me personally. I thank the Lord for the early missionaries who assisted the Spirit in bringing my ancestors into the Church. It has filled me with joy to read their conversion stories and great sacrifices and to know that my grandfathers and grandmothers busied themselves researching thousands of my ancestors, documenting the information by hand, submitting that information to the temple, and doing much of the temple work as well. How I love those men and women!

All of us, including me, must make renewed commitments to work on family history, one of the hard things we sometimes have to do. Like many, I have written my life history and assembled scrapbooks. But I must yet do more in searching after my kindred dead. I have renewed my commitment to the Prophet Joseph's inspirational call to redeem the dead:

> Brethren, shall we not go on in so great a cause? Go forward and not backward. Courage, brethren; and on, on to the victory! Let your hearts rejoice, and be exceedingly glad. Let the earth break forth into singing. Let the dead speak forth anthems of eternal praise to the King Immanuel, who hath ordained, before the world was, that which would enable us to redeem them out of their prison; for the prisoners shall go free.
>
> Let the mountains shout for joy, and all ye valleys cry aloud; and all ye seas and dry lands tell the wonders of your Eternal King! And ye rivers, and brooks, and rills, flow down with gladness. Let the woods and all the trees of the field praise the Lord; and ye solid rocks weep for joy! And let the sun, moon, and the morning stars sing together, and let all the sons of God shout for joy! And let the eternal creations declare his name forever and ever! And again I say, how glorious is the voice we hear from heaven, proclaiming in our ears, glory, and salvation, and honor, and immortality, and eternal life; kingdoms, principalities, and powers!
>
> Behold, the great day of the Lord is at hand; and who can abide the day of his coming, and who can stand when he appeareth? For he is like a refiner's fire, and like fuller's

> soap; and he shall sit as a refiner and purifier of silver, and he shall purify the sons of Levi, and purge them as gold and silver, that they may offer unto the Lord an offering in righteousness. Let us, therefore, as a church and a people, and as Latter-day Saints, offer unto the Lord an offering in righteousness; and let us present in his holy temple, when it is finished, a book containing the records of our dead, which shall be worthy of all acceptation. (D&C 128:22–24)

May these prophetic words move us to action—in fact, I hope some of you have already stopped reading and opened newfamilysearch.org! We each gain a more sure testimony of the power and importance of the redemption of the dead when we put aside some of our other cares and concerns and immerse ourselves in the work of becoming saviors on Mount Zion.

Further Study

As we ponder the importance of the redemption of the dead, it will be particularly helpful to understand more about Elijah, his keys, and the great prophetic and powerful turning of the hearts. The following resources will help further your study:

- Lds.org—Scriptures—Study Helps—Elijah
- Lds.org—Teachings—Gospel Topics—Priesthood Keys, Family History, and associated topics
- Lds.org—Resources—Sunday School—Leader Resources—Lesson Preparation—Lesson 39, "The Hearts of the Children Shall Turn to Their Fathers"

CHAPTER 18

Family History—The Challenge

I CHALLENGE YOU TO BEGIN your family history work today. I hope the previous chapter provided enough insight into Elijah's great mission that you have some motivation to start doing this important work. Now I'd like to teach you how to get started—because if I motivate you without training you, I frustrate you, and if I train you without motivating you, I bore you. I'll conclude this chapter with some prophetic counsel that I hope will top off your motivation.

How to Get Started

There is *much* to learn, and the procedure for doing family history work is always changing—sometimes quite a lot—over time. But remember this: there is joy in change. Be grateful for it! We believe in continuous revelation, and that also applies to the Family History Department of the Church. Their work is inspired. After all, where would we be without computers and the programmers who help us in the magnificent journey of redeeming our dead? (We'd be back to the pencil and paper I used when I was a boy!) This undertaking can be fun—so let's be positive and full of faith.

Let's start this journey the same way we start any other journey: one step at a time. I'll provide the basics, and once you're ready for more, you can get detailed training from your ward or branch family history consultant, at a family history center, or online. And should the steps change after this book is published, simply consult your ward family history consultant.

The first step is to get registered. Here's how:

Go to www.familysearch.org and click Sign In.

Click Create an Account, and fill in the information it asks for. If you are a member of The Church of Jesus Christ of Latter-day Saints, answer yes for that question, and the system will create an LDS Account for you. If you are not, answer no for that question; the system will create a FamilySearch account for you. Different resources are available to those with LDS accounts than those with FamilySearch accounts, but Family Tree and most resources are available for both for free. If you are still a little nervous, simply go to your family history center, call your ward family history consultant, or call toll-free 866-406-1830 for help. Although some use this number as a last resort, I usually use it first because it's simply a phone call away and everybody on the other end is *so* willing to help.

If you would like to take advantage of the Family Tree training materials to learn how to use the site, regardless of whether you are signed in, click Get Help on any page and then select Product Support.

Click Family Tree (the big button), and you will find the Family Tree Quick Start Guide. I'd encourage you to print the Quick Start Guide so you can refer to it away from your computer or when you are at a family history center. The information it contains is vital should you have any questions.

Now that you are registered, you are ready to get started.

A user's guide, the Family Tree Reference Manual, is available for Family Tree at https://familysearch.org/treetraining under More Training Videos. It explains everything. It's tempting to feel overwhelmed by all of the information, but don't let yourself feel that way. For now, just get started—save the user's guide on your desktop so you can refer to if you have a question.

The Get Help section also features some excellent video lessons. If you want to spend a few minutes to review them, you will be well prepared for what happens next.

Sign in at www.familysearch.org by using the username and password you set up when you registered. Once you are signed in, four basic sections are available to you: Family Tree, Photos, Search, and Temple (if you are a member of the Church).

Family Tree section. In this section, you can use the family pedigree resource to follow your pedigree back several generations. There are three views: Portrait, Traditional, and Fan Chart. Portrait view gives you a top-down, four-generation descendant view, including any pictures that have been submitted. Traditional view is your standard four-generation, bow-tie pedigree view. Fan Chart is a view of your ancestry in a five-generation fan, with one generation of descendants. This is interactive and can be repainted for any ancestor.

This is the area where you will search for ancestors and their descendants, as well as the area where you can add information and check on which temple ordinances have been completed. If an ancestor has not had a temple ordinance performed, a picture of the temple with a green arrow appears. When you click that symbol, a form enables you to select the names and ordinances that need to be completed for that person; it subsequently prints a Family Ordinance Request form that you take to the temple. At the temple, your family file cards will be printed, and you can then do the temple work. You will become a "savior on Mount Zion." This is where the journey really gets exciting!

There are a few other resources in the Family Tree section:

• The Find capability allows you to search for family members not yet connected to the tree; you can then connect them or merge them if they are duplicates. You can search for your ancestors by name or by number. (You'll learn more about numbers later.)

• The Watch List lets you select ancestors you want to track—you'll be alerted by e-mail if someone changes the information in Family Tree for that ancestor. This function lets you collaborate with others in "growing" your family tree.

Photos section. The Photos section is listed at the top of the web page, next to Family Tree. In the Photos section, you can:

Submit photos of your ancestors and connect them to your ancestor in Family Tree.

See and download photos that others have submitted; when you find them, the system will tell you how you are related.

Submit stories of your ancestors, connect a photo to the story, and tie it all together to your ancestor in Family Tree.

Submit documents of your ancestors and have them appear as sources for the events in their lives, connected to Family Tree, so that your extended family can see the actual documentation image that you have provided.

This section has been one of the most exciting recent additions to FamilySearch, allowing families to capture the live stories, experiences, and pictures of their family and share them with others.

Search section. The Search section is listed at the top of web page, next to Photos. In the Search section, you can access:

• Records: This area contains the images and indexes of historical records the Church is making available from the Family History collections of microfilm and digital images. There are now more than three billion names in this section.

- Genealogies: This area contains genealogies submitted to the Church through the Ancestral File and the Pedigree Resource File.
- Catalog: This area contains the Family History Library Catalog, an index to collections of the department.
- Books: This area lists an expanding collection of family history and genealogical publications; the Church, as well as other libraries and archives, is digitizing and publishing these books for free. There are already more than fifty thousand books online, with tens of thousands more to come.

Wiki. This area used to be the Learn section. This section brings up a wealth of information about how to do family history work. Three areas will enable you to learn, discover, and explore as you attempt to find your ancestors.

- The Research Wiki area contains an online encyclopedia about everything genealogical, from how to find records in a specific geographical area to how to find blank entry forms for census records.
- The Research Courses area contains courses on how to do genealogical research. It includes online videos where you will be instructed by Family History Library workers or their partners, such as the New England Historical and Genealogical Society.
- The Discussion Forums area lets you connect with other researchers whose interests are similar to yours, and it enables you to participate in online discussions in which you can share knowledge and ask for help.

Temple section. The Temple section is listed at the top of web page, next to Search. The Temple area keeps track of the temple work you are performing and lets you decide whether to provide your own proxies, turn the names over for the temple to provide proxies, or "unreserve" the names so other family members can do the work.

If you find that you need help and want to work with someone close to you, click on Get Help, then click Visit Us. A box will let you search for a nearby family history center where you can access additional help and assistance; this is often where your ward or branch family history consultant serves. At these locations, you have free access to many family history resources that would normally require a subscription, such as Ancestry.com.

By clicking the FamilySearch logo at the top left of the web page, you will be taken to the home page. There you will see picture pane that changes periodically and highlights six key features that can aid you in accomplishing the family history work you desire to focus on. I've already introduced the first four. The fifth is the Indexing section, and the sixth is a new feature, the Family Booklet, which is primarily for those without the benefit of technology.

Indexing section. This section is a launching point to the indexing site. Here you can sign up and participate in the FamilySearch indexing program, which creates the name indexes from the vast image collection of the Family History Department. Family history indexing is basically the process of extracting names, dates, locations, and other recorded information from digital images of historical documents. This extracted information is then used to facilitate research and provide data to be processed for temple work. It is vital to the work of redeeming the dead.

When you participate in indexing, you are helping prepare records to be processed for temple ordinances. Every ward and branch has a family history consultant or an indexing specialist who can get you set up for indexing. My family history consultant came to my home and showed me what to do—and that very night I did a batch of names. You can do it that easily too.

Blog. For those involved in social media, the Family History Department also sponsors and moderates a blog. This section is available from every page on the website by going to the bottom of a page and clicking Blog, which is right next to Feedback. This section is basically an ongoing online dialogue among representatives of the Family History Department about things that are happening in all areas of the work. Feel free to follow along, post your own comments, and share your views and contributions.

Now that you know what's available to you, go back to Family Tree and click on the different functions to become familiar with them. Don't miss the available training materials in the Get Help section. You might want to choose an ancestor's name to find out what you can do as you learn what's available. As I was writing this chapter, I randomly searched for Mathias Jolley, one of my ancestors. Lo and behold, there was a Mathias Jolley born in 1690 in England. When I clicked the Temple symbol, it read, Request Ordinances. I also found the names of lots of people who are working on my line—people I can contact to see how they are doing in their research of Mathias Jolley.

Don't forget your ward or branch family history consultant. They are eager to help with whatever you're able to do. If you need to do your work early in the morning or during the late hours of the evening, you can call the Church family consultant number; people are on staff around the clock to offer help and answer questions. The number for those in the United States is 866-406-1830 (an easy number to remember—the year the Church was officially organized). Should this number ever change, or if you'd like to find numbers for other locations in the world, simply consult the Church's website at familysearch.org. The first night I phoned, it was at 3:00 a.m.; someone in England answered and helped me over the hump. I hit another glitch at 6:00 a.m., and a sweet American sister helped me finish the process. Six names were now ready for their work to be done.

Concerning our duty to seek after our dead, President Howard W. Hunter said, "From Joseph Smith the Prophet to our present-day prophet, seer, revelator, and president we have been admonished to seek after our dead and perform for them those ordinances which are needed for their exaltation in the celestial kingdom of God" (*THWH*, 231). The Prophet Joseph Smith was even more emphatic: "Those Saints who neglect [ordinances] in behalf of their deceased relatives, do it at the peril of their own salvation" (*History of the Church*, 4:426).

President Hunter continued,

> With regard to temple and family history work, I have one overriding message: This work must hasten. The work waiting to be done is staggering and escapes human comprehension. Last year we performed proxy temple endowments for about five and a half million persons, but during that year about fifty million persons died. This might suggest futility in the work that lies before us, but we cannot think of futility. Surely the Lord will support us if we use our best efforts in carrying out the commandment to do family history research and temple work. . . . There is no work equal to that done in the temple. The objective of family history work is to make the blessings of the temple available to all people, living and dead. As we attend the temple and perform work for the dead, we acquire a deep sense of alliance with God and a better understanding of his plan for the

> salvation of the human race. We learn to love our neighbors as ourselves. Truly there is no work equal to that done in the temple. (*THWH*, 234)

When prophets speak, the debate is over. We then choose to obey and receive the promised blessings—or disobey and forfeit those blessings. I realize all of us have much to do, but let us *all* set some goals and make some plans. It's surprising how much can be accomplished in as little as one or two hours a week. Let us now go forward in redeeming the dead, that all mankind may enjoy all the blessings promised by our loving Heavenly Father and our Savior Jesus Christ.

Further Study

Following are some great resources to inspire you in the work:

- Lds.org—Teachings—Gospel Topics—Baptisms for the Dead, Family History, Plan of Salvation, Temples, and associated topics
- Lds.org.—Resources—Sunday School—Leader Resources—Lesson Preparation—D&C Lesson Manual—Lesson 39, "The Hearts of the Children Shall Turn to Their Fathers," and Lesson 40, "Finding Joy in Temple and Family History Work"

Note: Because there will continue to be improvements, new features, and changes to FamilySearch, the website will change from time to time. A sure way of finding the help you need is to click on Help in the upper right and explore the options given there. If you still have a problem finding what you want, call the help number listed on the website or visit with your ward family history consultant.

Chapter 19

Additional Doctrines of the Temple

The Doctrine of Receiving

To receive indicates acknowledgment and acceptance of knowledge, a gift, or a blessing. If we are to receive the ordinances, covenants, and word of God, we must accept them and act upon them, else we have not truly "received." Receiving acknowledges that those things we have heard or learned are true. So when we are talking about the temple, to *receive* the temple covenants and ordinances means we take them into our very souls. Further, it often entails having an experience with the Holy Spirit.

Gratitude is likewise crucial to the act of receiving. Receiving and gratitude are dependent on each other. If we are not grateful, we cannot truly receive; and if we do not truly receive, we cannot feel the gratitude from that gift or blessing. And since gratitude is the catalyst to change, change will lie dormant if we do not receive—because the word of God, doctrines, principles, commandments, ordinances, covenants, gifts, blessings, or knowledge have not been accepted and received into our hearts: "For what doth it profit a man if a gift is bestowed upon him, and he receive not the gift? Behold, he rejoices not in that which is given unto him, neither rejoices in him who is the giver of the gift" (D&C 88:33).

When discussing the concept of receiving, it is also important to consider gratitude to the giver of a gift, else we commit the sin of ingratitude. President Ezra Taft Benson reminded us:

> The Prophet Joseph is reported to have said at one time that one of the greatest sins for which the Latter-day Saints would be guilty would be the sin of ingratitude. I presume most of us have not thought of that as a serious sin. There is a great tendency for us in our prayers—in our pleadings

> with the Lord—to ask for additional blessings. Sometimes I feel we need to devote more of our prayers to expressions of gratitude and thanksgiving for blessings already received. Of course we need the daily blessings of the Lord. But if we sin in the matter of prayer, I think it is in our lack of the expressions of thanksgiving for daily blessings. (*TETB*, 363)

It follows that gratitude must be one of the cardinal virtues of life.

Now we see why blessings are withheld and consequences follow when people do not receive the gospel; by contrast, when people receive and embrace the gift, they are blessed.

The Blessings of Receiving

The blessing of receiving the covenants and the ordinances of the priesthood and, hence, the temple is the blessing of becoming sons and daughters of God in the truest sense: "But verily, verily, I say unto you, that as many as receive me, to them will I give power to become the sons [and daughters] of God, even to them that believe on my name. Amen" (D&C 11:30). We likewise read, "Wherefore, as it is written, they are gods, even the sons of God" (D&C 76:58).

Further, we receive the promise of full fellowship with the Father: "And also all they who receive this priesthood *receive* me, saith the Lord; For he that *receiveth* my servants *receiveth* me; And he that *receiveth* me *receiveth* my Father; And he that *receiveth* my Father *receiveth* my Father's kingdom; therefore all that my Father hath shall be given unto him" (D&C 84:35–38).

While we remain in mortality, we are promised direction in our daily lives: "For behold, again I say unto you that if ye will enter in by the way, and receive the Holy Ghost, it will show unto you all things what ye should do" (2 Ne. 32:5).

Consequences of Not Receiving

While sublime blessings are connected with the act of receiving the covenants, ordinances, and teachings of the gospel into our souls, the inverse is also true. Blessings that God is anxious and willing to give us will be withheld if we do not receive them: "And wo be unto him that will not hearken unto the words of Jesus, and also to them whom he hath chosen and sent among them; for whoso *receiveth* not the words of Jesus and the words of those whom he hath sent *receiveth* not him" (3

Ne. 28:34). We also read, "For strait is the gate, and narrow the way that leadeth unto the exaltation and continuation of the lives, and few there be that find it, because ye *receive* me not in the world neither do ye know me" (D&C 132:22).

When we *receive* knowledge and blessings of this magnitude, we should show great gratitude by accepting and *receiving* them. And then we must be obedient to what we have received. If we do not receive, we cannot receive the associated blessing that comes with the acceptance.

Preparation for the Bridegroom

The parable of the king's son (see Matt. 22:1–14) and the parable of the ten virgins (see Matt. 25:1–13) teach two important doctrines about ordinances and covenants. The king sent his servants to invite the guests to the marriage of his son. But "they made light of it, and went their ways, one to his farm, another to his merchandise" (v. 5). The invited guests even slew the servants. The king, who was very angry, "destroyed those murderers, and burned up their city" (v. 7).

The king again sent out his servants to extend invitations to the marriage feast, but this time he instructed them to invite all who would come, "both bad and good" (v. 10). On seeing that one of the guests was not wearing a "wedding garment" (v. 11), the king had the man bound and taken away, to be cast out. Then follows the verse we all know well: "For many are called but few are chosen" (v. 14). This bridegroom's wedding symbolizes the ushering in of the millennial reign and eventually entering into the actual presence of the Father.

The marriage theme is also rehearsed in the book of Revelation, where allusion to the temple is more specific: "Let us be glad and rejoice, and give honour to him: for the marriage of the Lamb is come, and his wife hath made herself ready. And to her was granted that she should be arrayed in fine linen, clean and white: for the fine linen is the *righteousness of saints*. And he saith unto me, Write, Blessed are they, which are called unto the marriage supper of the Lamb. And he saith unto me, These are the true sayings of God" (19:7–9).

The parable of the ten virgins carries the same message. Of the ten virgins who went out to meet the bridegroom, five were "wise" and took oil in their lamps. The other five were "foolish" and failed to take oil with them; instead, they "slumbered and slept" (v. 5) while the bridegroom tarried. Lacking oil, the foolish virgins asked the wise virgins to give them some oil, but the wise virgins said they did not have enough to share. While the foolish virgins were gone in search of oil, the bridegroom came and shut them out from the wedding, saying, "I know you not" (v. 12).

The end of the parable warns us, "Watch therefore, for ye know neither the day nor the hour wherein the Son of man cometh" (v. 13).

As a child, I thought it unkind of the wise virgins to not share their oil. But President Spencer W. Kimball clarified the principle for me: "The foolish [virgins] asked the others to share their oil, but spiritual preparedness cannot be shared in an instant. . . . This was not selfishness or unkindness. The kind of oil that is needed to illuminate the way and light up the darkness is not shareable. . . . In our lives the oil of preparedness is accumulated drop by drop in righteous living" (*Faith Precedes the Miracle*, 255–256).

Surely the oil is symbolic of the Holy Ghost, which brings light into our lives—individually. A verse in the book of Acts seems to confirm the doctrine of anointing. Peter, the head Apostle, on receiving a witness to take the gospel to the Gentiles, preached that "God anointed Jesus of Nazareth with the Holy Ghost and with power: who went about doing good; . . . for God was with him" (Acts 10:38). The Holy Ghost will indeed lead us to do good and will in a very real way prepare us for the coming of the Bridegroom in our own lives.

The lesson is clear: righteousness, faithfulness in keeping our garments clean, and observing our temple covenants are the requirements to come into the presence of our Father: "If you keep my commandments and endure to the end you shall have eternal life, which gift is the greatest of all the gifts of God" (D&C 14:7).

Keeping the Covenants and Obeying the Commandments

Keeping our covenants is critical to being worthy to receive the promised blessings of the temple, and the spirit in which we keep those commandments is what makes the difference: "Verily I say unto you, all among them who know their hearts are honest, and are broken, and their spirits contrite, and are willing to observe their covenants by sacrifice—yea, every sacrifice which I, the Lord, shall command—they are accepted of me" (D&C 97:8). Do we keep our covenants with a cheerful attitude, or do we obey grudgingly?

We should never be casual about or take lightly the sacred covenants we have made with the Lord. Many of the early Saints in Kirtland failed to realize the sacred nature of their promises:

> And your minds in times past have been darkened because of unbelief, and because you have treated lightly the things you have received—
>
> Which vanity and unbelief have brought the whole church under condemnation.
>
> And this condemnation resteth upon the children of Zion, even all.
>
> And they shall remain under this condemnation until they repent and remember the new covenant, even the Book of Mormon and the former commandments which I have given them, not only to say, but to do according to that which I have written. (D&C 84:54–57)

The ultimate, quintessential promise is extended to the faithful Saints who keep their covenants with the correct spirit:

> And if your eye be single to my glory, your whole bodies shall be filled with light, and there shall be no darkness in you; and that body which is filled with light comprehendeth all things.
>
> Therefore, sanctify yourselves that your minds become single to God, and the days will come that you shall see him; for he will unveil his face unto you, and it shall be in his own time, and in his own way, and according to his own will.
>
> Remember the great and last promise which I have made unto you; cast away your idle thoughts and your excess of laughter far from you. (D&C 88:67–69)

The concept of being filled with light all but defies mortal understanding, yet the results are clear: we will comprehend all things. Let us press forward, that we may be sanctified in this incredible journey. Seeing more clearly, feeling more deeply, becoming more godlike—these are the source of hope and joy in mortality. It is why we came to this Earth; it is what the Father ordained for us. The blessings are ours to claim, if only we will "see."

Temple Texts: The Celestial Law

John W. Welch's landmark work *The Sermon at the Temple and the Sermon on the Mount: A Latter-day Saint Approach* presents persuasive evidence that the scriptures provide two marvelous "temple texts": first, the Sermon on the Mount, as recorded in Matthew 5–7; and second, Jesus's sermon given "round about the temple" and recorded in 3 Nephi 12–14. These texts are the new law and new covenant (or a "new testament"), such as what is contained in a temple endowment. It makes perfect sense that Jesus would come to a mount (symbolic of a temple) and to His house to teach the law by which all men must live in order to enter the kingdom of heaven. Brother Welch explained these temple texts to me and wrote the following section for this book:

Authority from God

Standing behind everything that is said and done in the temple is the power and authority of God administered by virtue of the keys held by His authorized priesthood leaders. It is by the power of this authority that solemn promises can be made and relied on. A person with authority also speaks firmly, for penalties and consequences follow noncompliance. In the Sermon on the Mount and at the temple, we see Jesus speaking with this same authority, extending promises from beginning to end. His sermon begins with solemn promises. We call these the Beatitudes. They are promises, not mere assertions of opinion or psychological assessments. In the Beatitudes, Jesus is not saying, "In my view, happy are the meek." The Beatitudes, like the promises extended in the temple, are solemn assurances of future rewards. They actually read: "Blessed *will be* the poor in spirit, for theirs will be the kingdom of heaven." "Blessed *will be* the merciful, for they shall receive mercy." "Blessed *will be* the peacemakers, for they shall be called the children of God." The future tense in each of these Beatitudes assures us that the unstated verb of being in the opening clause should be understood in the future tense as well. These are promises, not just idle platitudes, and these promises come from someone who has the power and authority to make good on them.

In the middle of the Sermon on the Mount, Jesus speaks explicitly of promised rewards: "If ye love them which love you, what *reward* have ye?" [Matt. 5:46]. "Pray to thy Father which is in secret; and thy Father which seeth in secret shall *reward* thee openly" [Matt. 6:6]. At the end of the Sermon, even more promises are extended: "Ask and it shall be given you; seek, and ye shall find" [Matt. 7:7]. "What man is there of you, whom if his son ask for bread, will he give him a stone? If ye then being evil know how to give good gifts unto your children, how much more shall your Father which is in heaven give good things to them that ask him?" [Matt. 7:9–11].

Rewards are nice, but one must also notice that the face of authority signals warnings. Penalties will follow misconduct. With authority, Jesus lays out some extremely dire consequences: "But if the salt have lost his savour . . . it is thenceforth good for nothing, but to be cast out and to be trodden under foot of men" [Matt. 5:13], one of the most humiliating, literal, and demeaning punishments known to the ancient world. "Whosoever therefore shall break one of these least commandments, and shall teach men so, he shall be called *the least* in the kingdom of heaven" [Matt. 5:19]. "Except your righteousness shall exceed the righteousness of the scribes and Pharisees, ye shall *in no case* enter into the kingdom of heaven" [Matt. 5:20]. "That whosoever is angry with his brother without a cause shall be in danger of the judgment . . . but whosoever shall say, Thou fool, shall be in danger of hell fire" [Matt. 5:22]. "If ye forgive not men their trespasses, neither will your Father forgive your trespasses" [Matt. 6:15]. "Not every one that saith unto me, Lord, Lord, shall enter into the kingdom of heaven; but he that doeth the will of my Father which is in heaven" [Matt. 7:21]. To Satan and those who do his bidding, God will say, "Depart from me, ye that work iniquity" [Matt. 7:23]—for the sandy-footed house or kingdom of the foolish man will ultimately suffer great and total destruction.

These warnings of future divine judgment separate Jesus's Sermon on the Mount and sermon at the temple from the realm of theology and place it in the world of revelation. Authoritatively imposed divine penalties are not the diet of philosophers and moralists. Something much more than just good moral instruction is going on in the gospel of Jesus Christ, in His sermons, and at His temple. And yet, in addition, none of these experiences leaves people quivering with fear at the prospect of punishment, for the faces of the Savior and His holy servants are filled with eternal goodness, light, and love.

In the temple, people learn by practice, repetition, role modeling, emulating, rehearsing, and enablement. We call these actions *sacred ceremony*. Practice makes perfect. Planning and committing ahead enables success when the tests of life come. What we need is to be shown the way by one who knows the way and can walk us through the process of eternal progression. As we look at the face of that escort who initiates us to this process, we see a face of invitation beckoning us to commit to follow, to do what we are told. This is a face of things that can be taught to others in words and actions, even though much is communicated only by veiled messages and subtle innuendos. There are pregnant pauses and revealing inflections in the presentation, which highlight coded language, words, and concepts that are known only to those who have been brought into the Master's true vocabulary and sublime discourse.

Temple or ritual texts are intended to be repeated over and over. Ritual or ceremonial texts acquire meanings all their own, beyond the words they contain. Those meanings signal belonging, group identity, and loyalty. We all have our daily rituals, of course, that we perform as we go through each day, coded things we say and do, whose true meanings are known only to our family and close associates. Those kinds of rituals are mundane or casual, but other rituals become sacred when they are formally performed in holy places with celestial goals in mind.

Again, the text in the Sermon on the Mount offers us a public example of words carrying sacred meaning. These scriptures can be profitably memorized and repeated in moments of meditation. They lend themselves wonderfully to ritual. For example, the Golden Rule is known and repeated in moments of ethical decision-making. This saying is invoked to encourage ourselves and others to follow the Savior in all we do, to remember our baptismal covenant to bear one another's burdens, and to keep this greatest commandment, on which hangs all the law and the prophets.

The Lord's Prayer is another obvious example of a ritual text. It has been repeated in the Christian liturgy since the first century, as we know from an early handbook of priesthood ordinances and instructions known as the *Didache*. Initially, the Lord's Prayer was used as group prayer. It was not repeated by mere memorization, but it was used as a model for how the men and women in Christian communities should pray together.

Even the command or invitation or prediction found in the Sermon on the Mount, "Be ye therefore perfect," or "Ye shall be therefore perfect," is perfectly at home in a ceremonial setting. It invites us to go on, beyond the Aaronic order reflecting things that were said of old under the law of Moses, into a higher order of covenants, instructions, blessings, and powers. The word *perfect* is the translation of the Greek word *teleios*, which when used in ritual settings means "to go on to become fully and completely initiated and introduced into the sacred experience." The higher order, which is presented in Matthew 6, teaches rules about giving alms to the poor, laying up treasures not on Earth but in heaven, and dedicating ourselves to serving only one master. These requirements are very sacred, indeed. Many things in the Sermon on the Mount go hand in hand with a ritual experience. Fasting, washing, and anointing are mentioned in Matthew 6:16–17. Clothing the disciples is also mentioned. They are promised to be clothed in garments more glorious than those of Solomon, the great builder of the temple of Solomon. Finally, the Sermon prepares its listeners to pass through the Final Judgment and tells them what the test will be: "For with what judgment ye judge, ye shall be judged" [Matt. 7:2].

Certain parts of this experience need to be kept confidential. Jesus called those holy things pearls: "Give not that which is holy unto the dogs, neither cast ye your pearls before swine" [Matt. 7:6]. Those who violate this requirement, Jesus emphatically says, will be torn to pieces by the dogs and trampled under the feet of the pigs.

With all this, the hearers are prepared to make a threefold petition: to ask, seek, and knock. The text then speaks of passing through a narrow opening or gate on a narrow path that is mentioned just before a tree that produces good fruit. This tree and this way are symbolic references to the tree of life and the path that leads back to it in the Garden of Eden. And in the end, the righteous person is allowed to enter into the presence of God, while the wicked is told, *Depart. I never knew you.* Being recognized as one who "knew" God can certainly be understood as a reference to having entered into a covenant with God.

We can now understand why the Sermon on the Mount begins with that series of promises of ultimate blessings called the Beatitudes. They promise celestial glory. The first can be translated: "Exalted will be the poor in spirit, for theirs shall be the celestial kingdom." Another Beatitude promises a new name, for the peacemakers shall be called "the children of God," and "the pure in heart" shall "see God." And at the same time, we can understand why it ends with the short parable familiar from Primary: "Whosoever heareth these sayings of mine, and doeth them, I will liken him unto a wise man, which built his house upon the rock. But whosoever heareth these and does them not, is likened unto a foolish man who built his house on the sand." In the world view that prevailed in Jesus's day, the temple stood like a rock between the heavens and waters above and the primordial waters below. The temple withstood the waters of chaos, destruction, and darkness. The floods would indeed come up and the rains come, but those who build their house upon the principles and powers of the temple will not be overcome. (John Welch, personal papers)

This visionary explanation of the Savior's sermons is eye-opening and helps us realize the words of Christ speak clearly of the temple of our God. When we come to understand and appreciate these supernal truths, we will recognize the temple and the doctrines of the temple in many of the scriptural accounts of the prophets. Even the title of our Savior *Christ the Lord* is a significant link through the Atonement to the endowment in the house of the Lord. I'm deeply indebted to John Welch for this most insightful treatise.

The New Law

The Lord admonished the people of Nephi, "And behold, I have given you the law and the commandments of my Father, that ye shall believe in me, and that ye shall repent of your sins, and come unto me with a broken heart and a contrite spirit. Behold, ye have the commandments before you, and the law is fulfilled. Therefore come unto me and be ye saved; for verily I say unto you, that except ye shall keep my commandments, which I have commanded you at this time, ye shall in no case enter into the kingdom of heaven" (3 Ne. 9:19–20).

This charge surely speaks of being obedient to the commandments and offering the new sacrifice of a broken heart and contrite spirit.

Elder Bruce R. McConkie emphasized the importance of such obedience:

> That law by obedience to which men gain an inheritance in the kingdom of God in eternity is called celestial law. It is the law of the gospel, the law of Christ, and it qualifies men for admission to the celestial kingdom because in and through it men are "sanctified by the reception of the Holy Ghost," thus becoming clean, pure, and spotless (3 Ne. 27:19–21).

> "And they who are not sanctified through the law which I have given unto you, even the law of Christ," the Lord says, "must inherit another kingdom, even that of a terrestrial kingdom, or that of a telestial kingdom. For he who is not able to abide the law of a celestial kingdom cannot abide a celestial glory" (D. & C. 88:21–22). Those who have the companionship of the Holy Ghost and are guided thereby in their lives are "able to abide the law of a celestial kingdom," including the law of consecration or anything else the Lord might ask of them. They are the ones who—"united according to the union required by the law of the celestial kingdom" (D. & C. 105:1–5)—will build up Zion in the last days. (*Mormon Doctrine*, 117)

Obedience was the watchword for our missionaries in the England London South Mission when I served as mission president. Obedience is often called the first law of heaven, and rightly so. This is the essence of our test here upon the Earth; the Lord said, "And we will prove them herewith, to see if they will do all things whatsoever the Lord their God shall command them" (Abr. 3:25). It is through obedience that we demonstrate our love of God: "If ye love me, keep my commandments" (John 14:15).

The Importance of Prayer, Sacrifice, Feasting, and Living by the Word of God

The act of prayer and the principle on which it is based permeate the temple and the scriptures; in prayer we draw upon the powers of heaven. It is the foundational principle of a loving Heavenly Father who invites His children to seek Him. This concept is taught with great clarity and by example in the temple, where we express gratitude; seek light, truth, wisdom, and understanding; plead for direction and help; and seek strength and confirmation.

In the temple, we learn that we are to watch and pray always so as not to be led away into temptation. We learn that our Father answers our prayers by sending messengers, angels, prophets, leaders, teachers, and inspiration from the Holy Spirit. We learn that sometimes He answers swiftly and clearly, and sometimes we need to wait patiently and do more on our part. We learn that sometimes answers come through a stupor of thought and that sometimes the Lord simply says no. We learn that sometimes He indicates that alternatives are be okay, and sometimes He sends a parent, neighbor, friend, or leader with the message. We learn that sometimes an event occurs that answers our question or makes our problem solvable. We learn that sometimes our concern is trivial or the answer already clear, and the Lord simply does not need to be involved. But one point is made clear in all instances of teaching concerning prayer: We must pray always, with real intent, having faith, and coming before the Lord with a broken heart and contrite spirit. Then He will answer.

These principles and guidelines are taught clearly in the temple. Do our temple eyes discern there the doctrine of prayer and worship? Sometimes we miss the most elemental things if we do not approach them with the correct posture or spirit. As we come to see and understand the goodness of God, our prayers of gratitude and our needs will echo daily in the presence of our Heavenly Father. Our homes, as well as the temple, become sanctuaries because of our humble prayers.

Along with the commandments to pray and offer sacrifice, we are admonished to read and study the scriptures—ancient, modern, and living. Scriptures are the revealed words of God through the power of the Holy Ghost, be they to prophets of the past or the present: "And this is the ensample unto them, that they shall speak as they are moved upon by the Holy Ghost. And whatsoever they shall speak when moved upon by the Holy Ghost shall be scripture, shall be the will of the Lord, shall be the mind of the Lord, shall be the word of the Lord, shall be the voice of the Lord, and the power of God unto salvation. Behold, this is the promise of the Lord unto you, O ye my servants" (D&C 68:3–5).

As we come to understand the principles of prayer, sacrifice, and searching the scriptures, a multitude of truths beckon us to apply these to the temple, which then truly becomes a *house of learning*. If we prepare prayerfully to go to the temple and are willing to sacrifice for this privilege, the Holy Ghost will become our instructor as we listen to and observe the teachings carefully.

Happiness and the Temple

The symbolism in the temple consists of a multiplicity of meanings, layer upon layer, which means that we learn "line upon line, precept upon precept" each time we attend. The wonderful thing about those symbols is that as we grasp them, they come to form an increasingly coherent whole, all of them resonating one with another so as to connect and clarify all aspects of the Atonement. Indeed, that is exactly what happens in the course of the symbolic presentation of the endowment. The joy that comes from obedience to the laws and ordinances of the gospel is encompassed in the ordinances and covenants of the Lord's house. That is why Nephi, after building a temple in the New World, could say of his people that they now "lived after the manner of happiness" (2 Ne. 5:27).

Everything in our Father's perfect plan is designed for our happiness and to make it possible for us to return to God's presence. Under the law of Moses, the ark of the covenant housed in the Holy of Holies of the temple was a symbol of the presence of the Lord and was the focus of worship at that time. Likewise today, the culminating event of our mortal life is to symbolically return to the presence of God the Father. The converse is also true, as we learn from Nephi's pronouncement that the curse that came upon the Lamanites was their being cut off from the presence of God (see 2 Ne. 5:20)—which means, symbolically and literally, they could no longer participate in the ordinances of the priesthood in a temple of God.

Jesus's teachings to the Nephites as they gathered around the temple mount had a powerful and profound effect on those who heard and received the message: "And it came to pass that there was no contention in the land, because of the love of God which did dwell in the hearts of the people. And there were no envyings, nor strifes, nor tumults, nor whoredoms, nor lyings, nor murders, nor any manner of lasciviousness; and surely there could not be a happier people among all the people who had been created by the hand of God" (4 Ne. 1:15–16).

We often use the word *happiness* lightly, failing to appreciate the eternal significance of its true meaning. Happiness is always equated with returning to the presence of God. The endowment, the receiving of sacred ordinances and covenants, is the process that enables us to return to the presence of God and there enjoy never-ending happiness.

It is significant that one of the names of the plan of salvation is the "plan of happiness"; happiness is indeed the design of our existence. Our object is not the forbidden pleasures of the world, for wickedness never was happiness, and we are restored according to our works:

> And if their works are evil they shall be restored unto them for evil. Therefore, all things shall be restored to their

> proper order, everything to its natural frame—mortality raised to immortality, corruption to incorruption—raised to endless happiness to inherit the kingdom of God, or to endless misery to inherit the kingdom of the devil, the one on one hand, the other on the other—
>
> The one raised to happiness according to his desires of happiness, or good according to his desires of good; and the other to evil according to his desires of evil; for as he has desired to do evil all the day long even so shall he have his reward of evil when the night cometh. (Alma 41:4–5)

Learning the doctrines of God in the temple is exhilarating and fulfilling. My eyes and ears and heart have helped me come to understand eternal truths and blessings I would have thought impossible many years ago. These truths have enlarged my soul as I have come to see more clearly the meaning of the temple ceremony and as I have contemplated how we as Saints can grow together to become even as God is.

Chapter 20

The Temple as a Model for Teaching Our Families

Adam and Eve set the example for teaching our families:

> And in that day Adam blessed God and was filled, and began to prophesy concerning all the families of the earth, saying: Blessed be the name of God, for because of my transgression my eyes are opened, and in this life I shall have joy, and again in the flesh I shall see God.
>
> And Eve, his wife, heard all these things and was glad, saying, Were it not for our transgression we never should have had seed, and never should have known good and evil, and the joy of our redemption, and the eternal life which God giveth unto all the obedient.
>
> And Adam and Eve blessed the name of God, and they *made all things known unto their sons and their daughters.* (Moses 5:10–12)

"All things" certainly includes the plan of redemption as taught in the temple.

I am grateful for the pattern our first parents set as a clear example of instruction for us. We are to teach our children as we have been taught in the temple. Just as our personal growth extends from temple worship, so we can pass that same blessing on to our children.

I'd like to again defer to the insights of John Welch regarding using the temple as a template in teaching our children and our families. He wrote the following section specifically for this book to explain that important principle.

Using the Temple as a Template

Many times in life, it comes in handy to have a pattern, a stencil, or a blueprint. We sometimes call these models "templates," and we consult them often as we sew or build. By following a map or guidelines, we have a better chance of getting where we are trying to go.

In many ways, the temple is also a template. It is a scale model of the eternal world, of things in heaven and on Earth. It gives righteous patterns and guidelines to follow. This template can guide us in our most important decisions in life. How much guidance one gets out of the temple depends on how one sees the temple. If it is seen as a toolbox or road map, it will serve you well.

For example, in raising children, what better guide could one ask for than the model given of how God Himself instructed and raised Adam and Eve, and by extension all of their descendants? By seeing the temple this way, we might ask ourselves, what does God teach us in the temple, and in what order are those principles taught? Might this be a good way to teach our children?

Early in life, children should be taught the importance of their mortal bodies and the need to keep their bodies protected and clothed. Ordinary names become special and holy when we understand the value of each individual soul in the eyes of God. Even the youngest children can be taught to honor their family name. Keeping confidences is another principle young children can be taught.

Next, children can appreciate the beauties of the world and its miraculous orderliness. They can be taught about mountains and rivers, plants and animals, as well the fundamental existence of opposites in this world—light and dark, wet and dry, pleasure and pain—so they can learn by experience to distinguish good from evil and keep the commandment to be happy and have joy (see 2 Ne. 2:25).

In the next stage of childhood, the garden of life, one must be taught to make choices and use agency. There is a positive side to obedience when one thinks of all the things one can do. Of many things, one may freely eat (see Gen. 2:16). Here children are taught to find joy in good work, tending gardens, and in naming and caring for animals. But here one must also begin to recognize Satan's temptations, some of which are outright deceptions and others half-truths, but all are lies. If one succumbs, children here can learn that God will always find them.

He may ask, "Where are you going?" (see Moses 4:15), but He already knows the answer to such questions. By learning to take responsibility for the natural consequences of their actions and by making and keeping promises, children will be equipped to go out into the world and learn to recognize the voices that can or cannot be trusted.

This kind of thinking draws important lessons from every corner of the temple. In the temple, the Father teaches His children how to make sacrifices and to be unselfish, even if they do not understand why. He teaches the importance of giving thanks, of not doing everything for money, of returning and reporting, of knowing what is found in the scriptures, and of not taking the name of God in vain. With this, one is prepared to enter Young Men or Young Women, the level of the Aaronic Priesthood.

In preparing young people for serving missions and getting married, the model tells us that principles of morality, chastity, loyalty, dedication, and a yearning for spirituality are to be taught next. And with that, one is prepared to receive the Melchizedek Priesthood, reconcile with all people, be worthy to return home to God's presence, and marry for time and eternity.

Behind the idea of this model stand three concepts. The first is that each thing we see or hear in the temple is there to teach us some principle. Everything that is modeled or presented to us there is based on a true concept or principle. The second is that every true principle should be followed and put into practice. These things are not shown for our idle curiosity. We are expected to use what we learn in the temple to promote much righteousness. And third, things are intentionally and purposefully presented to us by this model in a particular order. The temple is a house of order. The order in which ideas are introduced in the temple makes sense developmentally in the lives of growing children and in many other settings as well. The order makes sense in our own personal development and maturation within our Church callings or our marriages. In other words, the things that come first in the temple are things we should work on first; the things that come next should be the focus of attention as we progress step by step. (John Welch, personal correspondence)

Every moment in the temple can be a learning moment, a glimpse of God's purposes beyond particulars of the ceremony. This is how our

Heavenly Father prepares His children to return to His presence. The temple is the means by which we receive the greatest of God's promised blessings. As we teach our children, we can follow a parallel pattern adapted to their level of understanding, as President Ezra Taft Benson counseled:

> I would like to direct my remarks to you parents and grandparents. I would like to share with you what I would hope you would teach your children about the temple.
>
> The temple is a sacred place, and the ordinances in the temple are of a sacred character. Because of its sacredness we are sometimes reluctant to say anything about the temple to our children and grandchildren.
>
> As a consequence, many do not develop a real desire to go to the temple, or when they go there, they do so without much background to prepare them for the obligations and covenants they enter into. I believe a proper understanding or background will immeasurably help prepare our youth for the temple. This understanding, I believe, will foster within them a desire to seek their priesthood blessings just as Abraham sought his. ("What I Hope You Would Teach Your Children about the Temple," *Ensign*, May 1986, 6)

The plan of happiness is all about families, and each family is a family of God. Parents have a solemn duty not only to love and care for their children but also to prepare them to receive the covenants and instruction of the temple.

How do we go about that preparation? As the *Encyclopedia of Mormonism* remarks, members of the Church can discuss everything about the temple except specific details regarding the temple ceremonies—the signs and tokens and the specific language of the ceremony and covenants, all of which are too sacred to discuss outside the temple. It is entirely appropriate to teach our children using the scriptures, the temple preparation course, statements from our prophets, and articles in the *Encyclopedia of Mormonism* itself. In this book, I have made every effort to follow that guideline. I have also drawn heavily from the scriptures for insights and understanding that will help us appreciate the significance of the temple in our lives.

CHAPTER 21

An Invitation to Come to the House of the Lord

THE LORD HAS INVITED US to come to His house that we might be endowed with power. The First Presidency has emphasized the importance of the temple—and all of its lifesaving ordinances and covenants, knowledge of the mysteries of godliness, and knowledge of God—as being one of the most paramount topics on which Church leaders should focus.

The following admonition from a leadership training document the First Presidency wrote leaves no doubt as to leaders' and parents' responsibilities in regard to the place of the temple in Heavenly Father's children's lives. To accomplish the mission of the Church,

> leaders should encourage every member to *receive all essential priesthood ordinances, keep the associated covenants, and qualify for exaltation and eternal life.* Church leaders should use priesthood quorums, auxiliaries, and stake and ward councils to help produce the following results:
>
> **Families:** Teach the preeminence of the home and family as the basic organizational unit of the Church. *Emphasize the place of the higher priesthood in helping individuals and families qualify for exaltation* (see D&C 84:19–22). Encourage each family member—parents and children—to study the scriptures, pray regularly, and live the gospel of Jesus Christ.
>
> **Adults:** *Encourage each adult to be worthy to receive the ordinances of the temple. Teach all adults to identify their ancestors and perform vicarious temple ordinances for them.*
>
> **Youth:** Help prepare each young man to receive the Melchizedek Priesthood, *to receive the ordinances of the temple*, and to be worthy to serve a full-time mission. Help prepare

> each young *woman to be worthy to make and keep sacred covenants and receive the ordinances of the temple.* Strengthen youth through participation in meaningful activities.
>
> **All Members:** *Help priesthood and auxiliary leaders, ward councils, ward and full-time missionaries, and members work cooperatively in a balanced effort to rescue individuals,* strengthen families and Church units, increase priesthood activity, and gather Israel through conversion, retention, and activation. Teach members to provide for themselves and their families, and assist the poor and needy in the Lord's way. (*Handbook 2: Administering the Church*)

This revelatory statement emphasizes the importance of the temple in our lives as a way of empowering us to perfection and fulfilling the Prophet Joseph Smith's prophetic vision concerning our dead. The Prophet stated, "The greatest responsibility in this world that God has laid upon us, is to seek after our dead." He then added that because we cannot be saved without them, "it is necessary that those who have gone before and those who come after us should have salvation in common with us, and thus hath God made it obligatory to man" (*Times and Seasons*, 5:616).

Everything about the gospel points to the temple and the exalting blessings all mankind are to receive there. This is the work in which we are engaged—that all mankind may receive the ordinances of the temple and thus have the opportunity to return to the presence of our Heavenly Father.

The Invitation

The Lord does not *assign* us to come to His house; we are *invited* to come so He can endow us with power and the Holy Ghost. No one on Earth keeps a record of our attendance. No one will ask us if we have been to the temple or require us to account for the number of ordinances we have completed. Temple worship is a sacred agreement between us and the Lord. It is up to us to choose to accept His invitation.

When we choose to go to the temple, we choose to separate ourselves from the world. That separation is represented by our exchanging our clothes of the world for clothing of white, a symbol of cleanliness and purity. In the Lord's house, we are all alike, for the Lord is no respecter of persons. All can receive the same blessings through faithfulness.

Our agency is what gives us the right to choose to go to and worship in the temple. The Lord wants to endow us with power, but we must accept that gift, "that ye might escape the power of the enemy, and be gathered unto me a righteous people, without spot and blameless—Wherefore, for this cause I gave unto you the commandment that ye should go to the Ohio; and there I will give unto you my law; and there you shall be endowed with power from on high" (D&C 38:31–32).

The continual reminders we receive about building temples and gathering the Lord's people confirms the emphasis the Lord puts on building temples. Building temples is for more than redeeming the dead. It is also for giving the precious gift of enlightenment and power. The Lord Himself says, "Yea, verily I say unto you, I gave unto you a commandment that you should build a house, in the which house I design to endow those whom I have chosen with power from on high" (D&C 95:8). "And ye are to be taught from on high. Sanctify yourselves and ye shall be endowed with power, that ye may give even as I have spoken" (D&C 43:16).

The temple is for the perfecting of the Saints and the empowering of those who proclaim the gospel. The temple is the focus of the gospel and the key to exaltation and eternal lives. This is the place where we make covenants and receive ordinances so we can receive a life like that of our Heavenly Parents. This is why we look to the temple—that we may receive all that our Father has.

With all of that in mind, would we not now seek to go to the temple more often?

We have been given a charge to sanctify ourselves. Though all blessings are gifts from God, we are to magnify them and work out our own salvation so as to be clean, pure, and holy. We are instructed, "Come unto the Lord with all your heart, and work out your own salvation with fear and trembling before him" (Morm. 9:27). We should be prepared to learn the eternal truths of the temple, which knowledge will give us power to do good:

> That they themselves may be prepared, and that my people may be taught more perfectly, and have experience, and know more perfectly concerning their duty, and the things which I require at their hands. And this cannot be brought to pass until mine elders are endowed with power from on high. For behold, I have prepared a great endowment and blessing to be poured out upon them, inasmuch as they are faithful and continue in humility before me (D&C 105:10–12).

Then we too will feel like the Saints who were endowed prior to the exodus from Nauvoo. We will rejoice when we come to realize the extent and power of the blessings with which we will be endowed: "Yea the hearts of thousands and tens of thousands shall greatly rejoice in consequence of the blessings which shall be poured out, and the endowment with which my servants have been endowed in this house" (D&C 110:9).

These scriptures are a plea by our Heavenly Father and our Savior to Their beloved children to please come to Their house, where we make sacred covenants and receive sacred ordinances that will endow us with knowledge, wisdom, protection, and an abundance of the Spirit. Such things will enable us to better prove ourselves worthy during our mortal journey. What love, kindness, and concern—what an expression of mercy and grace, doing all of this for us so we can have eternal life!

Prophets in modern times have promised us blessings for devoted temple worship. President Gordon B. Hinckley said:

> I hope that everyone gets to the temple on a regular basis. I hope your children over 12 years of age have the opportunity of going to the temple to be baptized for the dead. If we are a temple-going people, we will be a better people, we will be better fathers and husbands, we will be better wives and mothers. I know your lives are busy. I know that you have much to do. But I make you a promise that if you will go to the house of the Lord, you will be blessed; life will be better for you. Now, please, please, my beloved brethren and sisters, avail yourselves of the great opportunity to go to the Lord's house and thereby partake of all of the marvelous blessings that are yours to be received. ("Excerpts from Recent Addresses of President Gordon B. Hinckley," *Ensign*, Jan. 1998, 73)

President Hinckley likewise explained the power of true conversion when he said, "There is the motivation that comes of true conversion. When there throbs in the heart of an individual Latter-day Saint a great and vital testimony of the truth of this work, he will be found doing his duty in the Church. . . . He will be found in attendance at the temple as frequently as his circumstances will permit" (Regional Representatives' Seminar, Apr. 6, 1984).

President Hinckley has admonished us, "I would hope that we might go to the house of the Lord a little more frequently. . . . In this noisy, bustling, competitive world, what a privilege it is to have a sacred house where we may experience the sanctifying influence of the Spirit of the Lord" ("Closing Remarks," *Ensign*, Nov. 2004, 104–105).

One day as we were talking, O. Dewey Bennett, my counselor in the Manti Temple presidency, mused, "Would it ever have been a convenient time to build the Kirtland Temple?" We discussed the implications of the fact that the early Saints built the temple during a period of much tribulation and poverty. That served as a launching place for a discussion of the fact that the events and activities that bring such spiritual power into our lives are rarely accomplished without great sacrifice—and are never convenient.

Was it convenient for the Prophet Joseph to be persecuted? Incarcerated? Tarred and feathered?

Was it convenient for the Saints to build the Nauvoo Temple?

Was it convenient for the Saints to leave Nauvoo in the dead of winter, to line their wagons up along Parley Street, where they waited for days to cross the mighty Mississippi River?

Was it convenient for the Saints to cross the plains?

Was it convenient for the Willie and Martin handcart companies to be stranded on the frozen trail, where so many died?

Was it convenient for the Saints to build the Salt Lake, St. George, Logan, and Manti Temples?

Most of all, was it convenient for the Lord God, our Savior Jesus Christ, to suffer with such agony in Gethsemane and later die on the cross? This crowning event in the perfect plan of our Heavenly Father was wrought with a price we cannot comprehend, although we can be grateful for it. His sacrifice demonstrates the great love our Savior has for us.

We learn from the Savior Himself that His sacrifice and Atonement makes it possible to repent—and, as a result, brings a great responsibility upon us to repent:

> Therefore I command you to repent—repent, lest I smite you by the rod of my mouth, and by my wrath, and by my anger, and your sufferings be sore—how sore you know not, how exquisite you know not, yea, how hard to bear you know not.
>
> For behold, I, God, have suffered these things for all, that they might not suffer if they would repent;

> But if they would not repent they must suffer even as I;
> Which suffering caused myself, even God, the greatest of all, to tremble because of pain, and to bleed at every pore, and to suffer both body and spirit—and would that I might not drink the bitter cup, and shrink—
> Nevertheless, glory be to the Father, and I partook and finished my preparations unto the children of men.
> Wherefore, I command you again to repent, lest I humble you with my almighty power; and that you confess your sins, lest you suffer these punishments of which I have spoken, of which in the smallest, yea, even in the least degree you have tasted at the time I withdrew my Spirit. (D&C 19:15–20)

We all need to repent, especially in regard to temple work. There will never be a convenient time—but just as it was not "convenient" for the Savior to perform His infinite Atonement, inconvenience cannot excuse our delinquency.

When we read of the Lord not wanting to drink of the bitter cup when so much pain and suffering were involved, we begin to grasp the price He paid—the ultimate inconvenience. Yet, in our Savior's sacrifice and suffering, we receive the ultimate gift of forgiveness through repentance and eternal life through obedience. How grateful we should be! How changed we should become! Is it too much for our prophets to ask us to redouble our efforts in regard to redeeming the dead?

As we try to make time to attend the temple, we should expect opposition—it is part of the Father's perfect plan. Temple worship will almost never be convenient; it calls for obedience, for consecration, and for sacrifice, as Latter-day Saints in many parts of the world exemplify. In times past, it was extremely difficult in many areas to simply get to the temple. Things are improving, but consider the following:

Saints in Honduras and Nicaragua spend fourteen to thirty-two hours of travel on a bus to get to the temple.

Saints in Thailand must plan for nearly a year to travel the 1,370 miles to the Manila Temple.

Brazilian Saints in the heart of the Amazon travel 3,890 miles by canoe and by bus to attend the temple.

Temple work will not always be convenient, but it will always be lifesaving and exalting. And while we may not be persecuted, jailed unjustly, or driven from our homes, while we may not have to travel for days to enjoy the privilege of worship in the house of the Lord, we *will* have to make sacrifices. Let us set some goals and make some plans to obtain the blessings of temple worship and redeem the dead. It is our personal choice—"That every man may act in doctrine and principle pertaining to futurity, according to the moral agency which I have given unto him, that every man may be accountable for his own sins in the day of judgment" (D&C 101:78).

Moral agency carries with it such responsibility and accountability for our choices. The prophet Brigham Young spoke to this very point:

> What do you suppose the fathers would say if they could speak from the dead? Would they not say, "We have lain here thousands of years, here in this prison house, waiting for this dispensation to come? Here we are, bound and fettered, in the association of those who are filthy?" What would they whisper in our ears? Why, if they had the power the very thunders of heaven would be in our ears, if we could but realize the importance of the work we are engaged in. All the angels in heaven are looking at this little handful of people, and stimulating them to the salvation of the human family. So also are the devils in hell looking at this people, too, and trying to overthrow us, and the people are still shaking hands with the servants of the devil, instead of sanctifying themselves and calling upon the Lord and doing the work which he has commanded us and put into our hands to do. When I think upon this subject, I want the tongues of seven thunders to wake up the people. Can the fathers be saved without us? No. Can we be saved without them? No, and if we do not wake up and cease to long after the things of this earth, we will find that we as individuals will go down to hell, although the Lord will preserve a people unto himself. Now we are ready to give endowments, do you have any feelings for those who have died without having the Gospel? (*DBY*, 305)

I encourage you to make the inconvenient choice and to call down the blessings of heaven on you, your ancestors, and your posterity. The work of redeeming the dead is both sacred and solemn. It is temple work. It is the Father and the Savior's work. It is *our* work.

The feelings I have while in the temple let me know I am in the Lord's house. I feel peace. I look forward to attending the temple. When things in my everyday life get overwhelming, it is a refuge. It is a safe place, a holy place. While serving in the Manti Temple, I had the joy of simply being in the temple for thousands of hours. They were hours full of joy and peace. Yes, there were some harried moments in trying to make everything in the schedule work out, but even then, the tender mercies and miracles of the Lord always made everything work out. As workers, we would discuss how the Lord's hand made sure that His house was a house of order—a house of prayer, a house of revelation, a house where His presence and glory were felt.

My cup runs over with gratitude for the goodness of God in blessing His children through the ordinances and covenants of the greater priesthood and through the great vicarious work in His holy house.

Chapter 22
Temple Worthiness and Attendance

All blessings from God are granted to us based on our obedience and worthiness. Worthiness to enter the house of the Lord is a symbol of our membership in the kingdom of God. Temple worship is part of maintaining our temple worthiness, and it should be our continual goal.

We learn from the *Encyclopedia of Mormonism* that

> the bishop, who is responsible as a judge in Israel (D&C 107:72, 74, 76), conducts the initial [temple recommend] interview. He seeks to discern personal worthiness and standards of Christlike living and counsels appropriately with those whose lives are in need of any change or repentance. It is considered a serious matter to become prepared to receive the covenants, ordinances, and blessings of the temple. Questions are asked to ascertain one's faith in God the Eternal Father, in his Son Jesus Christ, and in the Holy Ghost; and inquiry is made regarding the person's testimony of the restored gospel and loyalty to the teachings and leaders of the Church. Worthiness requirements include being honest, keeping the commandments, such as chastity—sexual continence before marriage and fidelity within marriage—obeying the laws of tithing and the Word of Wisdom, fulfilling family responsibilities, and avoiding affiliation with dissident groups. The First Presidency often emphasizes that it is a solemn responsibility for a bishop or stake president to conduct a temple recommend interview. An equal responsibility rests upon the person who is interviewed to respond to questions fully and honestly [*Ensign*, Nov. 1978, 40–43]. One practical

> purpose of the recommend interview is to help the applicant be adequately prepared to commit to the way of life the temple covenants will require. (4:1446)

Temple worthiness is a barometer of our righteousness. It is as if the oil of our lamps testifies of our righteousness. President Howard W. Hunter, in his short tenure as the President of the Church, emphasized temple worship:

> The temple should be our ultimate earthly goal. Let us truly be a temple-attending and a temple-loving people. We should hasten to the temple as frequently, yet prudently, as our personal circumstances allow. We should go not only for our kindred dead but also for the personal blessing of temple worship, for the sanctity and safety that are within those hallowed and consecrated walls. As we attend the temple, we learn more richly and deeply the purpose of life and the significance of the atoning sacrifice of the Lord Jesus Christ. Let us make the temple, with temple worship and temple covenants and temple marriage, our ultimate earthly goal and the supreme mortal experience. . . .
>
> The Lord desires that his people be a temple-motivated people. It would be the deepest desire of my heart to have every member of the Church be temple worthy. I would hope that every adult member would be worthy of—and carry—a current temple recommend, even if proximity to a temple does not allow immediate or frequent use of it. . . .
>
> May I encourage the adults who have current temple recommends to attend the temple on a regular basis. Make sure in your planning that you include a visit to the temple as often as personal circumstances will allow. I promise you that your personal spirituality, relationship with your husband or wife, and family relationships will be blessed and strengthened as you regularly attend the temple. (*THWH*, 236, 239, 241)

I testify that knowing that our eternal companions are worthy of a temple recommend reassures us of each other's faithfulness. It is a witness of our desire to serve the Lord and keep the commandments.

Elder Richard G. Scott also admonished the Saints to attend the temple frequently, encouraging them to set personal goals:

> Because I love you, I am going to speak to you heart to heart, without mincing words. I have seen that many times individuals have made great sacrifices to go to a distant temple. But when a temple is built close by, within a short time, many do not visit it regularly. I have a suggestion: When a temple is conveniently nearby, small things may interrupt your plans to go to the temple. Set specific goals, considering your circumstances, of when you can and will participate in temple ordinances. Then do not allow anything to interfere with that plan. ("Temple Worship: The Source of Strength and Power in Times of Need," *Ensign*, May 2009, 43–45)

As I reread Elder Scott's remarks, my thought was, *I can do better.* I immediately set a goal for the next year, and with the Lord's help, I accomplished it, with many visits to spare. Seeking to please the Lord always makes a goal more satisfying and a commitment easier to keep. Goals are a way to help us keep our covenants and obey the commandments. Elder Scott also testified in his talk that setting a goal worked for him—and I likewise testify that it worked for me. Let us all consider setting a goal.

We must come to understand as we progress in the gospel that temple worthiness and temple worship are matters of salvation, ones that matter most in life. Just as oxygen, food, clothing, and shelter are requisites to mortality, so temple worship is requisite to our spirituality and requisite to eternal life, because it is through the ordinances and covenants of the temple that we are appointed to exaltation.

The Hymns of the Temple

When we consider worthiness, we are well advised to turn to the scriptures, which teach of the attributes we should endeavor to cultivate as we prepare to cross the threshold of the temple. We might call the scriptures that describe these attributes "the hymns of the temple." The temple hymns are all about moral worthiness, the attributes of those who sought to enter the temple compound in ancient Israel, and the promised blessings that came from worshipping in those sacred precincts.

I am indebted to Donald Parry for my introduction to the "temple hymns." He has given me permission to quote his work and adapt it to our discussion (adapted from Parry, "Who Shall Ascend?" 729–742).

Hymns of the Temple, Psalm 15
A Psalm of David (Ps. 15:1–5)

The Question: "Lord, who shall abide in thy tabernacle? who shall dwell in thy holy hill?"

The Answer: "He that walketh uprightly, and worketh righteousness, and speaketh the truth in his heart. *He that* backbiteth not with his tongue, nor doeth evil to his neighbour, nor taketh up a reproach against his neighbour. In whose eyes a vile person is contemned; but he honoureth them that fear the Lord. He that sweareth to his own hurt, and changeth not. He that putteth not out his money to usury, nor taketh reward against the innocent."

The Promised Blessings: "He that doeth these *things* shall never be moved" from the Lord's holy house.

David simply asks the question, "Who can come to the temple of the Lord?" The answer is clear: those who are kind, loving, and otherwise Christlike. Among other things, those who are worthy to come to the temple strive to:

Walk uprightly, continuing toward perfection.

Work righteousness—do the good works they were foreordained to do.

Speak the truth in their hearts—their true self being manifested.

Hold others equal in their eyes and look down upon no one but rather love and nurture.

Give God honor—the Lord honors those who reverence Him.

Swear in their hearts—they are true and faithful to their promises.

Take no reward against the innocent—never take advantage of their status.

When we do these things, we *will not be moved* from the temple of our God nor from His presence—in other words, we will not lose our temple blessings. We will have the blessings of exaltation.

Hymns of the Temple, Psalm 24
The Psalm of David (Ps. 24:3–5)

The Question: "Who shall ascend into the hill of the Lord? or who shall stand in his holy place?"

The Answer: "He that hath clean hands, and a pure heart; who hath not lifted up his soul unto vanity, nor sworn deceitfully."

The Promised Blessings: "He shall receive the blessing from the Lord, and righteousness from the God of his salvation."

The question essentially asks, "Who can enter the temple and stand within the temple's holy precincts?" The answer is that those who are pure in heart and soul may enter. That includes those who, among other things, strive to:

Have clean hands—they are repentant and upright.

Have a pure heart—they act with real intent. There is no guile or deceit in their hearts, no ulterior motives. They seek the welfare of others. Their motives, affections, desires, and decisions are pure and reflect in their actions.

Have no vanity—there is in them no pride, no showiness, no seeking to esteem themselves above others.

When we do these things, we receive all the blessings our perfect and loving Heavenly Father stands ready to give us. Like His Son, Jesus Christ, we will receive "all that my Father hath" (D&C 84:38).

Hymns of the Temple, Isaiah 33
The Prophet Isaiah (Isa. 33:114–117)

The Question: "Who among us shall dwell with the devouring fire? Who among us shall dwell with everlasting burnings?" (*Everlasting burnings* and the *devouring fire* represent the presence of God.)

The Answer: "He that walketh righteously, and speaketh uprightly; he that despiseth the gain of oppressions, that shaketh his hands from holding of bribes, that stoppeth his ears from hearing of blood, and shutteth his eyes from seeing evil."

The Promised Blessings: "He shall dwell on high: his place of defence *shall be* the munitions of rocks: bread shall be given him; his waters *shall be* sure. Thine eyes shall see the king in his beauty: they shall behold the land that is very far off."

The question asks, "Who can dwell in the presence of God?" The answer says that those who follow the strait and narrow path by keeping all of God's commandments and covenants can dwell in His presence. They are those who, among other things, strive to:

Walk in righteousness and keep the commandments in purity.

Speak the truth—say what is just and true, what is kind and benevolent—in all conversation.

Do not accept bribes or rewards for engaging in any evildoings or activities.

Shut their eyes from evil—do not choose to behold or condone evil they may see.

If we do the things specified in these hymns of the temple, we will ultimately be exalted. Our Savior will be our rock, "our sure foundation," our protection (Hel 5:12), the bread of life and living water (see John 4:10; 6:35, 48, 51). We will see God in His glory and partake of our eternal lives in the celestial kingdom.

Each of these hymns speaks of the requirements and qualities we should ponder and seek to acquire so we can cross the threshold of the temple worthily, humbly, and gratefully. We need not be perfect—we simply have to be humble and offer a broken heart and a contrite spirit as our sacrifice. Then we can come to know the Lord, even as He is, as charity is bestowed upon the true followers of Christ, "that when he shall appear we shall be like him, for we shall see him as he is; that we may have this hope; that we may be purified even as he is pure. Amen" (Moro. 7:48).

CHAPTER 23
Preparing to Enter the Lord's Holy House

PRESIDENT GORDON B. HINCKLEY EXPLAINED, "What a unique and remarkable thing is a temple recommend. It is only a piece of paper with a name and signatures, but in reality it is a certificate that says the bearer is 'honest, true, chaste, benevolent, virtuous' and that he or she believes in doing good to all, that 'if there is anything virtuous, lovely, or of good report or praiseworthy,' he or she seeks after such" ("Keeping the Temple Holy," *Ensign*, May 1990, 51).

The temple recommend is all about worthiness to enter the house of the Lord. However, being able to pass a temple recommend interview is one thing; being fully prepared to worship in a spirit of thanksgiving and to partake of sacred ordinances and covenants is quite another. This personal preparation is vital to enjoying an uplifting and edifying experience. Those who are preparing to receive their own endowment should take a temple preparation class and carefully read the pamphlet *The Holy Temple* by President Boyd K. Packer.

When worshipping in the temple, we should be humble and grateful. We must go with the sacrifice of a broken heart and contrite spirit. We should prayerfully prepare ourselves, studying and feasting upon the word of God, pondering and meditating that the windows of heaven might be opened to us. Such is the way President Joseph F. Smith prepared when the vision of the dead opened to him. He said, "The eyes of my understanding were opened, and the Spirit of the Lord rested upon me, and I saw the hosts of the dead, both small and great" (D&C 138:11). He also saw "the building of the temples and the performance of the ordinances therein for the redemption of the dead" (D&C 138:54). May we also catch the spirit of this vital temple work as we prepare to worship the Lord in His holy house.

Too often we simply hop in our car and drive to the temple, perhaps even rushing so we can make the next session and not have to wait. Knowing that the Lord has invited us to His holy house, we might take the time to prayerfully prepare or even bring a "gift," as we would to a friend who invited us to dinner, as a token of our gratitude for the evening. The gift we bring to the Lord's house is our broken heart and contrite spirit, the required sacrifice.

Truman Madsen writes of an incident involving President David O. McKay that may remind us of our responsibility to personally prepare to enter the house of the Lord:

> On the occasion in Los Angeles, President McKay stopped everyone by saying: "This young lady came to me. She had had both experiences [entering the temple and joining a sorority], but said she had been far more impressed with her sorority." We gasped.
>
> President McKay was a master of the pause. He let that wait for several seconds and then said: "Brothers and sisters, she was disappointed in the temple. Brothers and sisters, I was disappointed in the temple." Then he finished his sentence: "And so were you." Then no one gasped. He had us.
>
> "*Why* were we?" he asked. And then he named some of the things. We were not prepared. How could we be, fully? We had stereotypes in our minds, faulty expectations. We were unable to distinguish the symbol from the symbolized. We were not worthy enough. We were too inclined quickly to respond negatively, critically. And we had not yet seasoned spiritually. Those are my words, but they cover approximately what he said. I will give you the quotation verbatim.
>
> This was a man, at that time eighty years of age, who had been in the temple every week for some fifty years, which gave him, I thought, some right to speak. He said: "I believe there are few, even temple workers, who comprehend the full meaning and power of the temple endowment. Seen for what it is, it is the step-by-step ascent into the Eternal Presence. If our young people could but glimpse it, it would be the most powerful spiritual motivation of their lives." . . .
>
> But there were three things amiss in me, and I dare suppose these may be amiss in some others. First, I hadn't

carefully read the scriptures about the temple. It had not occurred to me that there are over three hundred verses, by my count, in the Doctrine and Covenants alone that talk about the temple and the "hows," if you will, of preparation. I had not read what the Brethren had said to help us—I was unaware of those statements. Today we are well supplied with informative material in books such as *The House of the Lord*, by Elder James E. Talmage; *The Holy Temple*, by Elder Boyd K. Packer; and several articles in the *Encyclopedia of Mormonism*, volume 4.

Second, I was, I am afraid, afflicted with various kinds of unworthiness and not too anxious to change all that. Oh, we talk of it and we aspire. We want change, but we don't want it enough. We are (and I don't laugh at poor Augustine for saying this) like Augustine, who said in a prayer, "Oh God, make me clean, but not yet." We talk of sacrifice. The one the Lord asks of us *now* is the sacrifice of our sins—the hardest thing in the world to give up. There's still a certain bittersweet enjoyment. But His promise is crystal clear. "If you will purify yourselves, sanctify yourselves, I will bless you" (see D&C 88:74). And I'm afraid the postscript is: "And if you don't, I can't."

The third point is that I had a built-in hostility to ritual and to symbolism. I was taught by people both in and out of the Church—with good intention, I have no doubt—that we don't believe in pagan ceremony; we don't believe in all these procedures and routines; that's what they did in the ancient apostate church: we've outgrown all that. That in effect is throwing out the baby with the bath water. We're not against ordinances. God has revealed them anew. And I suspect they are as eternal as are what we often call eternal laws. There are certain patterns or programs, certain chains of transmission, which are eternal. Ordinances tie in with those, if they are not identical with them. God has so decreed, but that decree is based upon the very ultimate nature of reality. You *cannot* receive the powers of godliness, says the scripture, except through the ordinances (see D&C 84:20). That hadn't ever entered my soul. I thought our sacraments were a bit of an embarrassment and that sometimes we could do away with them. One day it suddenly became

> clear to me—this is the Lord's pattern of our nourishment. We need spiritual transformation. We can eat, if you will, receive, drink (the Lord uses all those images) the Living Fountain through ordinances. I pray that we will reach out for what is written, reach out for repentance, and reach out in the recognition that the ordinances are channels of living power. (*The Radiant Life*, 125–126)

The precious truths that Brother Madsen teaches can be applied to our lives as well.

Preparing to worship in the temple is a very personal, private act. We should not legislate what one should or should not do in particular detail but rather follow some principles of the gospel that will help us be in tune with the Spirit and not the world—principles that will bring us closer to God and make us more sensitive to the Spirit. They might include the following:

1. We can prepare prayerfully while pondering the blessings available from the Lord to all—both the living and the dead.

2. We can remember the covenants we have already made and promised to keep, such as the promises of always having the Spirit with us as we keep the commandments.

3. We can ponder gratefully the Atonement of the Lord while recognizing the goodness and mercy of God.

4. As we actually enter the house of the Lord, we can focus on our desire to become cleansed and sanctified so as to be taught eternal verities. Entering the presence of the Lord, even symbolically, requires us to make ourselves holy through the Atonement and the power of the Holy Ghost, as the Lord reminds us: "Now this [seeing the face of God] Moses plainly taught to the children of Israel in the wilderness, and sought diligently to sanctify his people that they might behold the face of God" (D&C 84:23).

5. In humility we can replace our fears and jealousies with charity as we increase in faith and knowledge. Then the veil shall be rent, and we shall "see" God, "not with the carnal neither natural mind, but with the spiritual" (D&C 67:10). Let us not consider this gift too lofty to attain, for we are divine children of God, even temples, for "the Spirit of God dwelleth in [you]" (1 Cor. 3:16–17; 6:19; D&C 93:35).

When we enter the temple, we literally cross the threshold into the house where the Lord dwells. The revelation on this point is clear: "And that all people who shall enter upon the threshold of the Lord's house may feel thy power, and feel constrained to acknowledge that thou hast sanctified it, and that it is thy house, a place of thy holiness" (D&C 109:13). As you prepare to enter the temple, I encourage you to read and reread section 109 of the Doctrine and Covenants, the Kirtland Temple dedicatory prayer. This glorious prayer brings much light and truth to worthy worship in the Lord's temple.

If we have entered the temple prepared and are alert and attentive to what happens there, we can take with us as we leave power, light, and the warm feelings of the Savior's loving arms, as expressed in the symbols of the covenants and ordinances we have just experienced. The temple experience can eventually become embedded in our beings. We will have gained increased knowledge that when applied gives us greater power to do good. We will leave having been clothed in the garment of the holy priesthood, "even with the robe of righteousness" (2 Ne. 9:14; 4:33; Isa. 61:10), as a reminder to keep our covenants and as a protection against temptation.

Chapter 24

Promised Blessings of Temple Worship

Temple worship is the term I have used to describe offering up to the Lord our thanksgiving for all things—including our own endowment and sealing to our eternal companion, participating in acts of vicarious service, and attending sealing, endowment, and initiatory sessions in the temple.

Temple worship, like all things associated with the temple and the gospel of Jesus Christ, is anchored in, is an appendage to, and is empowered by our Savior. His atoning sacrifice is typified so pervasively in the temple because He is in and through all things (see D&C 50:27; 63:59; 88:6, 41). This is the plan of our Heavenly Father: all things are done through His Son.

The way we worship indicates the state of our hearts. It represents our true feelings. We are what we worship, and we see that principle in the way we ourselves live and the way others live. We set our hearts upon the things that matter most to us, and this shows through our actions and our attitudes. It is through regular temple worship that we keep our perspective on the eternities and what matters most. It is like having our rudder for life set on the course for eternal life and returning to the presence of our Father and our Savior. The following are some key elements that will help us build a foundation upon which we can build our temple worship.

The Blessings of Receiving Ordinances and Making Covenants

Ordinances and covenants are administered by the power of the priesthood. *Covenants* are agreements or promises made with the Lord. *Ordinances* are sacred rites and ceremonies. Elder John A. Widtsoe taught, "An ordinance is an earthly symbol of a spiritual reality. It is usually also an act of symbolizing a covenant or agreement with the Lord. Finally, it is nearly always an act in anticipation of a blessing from heaven. An ordinance, then, is distinctly an act that connects heaven and earth, the spiritual and the temporal" (*Priesthood and Church Government*, 348).

The sacred ordinances and covenants of the temple bind us to our Savior and to our Heavenly Father and allow us to return to Their presence. The Prophet Joseph taught, "All men who become heirs of God and joint heirs with Jesus Christ will have to receive the fullness of the ordinances of his kingdom; and those who will not receive all the ordinances will come short of the fullness of that glory" (*HC*, 5:424).

If we do not fully receive the ordinances and covenants, we do not receive Christ, nor do we rejoice: "For what doth it profit a man if a gift is bestowed upon him, and he receive not the gift? Behold, he rejoices not in that which is given unto him, neither rejoices in him who is the giver of the gift" (D&C 88:33).

Temple worship is one critical way we offer reverent thanksgiving and accept the Lord's sacred ordinances and covenants. The Lord in turn gives us knowledge and an outpouring of the fulness of His Spirit. We offer a *living* sacrifice through our service to others and accept the goodness of God as we receive these sacred ordinances and covenants for ourselves.

The continual refreshing of our minds is paramount in our temple worship. We don't just enter into the covenants; we seek to live them in our daily lives. The temple empowers us to *live* covenants, not just *make* covenants. My wife taught me to ponder my covenants as I dress myself each morning in the sacred garment; it has been an eye-opening and empowering moment as I remember the purpose for the garment of the holy priesthood, "the robe of righteousness."

Oh, the goodness of God. Though our minds are finite and mortal, they are nevertheless able to grasp with gratitude the promised blessings, including a return to our Father and our Savior.

The challenge becomes this: What can we do to prepare to worship in the house of the Lord and thus partake of the promised blessings?

All the covenants and ordinances of the gospel are tied to blessings predicated on our obedience to the laws upon which those blessings are predicated (see D&C 130:20–21). So it is with the blessings of temple worship. We receive associated knowledge and understanding as it relates to eternal lives, and an understanding of any doctrine, principle, commandment, covenant, or ordinance fills us with gratitude, for we see in them God's promised blessings. That gratitude draws us to the Lord and creates within us a desire to change—to change our hearts, our attitudes, our behavior. We become truly motivated to become better, to become more. The promised temple blessings truly remind us of the power of temple worship.

The Blessing of the Atonement

In the endowment, we come to understand and appreciate the Atonement more fully. We begin to see that all things point to and typify Him (see 2 Ne. 11:4), that all things are an appendage to the infinite Atonement. It is through the Atonement that we are cleansed. Through the power of the Atonement, we are ultimately brought into the presence of the Father. In sum, the Atonement is the enabling power of the endowment, not only for us personally but vicariously for the salvation of all who did not receive these ordinances in this life.

As we center our minds and hearts on our Savior and truly internalize the temple covenants and teachings, the Atonement will become more efficacious in our lives.

The Blessing of the Fulness of the Holy Ghost

It is only in the temple that we can "receive a fulness of the Holy Ghost, and be organized according to [his] laws, and be prepared to obtain every needful thing" (D&C 109:15). The Holy Spirit of Promise, the Holy Ghost, ratifies all temple blessings. It is "that Spirit which leadeth to do good—yea, to do justly, to walk humbly, to judge righteously" (D&C 11:12). It is the Holy Ghost whose fruit "is love, joy, peace, longsuffering, gentleness, goodness, faith, Meekness, temperance" (Gal. 5:22–23). The Spirit (the Comforter) testifies of Christ (see John 15:26) and "shall teach you all things, and bring all things to your remembrance" (John 14:26). It sheds abroad the "love of God . . . in our hearts" (Rom. 5:5). We preach, teach, and speak by the power of the Holy Ghost (see 2 Pet. 1:21; D&C 68:3–7). We are "sanctified by the reception of the Holy Ghost" (3 Ne. 27:20).

Such words should inspire us to pray for the Spirit to be with us as a constant companion. But there is a price for this promised blessing. The Holy Spirit is bestowed upon those who love God and "purify themselves before Him" (D&C 76:116)—those who keep the commandments. The prophet Wilford Woodruff confirmed these principles: "You may have the administration of angels; you may see many miracles; you may see many wonders in the earth; but I claim that the gift of the Holy Ghost is the greatest gift that can be bestowed upon man" (*Teachings of the Presidents of the Church: Wilford Woodruff*, 46).

Brigham Young also emphasized the blessing of the fulness of the Holy Ghost when he said, "If the Latter-day Saints will walk up to their privileges and exercise faith in the name of Jesus Christ and live in the enjoyment of the fullness of the Holy Ghost constantly day by day, there is nothing on the face of the Earth that they could ask for that would not be given to them. The Lord is waiting to be very gracious unto this people and to pour out upon them riches, honor, glory, and power, even that they may possess all things according to the promises He has made through His apostles and prophets" (*JD*,11:114).

Let us yearn for the Holy Ghost in our lives. I have felt His Spirit, and it has transformed me. It leads me to do good, especially when I think of others rather than of myself. I have relied on my Comforter, the Holy Spirit, as a teacher throughout my life. He gives me the words to say and how to say them, as the Lord promised the Prophet Joseph the Holy Ghost would do: "And this is the ensample unto them, that they shall speak as they are moved upon by the Holy Ghost. And whatsoever they shall speak when moved upon by the Holy Ghost shall be scripture, shall be the will of the Lord, shall be the mind of the Lord, shall be the word of the Lord, shall be the voice of the Lord, and the power of God unto salvation" (D&C 68:3–4). This is the third time you have read these verses. I will read them again as I edit the book for the tenth time. That makes thirty times, and I never tire of them—instead, I stand in awe at the goodness of God for giving us this supernal gift of the Holy Ghost in our lives. What a responsibility! What a blessing! Gratitude flows from my heart unceasingly. This promise is to *all* faithful members of the Church (see D&C 68:7; 2 Ne. 32:5). As the prophet Joel pointed out, the Lord is no respecter of persons: "And it shall come to pass afterward, that I will pour out my spirit upon all flesh; and your sons and your daughters shall prophesy, your old men shall dream dreams, your young men shall see visions" (Joel 2:28).

The gifts of the Spirit can be ours as we qualify according to the will of God (see D&C 46:8–33; Moro. 10:8–19). Our Heavenly Father has given us a member of the Godhead to help us throughout our lives, in every hour of need, through our faithfulness—a humbling thought.

The Blessings of Instruction, Edification, and Revelation

If we go to the temple in an attitude of humility and prayer, we will be taught the doctrines, principles, ordinances, and covenants necessary to return to our Heavenly Father. The Lord describes His house as a house of learning (see D&C 109:8), where, according to Elder John A. Widtsoe, we are taught the doctrines of eternal life:

> The temple ordinances encompass the whole plan of salvation, as taught from time to time by the leaders of the Church, and elucidate matters difficult of understanding. There is no warping or twisting in fitting the temple teachings into the great scheme of salvation. The philosophical completeness of the endowment is one of the great arguments for the veracity of the temple ordinances. Moreover, this completeness of survey and expounding of the Gospel plan, makes temple worship one of the most effective methods in refreshing the memory concerning the whole structure of the gospel. Another fact has always appealed to me as a strong internal evidence for the truth of temple work. The endowment and the temple work as revealed by the Lord to the Prophet Joseph Smith fall clearly into four distinct parts: The preparatory ordinances; the giving of instruction by lectures and representations; covenants; and, finally, tests of knowledge. I doubt that the Prophet Joseph Smith, unlearned and untrained in logic, could of himself have made the thing so logically complete. ("Temple Worship," 12:58)

Elder Widtsoe also described the manner by which we are taught in the house of the Lord:

> The wonderful pedagogy of the temple service, especially appealing to me as a professional teacher, carries with it evidence of the truth of temple work. We go to the temple to be informed and directed, to be built up and to be blessed. How is all this accomplished? First by the spoken word, through the lectures and conversations, just as we do in the class room, except with more elaborate care, then by the appeal to the eye by representations by living, moving beings; and by pictorial representations [and, we would now add, filmed presentations] in the wonderfully

> decorated rooms. . . . Meanwhile the recipients themselves, the candidates for blessings, engage actively in the temple service. . . . Altogether our temple worship follows a most excellent pedagogical system. I wish instruction were given so well in every schoolroom throughout the land, for we would then teach with more effect than we now do. For these reasons, among many others, I've always felt that temple work is a direct evidence of the truth of the work reestablished by the Prophet Joseph Smith. It may be that the temple endowment and the other temple ordinances form the strongest available evidence of the divine inspiration of the Prophet Joseph Smith. ("Temple Worship," 12:59)

The Lord answers the prayers of those who come to the temple seeking inspiration and direction in their lives. Elder Widtsoe continues:

> I believe that the busy person on the farm, in the shop, in the office, or in the household, who has his worries and troubles, can solve his problems better and more quickly in the house of the Lord than anywhere else. If he will . . . [do] the temple work for himself and for his dead, he will confer a mighty blessing upon those who have gone before, and . . . a blessing will come to him, for at the most unexpected moments, in or out of the temple will come to him, as a revelation, the solution of the problems that vex his life. That is the gift that comes to those who enter the temple properly. ("Temple Worship," 12:63–64)

Temple worship and work are a wonderful opportunity to keep alive our spiritual knowledge and strength. Elder Widtsoe marveled at the power of the endowment:

> The mighty perspective of eternity is unraveled before us in the holy temples; we see time from its infinite beginning to its endless end; and the drama of eternal life is unfolded before us. Then I see more clearly my place amidst the things of the universe, my place among the purposes of God; I am better able to place myself where I belong, and I am better able to value and to weigh, to separate and to organize the common, ordinary duties of my life, so that the little things shall not

> oppress me or take away my vision of the greater things that God has given us. (*CR*, Apr. 1922, 97–98)

I testify to the truthfulness of Elder Widtsoe's insights. Through temple worship, we come to more clearly see life and our place in it. We learn of our divine nature and our ultimate destiny. The temple gives us hope and builds our faith. The Lord's holy house encourages us to come not only prepared and worthy but also with expectations of revelation and the knowledge of God; the mysteries of godliness unfold to us a little more fully every time we come prepared. We are enlightened with eternal truths that change our lives.

The mysteries of godliness teach us the ways to be godly, holy, and pure. We seek to become as our Gods are. That is our destiny. Godhood is not an ethereal, abstract doctrine; it is real and true. This was and is Heavenly Father's plan from the beginning—that we should have a life like that of our Heavenly Parents, with knowledge and power to do all things. Does this not motivate us to follow our Savior and keep the commandments? I want to be a worthy son!

The Blessing of Being Endowed with Power from on High

Our dispensation is a dispensation of temple building. We are engaged in aggressively building temples so the Lord can have a house where He can come to bless us with power and where all of God's children can have the opportunity to go forth so endowed: "And ye are to be taught from on high. Sanctify yourselves and ye shall be endowed with power, that ye may give even as I have spoken" (D&C 43:16; D&C 38:38).

The word *endow* as used in the New Testament comes from the Greek root *enduein*, meaning "to dress, clothe, put on garments, put on attributes, or receive virtue." The Lord commanded His Apostles to tarry in Jerusalem until they were "endued with power from on high" (Luke 24:49). The Lord, for the same reason, instructed the Brethren in this dispensation to tarry, that they might receive this power (see D&C 95:9).

The Blessing of Making Covenants and Receiving Ordinances That Qualify Us to Enter into the Presence of the Father

Brigham Young's teaching bears repeating: "Your endowment is, to receive all those ordinances in the House of the Lord, which are necessary for you, after you have departed this life, to enable you to walk back to the presence of the Father" (*DBY*, 416). It is our responsibility in this last and great dispensation to begin this great exalting work for those who have passed on. This vicarious work will continue through the Millennium so all of humankind who so wish can return to the presence of the Father and become "joint-heirs with Christ" (Rom. 8:17).

It is significant to note that all ordinances and covenants are performed individually—one temple patron or deceased person at a time. Each of us, living or dead, receives the signs and tokens that will allow us access to the Father's throne.

The Blessing of Becoming a Better People

Modern-day prophets have reminded us how the blessings of the temple help us become better people. President Gordon B. Hinckley stated,

> If every man in this church who has been ordained to the Melchizedek Priesthood were to qualify himself to hold a temple recommend, and then were to go to the house of the Lord and renew his covenants in solemnity before God and witnesses, we would be a better people. . . . So much of heartache and heartbreak would be avoided. . . . There would be a greater measure of appreciation and of mutual respect among us. And I am confident the Lord would smile with greater favor upon us. (*Ensign*, Nov. 1995, 53)

President Hinckley explained that the blessings of temple work lead to less selfishness, less contention, and less demeaning of others: "Those who come to the temples to do work for the dead generally know very little of those in whose service they labor. They expect no thanks for that service. They come out of a sense of love and duty. There is an absence of selfishness, except as they desire to refine and enhance their own spirituality in the process. If there were more temple work done in the Church, there would be less of selfishness, less of contention, less of demeaning others. The whole Church would increasingly be lifted to greater heights of spirituality, love for one another, and obedience to the commandments of God" (*TGBH*, 622).

I have witnessed this selfless service every day at the temple, but what is really observable is the way people act while in the house of the Lord. Loving-kindness is the watchword of temple workers. They always accommodate the patrons. "How can I help?" and "What can I do for you?" are typical phrases. Those who attend and worship in the temple experience these feelings, witness the love of God, and leave with overwhelming desires to be kind. *Just be kind* becomes the essence of a Spirit-directed life. Yes, husbands will be better husbands, and wives will be better wives, and mothers and fathers will perform their callings more diligently. The temple enlightens our minds and empowers us to be kind and to go about doing good.

Elder Joseph B. Wirthlin likewise talked about the plethora of blessings that come from worship in the house of the Lord:

> The ideals of faith, hope, and charity are most evident in the holy temples. There we learn the purpose of life, strengthen our commitment as disciples of Christ by entering into sacred covenants with Him, and seal our families together for eternity across generations. Receiving our own endowment in a temple and returning frequently to perform sacred ordinances for our kindred dead increases our faith, strengthens our hope, and deepens our charity. We receive our own endowment with faith and hope that we will understand the Lord's plan for His children, will recognize the divine potential within each of us as children of our Heavenly Father, and will be faithful to the end in keeping the covenants we make. Performing temple ordinances for the dead is a manifestation of charity, offering essential blessings to those who have preceded us, blessings that were not available to them during their mortal lives. We have the privilege of doing for them what they are unable to do for themselves. ("Cultivating Divine Attributes," *Ensign*, Nov. 1998, 27)

These are blessings we can claim as we regularly worship in the temple. If we go with an attitude to learn and become, we will learn and become "even as He is" (3 Ne. 27:27). As our minds rehearse the temple hymns, we will seek to prepare better, and in that preparation, we will become more holy. Our thoughts will be on how we behave toward others. Our lives will reflect the covenants we have made because we now seek to live those covenants. The Lord will always keep His promise to bless us and help us become all that God has ordained we should be.

Blessings of the Highest Order

In the temple, we receive blessings of the highest order. President John Taylor made this point clearly:

> The gospel, when introduced and preached to Adam after the fall, through the atonement of Jesus Christ, placed him in a position not only to have victory over death, but to have within his reach and to possess the perpetuity, not only of earthly, but of heavenly life; not only of earthly, but also of heavenly dominion; and through the law of that gospel enabled him (and not him alone, but all his posterity) to obtain, not only his first estate, but a higher exaltation on earth and in the heavens, than he could have enjoyed if he had not fallen; the powers and blessings associated with the atonement being altogether in advance of and superior to any enjoyment or privileges that he could have had in his first estate. (*The Gospel Kingdom*, 278)

One of these great blessings is eternal increase. We read in the scriptures that "in the celestial glory there are three heavens or degrees; And in order to obtain the highest, a man must enter into this order of the priesthood [meaning the new and everlasting covenant of marriage]; And if he does not, he cannot obtain it. He may enter into the other, but that is the end of his kingdom; he cannot have an increase" (D&C 131:1–4).

Another of these blessings is knowing that we can be "sealed up unto eternal life." We read of this, "The more sure word of prophecy means a man's knowing that he is sealed up unto eternal life, by revelation and the spirit of prophecy, through the power of the Holy Priesthood" (D&C 131:5). The Prophet Joseph Smith was likewise told, "And of as many as the Father shall bear record, to you shall be given power to seal them up unto eternal life. Amen" (D&C 68:12).

The President of the Church, and he alone administers the keys to this sealing power of uniting families eternally. Through revelation and by his authority, he confers this sealing power on other high priests in the Church, and they in turn bless the human family. This authority and power reaches into the eternities:

> All covenants, contracts, bonds, obligations, oaths, vows, performances, connections, associations, or expectations, that

> are not made and entered into and sealed by the Holy Spirit of promise, of him who is anointed, both as well for time and for all eternity, and that too most holy, by revelation and commandment through the medium of mine anointed, whom I have appointed on the earth to hold this power (and I have appointed unto my servant Joseph to hold this power in the last days, and there is never but one on the earth at a time on whom this power and the keys of this priesthood are conferred), are of no efficacy, virtue, or force in and after the resurrection from the dead; for all contracts that are not made unto this end have an end when men are dead. (D&C 132:7)

This is one of the "great and precious promises" to which the Apostle Peter urged the Saints of his day to "give diligence," that they might "make [their] calling and election sure" (2 Pet. 1:4, 10). The Prophet Joseph also encouraged the Saints to seek this blessing: "Oh! I beseech you to go forward, go forward and make your calling and your election sure" (*TPJS*, 366).

This more sure word of prophecy is empowering, as the Prophet Joseph taught:

> They [those seeking to have their calling and election made sure] then would want that more sure word of prophecy, that they were sealed in the heavens and had the promise of eternal life in the kingdom of God. Then, having this promise sealed unto them, it was an anchor to the soul, sure and steadfast. Though the thunders might roll and lightnings flash, and earthquakes bellow, and war gather thick around, yet this hope and knowledge would support the soul in every hour of trial, trouble and tribulation. Then knowledge through our Lord and Savior Jesus Christ is the grand key that unlocks the glories and mysteries of the kingdom of heaven. (*TPJS*, 298)

To have your calling and election made sure means simply that a man "is sealed up to eternal life" (D&C 131:5). This requires entering into the new and everlasting covenant of marriage and "whatsoever my servant hath put upon them, in time, and through all eternity; and shall be of full force when they are out of the world; and they shall pass by the angels, and the gods, which are set there, to their exaltation and glory in all things, as hath been sealed upon their heads, which glory shall be a fulness and a continuation of the seeds forever and ever" (D&C 132:19).

The Prophet Joseph explained the process of having our calling and election made sure:

> After a person has faith in Christ, repents of his sins, and is baptized for the remission of his sins and receives the Holy Ghost (by the laying on of hands), which is the first Comforter, then let him continue to humble himself before God, hungering and thirsting after righteousness, and living by every word of God, and the Lord will soon say unto him, Son, thou shall be exalted. When the Lord has thoroughly proved him, and finds that the man is determined to serve him at all hazards, then the man will find his calling and election made sure, then it will be his privilege to receive the other Comforter. (*TPJS*, 149)

The Holy Spirit of Promise is described as "another comforter":

> Wherefore, I now send upon you another Comforter, even upon you my friends, that it may abide in your hearts, even the Holy Spirit of promise; which other Comforter is the same that I promised unto my disciples, as is recorded in the testimony of John. This Comforter is the promise which I give unto you of eternal life, even the glory of the celestial kingdom" (D&C 88:3–4). I would exhort you to go on and continue to call upon God until you make your calling and election sure for yourselves, by obtaining this more sure word of prophecy, and wait patiently for the promise until you obtain it. (*TPJS*, 299)

The Prophet Joseph himself received this assurance: "I am the Lord thy God, and will be with thee even unto the end of the world, and through all eternity; for verily I seal upon you your exaltation, and prepare a throne for you in the kingdom of my Father with Abraham your father" (D&C 132:49).

The Prophet Joseph admonished us to seek for a more sure word of prophecy to know our calling and election is made sure: "Though they might hear the voice of God and know that Jesus was the Son of God, this would be no evidence that their election and calling was made sure, that they had part with Christ, and were joint heirs with Him. They then would want that more sure word of prophecy, that they were sealed in the heavens and had the promise of eternal life in the kingdom of God" (*TPJS*, 298).

This is given not only to special Saints but also to all of God's children. There is no competition, only the love of God as expressed to His children for their righteousness. This blessing can become an anchor to our souls, a sure and steadfast promise. It provides hope and knowledge that will support us through our mortal tribulations. It unlocks the mysteries of eternal verities.

The Blessing of the Garment, a Protection against Evil

The booklet the Church published on preparing to enter the temple explains, "The garment represents sacred covenants. It fosters modesty and becomes a shield and protection to the wearer" (*Preparing to Enter the Holy Temple*, 75). We learn much the same principle from Elder Carlos E. Asay:

> It is the special underclothing known as the temple garment, or garment of the holy priesthood, worn by members of The Church of Jesus Christ of Latter-day Saints who have received their temple endowment. This garment, worn day and night, serves three important purposes: it is a reminder of the sacred covenants made with the Lord in His holy house, a protective covering for the body, and a symbol of the modesty of dress and living that should characterize the lives of all the humble followers of Christ. ("The Temple Garment," *Ensign*, Aug. 1977)

It is written in the *Encyclopedia of Mormonism* that "the white garment symbolizes purity and helps assure modesty, respect for the attributes of God, and, to the degree it is honored, a token of what Paul regarded as taking upon one the whole armor of God (Eph. 6:13; cf. D&C 27:15). . . . Garments bear several simple marks of orientation toward the gospel principles of obedience, truth, life, and discipleship in Christ" (Marshall, 2:534).

Elder Carlos E. Asay, in his article concerning the garment, called attention to garments mentioned in the scriptures:

> Many references are found in the scriptures relating to garments and clothing. Enoch declared: "I beheld the heavens open, and I was clothed with glory" (Moses 7:3). Jacob spoke of a day of judgment when "we shall have a perfect knowledge of all our guilt, and our uncleanness, and our nakedness; and the righteous shall have a perfect knowledge of their enjoyment, and their righteousness, being clothed with purity, yea, even with the robe of righteousness" (2 Nephi 9:14). Isaiah rejoiced, saying, "God . . . hath clothed me with the garments of salvation, he hath covered me with the robe of righteousness" (Isa. 61:10). Alma referred to "all the holy prophets, whose garments are cleansed and are spotless, pure and white" (Alma 5:24). These and other prophetic statements suggest not only a cleanliness and purity within one's soul, but also a spotless covering over one's soul, signifying a life of goodness and devotion to God. ("The Temple Garment," 19)

The garment also acts as a protection for us. The First Presidency has reminded us, "Endowed members of the Church wear the garment as a reminder of the sacred covenants they have made with the Lord and also as a protection against temptation and evil. How it is worn is an outward expression of an inward commitment to follow the Savior" ("The Temple Garment," 19).

Surely, as we come to know and appreciate the garment of the holy priesthood, we will come to appreciate all of these things and more. It provides a covering for us; as we accept the Atonement, it covers our sins. Understanding its symbolism draws us closer to our Savior. Father, in His loving-kindness, provides this garment to bless and protect His children. Indeed, it is a robe of righteousness (see Isa. 61:10; 2 Ne. 4:33).

The Blessing of Symbolically Entering the Presence of God

We, being mortal and in a fallen state—a state of probation—are no longer in the presence of the Lord (see Alma 42:6–7, 9). However, as we purify our hearts and receive the Spirit, we are allowed to experience the glory of God. God's presence may occur in several different types of manifestations:

1. One could literally see God face-to-face, as described by Moses (see Moses 1:2).

2. One could see God by the quickening of the Spirit, through the spiritual mind (see D&C 67:10–12).

3. One could hear the voice of God audibly, as did Nephi (see 2 Ne. 31:15), or hear the voice of God in the heart and mind, as did Samuel the Lamanite (see Hel. 13:5). We also read that Adam and Eve, though cast out of the presence of God, heard His voice (see Moses 5:4).

4. One could feel the presence of God by being in His temples, where He dwells (see D&C 94:8).

Those with pure hearts may see the Lord simply by being in the temple. In His great condescension, the Lord said, "And inasmuch as my people build a house unto me in the name of the Lord, and do not suffer any unclean thing to come into it, that it be not defiled, my glory shall rest upon it; Yea, and my presence shall be there, for I will come into it, and all the pure in heart that shall come into it shall see God" (D&C 97:15–16).

The Lord promised Joseph Smith and others that if they stripped themselves of "jealousies and fears" and humbled themselves before Him, "the veil should be rent and you shall see me and know that I am" through their spiritual eyes (D&C 67:10). The same promise came to Joseph Smith when he and others were incarcerated in Liberty Jail: "Let thy bowels also be full of charity towards all men, and to the household of faith, and let virtue garnish thy thoughts unceasingly; then shall thy confidence wax strong in the presence of God; and the doctrine of the priesthood shall distill upon thy soul as the dews from heaven" (D&C 121:45).

The Lord explains how we can see Him: "And if your eye be single to my glory, your whole bodies shall be filled with light, and there shall be no darkness in you; and that body which is filled with light comprehendeth all things. Therefore, sanctify yourselves that your minds become single to God, and the days will come that you shall see him; for he will unveil his face unto you, and it shall be in his own time, and in his own way, and according to his own will" (D&C 88:67–68). When the Lord opens our eyes and our hearts are single to His glory, we begin to see Christ in the flowers, the streams, the mountains, and all of creation. Our souls swell with gratitude, for we understand that He made all things just for us.

We can also hear the voice of the Lord. As we pray, the Lord will speak to us by a still, small voice, which I myself have heard.

We are also able to feel the Lord's presence when we are on His errand: "And whoso receiveth you, there I will be also, for I will go before your face. I will be on your right hand and on your left, and my Spirit shall be in your hearts, and mine angels round about you, to bear you up" (D&C 84:88). Whenever we are in tune, we will feel His presence and will know of His concern for us.

These manifestations of the presence of the Lord come through the Spirit. Though we remain in the flesh, the Spirit enables us "to bear his presence in the world of glory" (D&C 76:118).

The Blessing of Being Perfected in Christ

The promised blessing of perfection through Jesus Christ is taught, symbolized, and made possible through the ordinances and covenants of the temple. Moroni exhorted us to "deny yourselves of all ungodliness" (Moro. 10:32), that we can become worthy to receive such a blessing. To deny ourselves of all ungodliness is to take upon us the attributes of godliness. We receive these perfecting ordinances and covenants in the temple by the power of the priesthood.

As we assist in the work of saving our dead, we also bring about our own perfection: "For their salvation is necessary and essential to our salvation. . . . They without us cannot be made perfect—neither can we without our dead be made perfect" (D&C 128:15).

The Blessing of the Power of Godliness

According to President Joseph F. Smith, the power of godliness, or the power to become like God, is particularly manifest in the higher ordinances in the temple. We read, "For if you keep my commandments you shall receive of his fulness" (D&C 93:20). The power of godliness is His divine nature. It is doing what He would do. It is living the Beatitudes and the commandments of God. It is being full of charity, which God bestows upon the true followers of His Son so that when He appears, we will be like Him (see Moro. 7:48)

This power is especially manifest in vicarious work for the dead as we, the living, make the sacred covenants and receive the sacred ordinances that enable them to come back into the presence of the Father too.

How and when do we manifest the power of godliness in our lives? Father's wonderful plan has patience built into it, so we receive such things a step at a time. We may find joy in the small and simple things a moment or a day at a time, for ultimately, they bring to pass what matters most: "And may God grant, in his great fulness, that men might be brought unto repentance and good works, that they might be restored unto grace for grace, according to their works" (Hel. 12:24).

The kingdom of God and Zion is all about people—so when we help anyone, we are contributing to the work of building up the kingdom of God, and we receive a bit of His power. These people may be our families, our neighbors, the people we are called to serve in our ward or branch, the poor, the ill, or those who are otherwise in special need, such as the widow or orphan.

The concept of godliness should not overwhelm us. Opportunities to serve abound. We need only seek them with a heart that desires to do good.

Blessing of Having the Mysteries of God Unfolded to Us

We are taught in the temple the mysteries of God. They are unfolded to us if we seek wisdom (see Alma 12:10; D&C 6:7, 11; 11:7).

In order to understand the mysteries—truth, light, doctrines, eternal verities—it is imperative that we give "heed and diligence" to the word. The condition of our heart determines the portion we receive: is it easily entreated? Does it, as King Benjamin asked his people, yield "to the enticings of Holy Spirit" (Mosiah 3:19)? According to Alma, the mysteries of God are imparted "unto the children of men . . . according to the heed and diligence which they give unto [God]" (Alma 12:9).

Because Laman and Lemuel hardened their hearts and failed to inquire of the Lord (see 1 Ne. 15:8–9), they could not know the things of the Lord, and they were thus swift to do iniquity and slow to remember the Lord their God. Their hearts were "past feeling" (1 Ne. 17:45). By their example, we learn that the mysteries of God come to those who are truly humble and yield their hearts to God.

Listening is another key requisite to receiving the mysteries. King Benjamin counseled his people to hearken when he admonished, "Open your ears that ye may hear, your hearts that ye may understand, and your minds that the mysteries of God may be unfolded to your view" (Mosiah 2:9). Then follows one of the most profound sermons ever given, portions of which an angel of God gave to King Benjamin. Among other things, it contains teachings about the all-important condescension of "the Lord Omnipotent . . . who shall come down from heaven among the children of men and dwell in a tabernacle of clay" (Mosiah 3:5). Knowledge of this blessing is in essence the message of the temple endowment, one of the mysteries of God.

The Blessing of Being Sealed as Eternal Families

Through the great sealing power restored by Elijah, countless hearts have turned and eternal families have been created (see Mal. 4:5–6; D&C 110:13–15). Through the Atonement, we not only become sons and daughters of Christ, but we also become organized and sealed families of God, a foundational principle in the great plan of happiness, the measure of our creation.

Orson F. Whitney wrote these comforting words:

> The Prophet Joseph Smith declared—and he never taught more comforting doctrine—that the eternal sealings of faithful parents and the divine promises made to them for valiant service in the Cause of Truth, would save not only themselves, but likewise their posterity. Though some of the sheep may wander, the eye of the Shepherd is upon them, and sooner or later they will feel the tentacles of Divine Providence reaching out after them and drawing them back to the fold. Either in this life or the life to come, they will return. They will have to pay their debt to justice; they will suffer for their sins; and may tread a thorny path; but if it leads them at last, like the penitent Prodigal, to a loving and forgiving father's heart and home, the painful experience will not have been in vain. (*CR*, Apr. 1929, 110)

Where can there be greater comfort than in the sealing of eternal families? Where can there be greater hope? Where can the power of God be manifest in greater abundance? That power can be manifest only in the house of the Lord. The temple is the only way. How blessed are we to have this knowledge. The goodness and mercy of God is always present in the sealing power of temple ordinances.

Elder Richard Winkel of the Seventy brings this principle to the personal family level:

> When you come to the temple you will love your family with a deeper love than you have ever felt before. The temple is about families. As my wife, Karen, and I have increased our temple service, our love for each other and for our children has increased. And it doesn't stop there. It extends to parents, brothers and sisters, aunts, uncles, cousins, forebears, and especially our grandchildren! This is the Spirit of Elijah, which is the spirit of family history work; and when inspired by the Holy Ghost, it prompts the turning of the hearts of the fathers to the children and the hearts of the children to the fathers. Because of the priesthood, husbands and wives are sealed together, children are sealed to their parents for eternity so the family is eternal and will not be separated at death. . . . Let's become a temple-attending and temple-loving people. I bear testimony that the temple is about families. I also testify that everything in the temple testifies of Jesus Christ. His example of love and service is felt there. The temple is His holy house. I know that He is the Son of God, our Savior, our Redeemer, our Mediator, and our Advocate with the Father. He loves us and wants our families to be happy and to be together forever. He wants all of us to be active in His temple. ("The Temple is about Families," *Ensign*, Nov. 2006, 9, 11)

I echo the words of Elder Winkel. It is true that our hearts turn to our fathers, but this also applies to our living families. My mind and heart are always on family when I worship in the temple. The entire purpose of the temple is to exalt the family of God and to bring about the sealing of families for time and eternity. Let us look to the temple, for within those sacred walls lie the knowledge and blessings of eternal lives.

The Blessing of Redeeming Our Deceased Forbears

The work of redeeming the dead is so important that the angel Moroni appeared to the boy prophet nearly seven years before the Church was organized and quoted the prophet Elijah, noting the fate of the Earth if we failed to do this great work: "Behold, I will reveal unto you the Priesthood, by the hand of Elijah the prophet, before the coming of the great and dreadful day of the Lord. And he shall plant in the hearts of the children the promises made to the fathers, and the hearts of the children shall turn to their fathers. If it were not so, the whole earth would be utterly wasted at his coming" (D&C 2:1–3). Years later, referring to the word *turn*, Joseph said that it should be translated as "bind" or "seal."

When the Savior visited the American continent approximately two hundred years after the Nephites arrived, He gave the Nephites those same words of Malachi (see 3 Ne. 24–25). Surely the Lord has impressed upon us the imperative nature of the salvation of all His children, living and dead.

The urgency of this work has become evident in the last few decades, with emphasis on indexing existing family records and especially on engaging the youth of the Church in that work. That program enables the Saints, old and young alike, to become saviors on Mount Zion.

The Blessing of Becoming Saviors on Mount Zion

The Prophet Joseph taught the Saints how they could become saviors on Mount Zion: "How are they to become saviors on Mount Zion? By building their temples . . . and going forth and receiving all the ordinances . . . in behalf of all their progenitors who are dead. . . . And herein is the chain that binds the hearts of the fathers to the children, and the children to the fathers, which fulfills the mission of Elijah" (*TPJS*, 330).

President Joseph Fielding Smith, in the dedicatory prayer of the Provo Temple, likewise reminded the Saints that they were to become saviors on Mount Zion when he said:

> We thank thee that thou didst reveal unto us thy priesthood, even the sealing power, by the hand of Elijah the prophet, so that in this temple and all thy other holy houses thy faithful saints may be endowed with power from on high and may enter into those everlasting covenants which open the door to the receipt of all of the blessings of Abraham, Isaac, and Jacob, and all the holy prophets. Thou knowest, O Father, that we seek these blessings, not only for ourselves and our descendants, but also for our forebears; for thou hast said that we, as saviors on Mount Zion, have power to save and redeem our worthy dead. ("Provo Temple Dedicatory Prayer," *Ensign*, Apr. 1972)

President Gordon B. Hinckley compared temple work to the mission of the Savior Himself: "I think that vicarious work for the dead more nearly approaches the vicarious sacrifice of the Savior Himself than any other work of which I know. It is given with love, without hope of compensation, or repayment or anything of the kind. What a glorious principle" ("Excerpts from Recent Addresses of President Gordon B. Hinckley," *Ensign*, Jan. 1998, 73).

The prophets confirm what the scriptures testify: "And now, my dearly beloved brethren and sisters, let me assure you that these are principles in relation to the dead and the living that cannot be lightly passed over, as pertaining to our salvation. For their salvation is necessary and essential to our salvation, as Paul says concerning the fathers—that they without us cannot be made perfect—neither can we without our dead be made perfect" (D&C 128:15).

Vicarious work in the temples for those beyond the veil is one of the most Christlike services we can perform. It is part of our perfection process, for "their salvation is necessary and essential to our salvation, as Paul says concerning the fathers—that they without us cannot be made perfect—neither can we without our dead be made perfect" (D&C 128:15). Vicarious work is exalting work. But it is *work*. It takes time and effort. We need to sacrifice for our kindred dead by giving our time and talents so that they can be redeemed. It may not be convenient, but it is required of us. And as we perform that work, we too will become saviors on Mount Zion.

The Blessing of Preparing Ourselves to Enter the Gate to Heaven

The Old Testament patriarch Jacob, on awakening from the dream in which he saw a ladder reaching to heaven, exclaimed, "This is none other but the house of God, and this is the gate of heaven" (Gen. 28:17). President Marion G. Romney explained the dream of Jacob's ladder:

> As, in his dream, Jacob saw himself on the earth at the foot of the ladder which reached to heaven where the Lord stood above it, and also beheld the angels ascending and descending thereon, he realized that the covenants he there made with the Lord were the rungs on the ladder which he himself would have to climb in order to obtain the promised blessings—blessings that would entitle him to enter heaven and associate with the Lord.

> It was because he had met the Lord there and entered into covenants with him there that Jacob considered the site so sacred that he named the place Bethel (the house of the Lord) and said of it: "This is none other but the house of God, and this is the gate of heaven" (Gen. 28:17). . . .
>
> Temples are to us all what Bethel was to Jacob, and more. They are also the gates to heaven for all our kindred dead. That we will do our duty in bringing our loved ones through them, I humbly pray. (*Look to God and Live*, 239–240)

The beginning ordinance on our journey back to God is baptism, when we pledge that we are willing to take upon ourselves the name of Christ (see D&C 20:37) and begin the process of putting on Christ (see Gal. 3:27). To *put on Christ* means to cover ourselves with Christ. We accept Him as our Savior, and in that process the Atonement covers us and our sins. We seek to emulate Him and be like Him as we have been commanded to do (see 3 Ne. 12:48; 27:27). We put on His attributes and take upon ourselves His divine nature. It is in the temple that we complete these two great acts, and through our faithfulness we become perfect in Him by the power of the infinite and eternal Atonement. President Lorenzo Snow, in his dedicatory prayer in the Manti Temple, said that the temple would serve the Saints "as one of the gates of heaven, opening into the straight and narrow path that leads to endless lives and eternal dominions" (Manti Temple Dedicatory Prayer, May 21, 1888).

This knowledge gives us direction and hope for the eternities. This changes the way we treat life and helps us come to know what matters most. Instead of looking for self-gratification, we look for fulfillment through service to our God and our fellowman. This knowledge motivates us to prepare every needful thing, including preparing to meet our God: "For behold, this life is the time for men to prepare to meet God; yea, behold the day of this life is the day for men to perform their labors" (Alma 34:32). "Where there is no vision, the people perish" (Prov. 29:18), but a vision of the eternities and the possibility of being with our Father changes the way we live.

The Blessing of Coming to Know God and Jesus Christ

By receiving in the temple instruction in the plan of salvation and by taking upon ourselves the images of the Crucifixion, we come to know Christ more fully. "And this is life eternal, that they might know thee the only true God" (John 17:3). All that transpires in the temple is a vivid reminder of the Atonement and a demonstration of Christ's love for us, "even that he layeth down his own life that he may draw all men unto him" (2 Ne. 26:24).

It is in this knowledge of God that we will know Him and He will know us. When we seek to understand the character of God, we will understand Him. We will worship Him and seek for our lives to align with His will. Thus, by knowing God, we will follow His commandments, and by obedience to His laws and ordinances, we will qualify for eternal life, all through the grace of God and His goodness.

Elder Bruce R. McConkie taught, "Thus to know God man has but to know himself. By introspective search in his own soul, man comes to a degree of understanding of God, including Deity's character, perfections, and attributes. As Joseph Smith said, 'If men do not comprehend the character of God, they do not comprehend themselves'" (*Sermons and Writings of Bruce R. McConkie*, 13).

As we diligently seek to know the Lord through humble prayer and seeking answers to the questions of life, we can hear the soft and gentle voice coming into our minds and hearts that testifies of His goodness and love. God and His Son stand waiting at the door; it is up to us to open the door and partake of Their goodness. God is our Father. He lives. Jesus is our Savior, and He atoned for our sins. We are Their sons and daughters.

This is the joy of life. We can have a personal relationship with our Heavenly Father and our beloved Savior. We can know Them. We can and will return to Their presence.

The Blessings of Being Crowned with Glory, Immortality, and Eternal Life

The Lord, in defining the conditions of the new and everlasting covenant of marriage, alluded to the blessing of the sealing ordinances of the temple: "Ye shall come forth in the first resurrection; and if it be after the first resurrection, in the next resurrection; and shall inherit thrones, kingdoms, principalities, and powers, dominions, all heights and depths" (D&C 132:19). Surely Alma also had in mind temple ordinances when he preached to the Saints in the city of Gideon: "And may the Lord bless you, and keep your garments spotless, that ye may at last be brought to sit down with Abraham, Isaac, and Jacob, and the holy prophets who have been ever since the world began, having your garments spotless even as their garments are spotless, in the kingdom of heaven to go no more out" (Alma 7:25).

All the scriptures that describe the multiplicity of blessings available in the temple make it clear that the temple is the only path back to our Father in Heaven. Receiving the temple ordinances and keeping our temple covenants make available all the blessings of God.

Our finite minds have difficulty comprehending the magnitude of our Father's blessings. It may be overwhelming, but there is one thing we can do with ease, and that is feel grateful for the goodness of God. We must never forget what the Lord has said: "For my thoughts are not your thoughts, neither are your ways my ways, saith the Lord. For as the heavens are higher than the earth, so are my ways higher than your ways, and my thoughts than your thoughts" (Isa. 55:8–9). With this in mind, let us be patient and accept the blessings of God, even though we don't yet understand the magnificence of it all.

CHAPTER 25

Perfection through Christ the Lord

IN THE TEMPLE, WE BUILD on all the ordinances and covenants we have previously entered into. It is in the temple that we are ultimately able to follow the admonition of Moroni: "Yea, come unto Christ, and be perfected in him, and deny yourselves of all ungodliness; and if ye shall deny yourselves of all ungodliness, and love God with all your might, mind and strength, then is his grace sufficient for you, that by his grace ye may be perfect in Christ; and if by the grace of God ye are perfect in Christ, ye can in nowise deny the power of God" (Moro. 10:32–33). Perfection and being complete comes in and through the Lord Jesus Christ.

A dear friend of mine who was trying with all her heart to become complete began to be troubled by the scripture that says, "We shall be brought to stand before God, knowing even as we know now, and have a bright recollection of all our guilt" (Alma 11:43). She felt she had repented of those things she had done wrong but worried that she would be caught unaware by something she had forgotten. She could picture herself standing before the Lord, consumed by a "bright recollection" of a misdeed that would keep her from His presence—the most miserable thing she could imagine.

After offering repeated desperate prayers, she at last went to the temple, pleading with the Lord that she could know of anything that would keep her from becoming whole and complete. Hours later, as she walked toward the door of the temple following worship that included the initiatory and the endowment, she saw a woman standing against the wall, waving to her. My friend remembered her as one of the workers who had served her in the initiatory, and responded to her invitation to approach.

"Oh, sister," the worker said, "when I was set apart as a temple worker, I was told that I would be privileged have many spiritual experiences with those I serve in the temple. That happened today when I served you. I felt that the Lord was so pleased with you and your life. You radiated such purity that you inspired me."

My friend was humbled and amazed that the Lord had answered her pleading prayer in such a direct and unmistakable way. She felt complete, holy, and clean, a blessing she received through the Atonement and through participating in temple worship. All who participate in a like manner with a repentant heart can enjoy that same promise.

This great blessing is what life is all about. It is about being forgiven through the Lamb of God as we repent with all our heart, might, mind, and strength (see D&C 109:34), that we can be perfected in Christ. This is to deny ourselves of all ungodliness. We offer our sacrifice of a broken heart and contrite spirit in baptism, as we partake of the sacrament, as we continually repent, and as we worship in the house of the Lord. We become forgiven and are made clean, pure, holy, sanctified, perfected, and complete through our Beloved Savior. He is the only way.

We begin the process of coming unto Christ as Nephi instructed: "Wherefore, my beloved brethren, I know that if ye shall follow the Son, with full purpose of heart, acting no hypocrisy and no deception before God, but with real intent, repenting of your sins, witnessing unto the Father *that ye are willing to take upon you the name of Christ, by baptism*—yea, by following your Lord and your Savior down into the water, according to his word, behold, *then shall ye receive the Holy Ghost*; yea, then cometh the baptism of fire and of the Holy Ghost; and then can ye speak with the tongue of angels, and shout praises unto the Holy One of Israel" (2 Ne. 31:13.).

It is through baptism and receiving the Holy Ghost that we start coming unto Christ, and we renew that commitment each week as we partake of the sacrament, "that they may eat in remembrance of the body of thy Son, and witness unto thee, O God, the Eternal Father, *that they are willing to take upon them the name of thy Son, and always remember him, and keep his commandments which he hath given them, that they may always have his Spirit to be with them*" (Moro. 4:3; D&C 20:77). We are truly "*willing to take upon [us] the name of Jesus Christ, having a determination to serve him to the end*, and truly manifest by [our] works that [we] have received of the Spirit of Christ unto the remission of [our] sins . . . [and] be received by baptism into his church" (D&C 20:37). This willingness to take upon us the name of Christ and to receive the Holy Ghost is but a type and a shadow that leads to greater things the Lord seeks to bestow upon us in His holy house. This is demonstrated by the fact that baptism is the ordinance and covenant of salvation, whereas the temple ordinances and covenants are the covenants of exaltation (see Bible Dictionary, "Abraham, covenant of"). The Lord seeks to endow us with power from on high in His holy house.

In the temple, we receive all the ordinances and covenants necessary to return to our Heavenly Father's presence. The blessings of the temple help us in our daily life by endowing us with profound knowledge, empowering ordinances and covenants, and the protection of the garment of the holy priesthood. As we speak of the garment and of Christ and His infinite Atonement, let us notice the parallels between them.

This is significant in regard to the symbolism of the garment. In the temple, we receive the garment of the holy priesthood (after the Order of the Son of God) to cover us and protect us from temptation and evil. The garment is a covering in our fallen and sinful state, and when we wear it, the Savior is able to protect and nurture us in all things through the enabling power of the Atonement (see Alma 7:11–12). His infinite Atonement *covers* and redeems us from that fallen state and our sins (see Isa. 61:10; Rev. 3:18; 2 Ne. 9:14; 4:33), and only His infinite Atonement can do this. Only our Savior can redeem us.

The garment is the armor of Christ that we put on, even the robe of righteousness that provides us with protection in the war against Satan. Christ the Lord is our armor and our strength (see Eph. 6:11–17; Alma 26:11–12; D&C 27:15–18). Only He can protect us. As mentioned earlier, the garment bears simple marks that remind us of our discipleship to Christ and that serve as an outward expression of an inner commitment to follow Him through the covenants we have made with Him. When we follow Christ, we become His disciples. The ordinance of being clothed in the garment of the holy priesthood is necessary to protect us and help us remember to keep our temple covenants, which remembrance leads to exaltation. We become perfected through Christ the Lord, the great Redeemer, the nurturer and Savior of our souls (see 2 Ne. 2:26; 4:31; Mosiah 13:33; 15:12; Alma 7:11–12). Christ, through His infinite Atonement, is the author and finisher of our faith (see Heb. 12:2). He sanctifies and justifies us as our garments are made clean through His blood.

We will plead like Nephi of old when he exclaimed, "O Lord, wilt thou encircle me around in the robe of thy righteousness! O Lord, wilt thou make a way for mine escape before mine enemies! Wilt thou make my path straight before me! Wilt thou not place a stumbling block in my way—but that thou wouldst clear my way before me, and hedge not up my way, but the ways of mine enemy" (2 Ne. 4:33). Christ covers us in every way, whether it be through the enabling power of the Atonement or in the robes of His righteousness. He is always there helping us become perfected through Him.

This is the way God our Father has ordained it to be. It is through the grace and goodness of God the Father that He gave us His Son. In the temple, we make the Son's Atonement efficacious in our lives as we receive Him through the ordinances and covenants and through our obedience to His commandments. We deny ourselves of ungodliness as we symbolically take upon ourselves Christ's divine nature by faithfully honoring our covenants and by being clothed in the garment of the holy priesthood. As the Apostle Peter promised the Saints of his day, "Brethren, give diligence to make your calling and election sure: for if ye do these things, ye shall never fail" (2 Pet. 3:10; verses 3–9).

King Benjamin echoed this same promise when he gave his people a name whereby they would be called:

> And now, because of the covenant which ye have made ye shall be called the children of Christ, his sons, and his daughters; for behold, this day he hath spiritually begotten you; for ye say that your hearts are changed through faith on his name; therefore, ye are born of him and have become his sons and his daughters.
>
> And under this head ye are made free, and there is no other head whereby ye can be made free. There is no other name given whereby salvation cometh; therefore, I would that ye should take upon you the name of Christ, all you that have entered into the covenant with God that ye should be obedient unto the end of your lives. (Mosiah 5:7–8)

Unfailing Gratitude and Charity

The temple is the grand key to receiving and accepting Christ and His Atonement. As we are drawn to Him, we come to understand and appreciate His infinite sacrifice and Atonement and everything He suffered, from Gethsemane to Golgotha. When we come to understand and accept the promises in the temple, we become filled with gratitude, which is the catalyst for change and all spiritual growth and progress. It is gratitude that draws us to Christ. Gratitude bears record of our love for Him. It acknowledges His hand in all things. "Gratitude is a divine principle," President Gordon B. Hinckley explained. "The Lord has declared through revelation: 'Thou shalt thank the Lord thy God in all things. . . . And in nothing doth man offend God, or against none is his wrath kindled, save those who confess not his hand in all things" ("With All Thy Getting Get Understanding," *Ensign*, Aug. 1988, 2).

Indeed, as we develop temple eyes and hearts, our souls become consumed with gratitude, which is part of the mighty change, the real spiritual growth—that is, "becoming"—that Alma described:

> And now, my brethren, I wish from the inmost part of my heart, yea, with great anxiety even unto pain, that ye would hearken unto my words, and cast off your sins, and not procrastinate the day of your repentance;
>
> But that ye would humble yourselves before the Lord, and call on his holy name, and watch and pray continually, that ye may not be tempted above that which ye can bear, and thus be led by the Holy Spirit, becoming humble, meek, submissive, patient, full of love and all long-suffering;
>
> Having faith on the Lord; having a hope that ye shall receive eternal life; having the love of God always in your hearts, that ye may be lifted up at the last day and enter into his rest. (Alma 13:27–29)

This is part of the perfection we experience as we enter into His rest.

Surely the temple is the ultimate fulfillment of being perfected in Christ, for He is the only way. Through the ordinances of the temple, the strength and enabling power of the Atonement brings about a divine nature in us. Through the covenants we make in the temple, our lives—our eternal lives—become linked to the Atonement, and we become one with the Father and the Son.

The temple is the place where the magnificence of the fulness of God's blessings comes to us. This is where we make the covenants of exaltation associated with the highest degree of glory. This is where we learn about eternal lives and about becoming like our Father. We may not understand all things at once, but through frequent attendance and a genuine desire to understand the ordinances of the temple, we can grow and obtain understanding—line upon line, grace upon grace.

Change must become a constant in our lives. If we don't move forward, we will remain static or even move backward. Ours is the task to move steadily toward perfection. If we slip a step, we must repent and give thanks for the Atonement of Christ, then right our wrong and start moving upward once more on the path to exaltation. This is the promise of the temple—the only way. As we understand and appreciate the doctrines, ordinances, and covenants of the temple, we can become new beings—sanctified, justified, and holy, without blemish. The Atonement, as presented in the endowment, will capture our souls. Having received the image of Christ in our bodies and our countenances, we can be spiritually born again.

This exalting process begins by our becoming worthy to enter the Lord's holy house. Worthiness comes through diligence in our prayers, searching diligently the word of God, and hearkening to our living prophets, which lead to living by the word of God. When we live by the word of God, we keep our temple covenants, and we wear the cloak of protection from temptation and evil.

Charity

Perhaps the ultimate crown of temple worship is the virtue of charity, which becomes the guiding force of all our actions. Charity, more than any other virtue, has the power to make us like our Savior. The Prophet Joseph taught that "love is one of the chief characteristics of Deity, and ought to be manifested by those who aspire to be the sons of God. A man filled with the love of God is not content with blessing his family alone, but ranges through the whole world, anxious to bless the whole human race" (*TPJS*, 174). Such love is the essence of godliness, for when we truly love, we seek for and serve all people. Just as "God anointed Jesus of Nazareth with the Holy Ghost and with power, who went about doing good," we too can be anointed with power and go about "doing good" (Acts 10:38), following the example of our Savior.

As we develop pure charity, our will becomes His will. Our desires become His desires. We yield our heart unto God (see Hel. 3:35). We exercise our will with an eye single to the glory of God. All our mental capacities become focused on the things of the Lord. We dedicate our physical and spiritual capacities and talents to pleasing God.

The charitable service that relates to the temple is the redemption of the dead, as the Apostle Paul wrote concerning the Israelites who escaped Egypt—"that they without us should not be made perfect" (Heb. 11:40). This principle also applies to our day—"neither can we without our dead be made perfect" (D&C 128:15).

This is the great work of charity in our temples, which work Moroni describes: "And charity suffereth long, and is kind, and envieth not, and is not puffed up, seeketh not her own, is not easily provoked, thinketh no evil, and rejoiceth not in iniquity but rejoiceth in the truth, beareth all things, believeth all things, hopeth all things, endureth all things" (Moro. 7:45). Mormon then admonishes us with these inspired words: "Wherefore, my beloved brethren, if ye have not charity, ye are nothing, for charity never faileth. Wherefore, cleave unto charity, which is the greatest of all, for all things must fail— But charity is the pure love of Christ, and it endureth forever; and whoso is found possessed of it at the last day, it shall be well with him" (Moro. 7:46–48). This is the gospel principle that leads those who attend and worship in the temple—especially the temple workers who spend countless hours accommodating those of us who choose to carry out this charitable service.

I leave you with my testimony that the temple is the only way, and it is available to us only through Christ the Lord. The love of God the Father and our Savior Jesus Christ is ever evident as They gather Their children in Their holy house. It is in the house of the Lord that They can come and dwell, that we may be endowed with power from on high and receive the precious covenants and ordinances that lead to eternal lives and exaltation.

Appendix

The History and Significance of Temples

Over the last one hundred years or so, the temple has become a major focus among Jewish and Christian biblical scholars, students of other religions, and secular scholars. These scholars have discovered that temple-like edifices and other sacred "spaces" are common among nearly all religious groups, ancient and modern. Several Latter-day Saint scholars have likewise turned their attention to the history and meaning of temples and temple building.

While for Latter-day Saints the temple experience is enriched largely through obedience, the Spirit, and temple work itself, many find additional meaning and inspiration in the study of what scholars say about the history and significance of temples in ancient Israel, in the early Christian Church, and among the Latter-day Saints.

Following is a lightly annotated list of books by Latter-day Saint scholars as well as other temple-focused scholars from which additional information is available.

Barker, Margaret. *Temple Theology, An Introduction.* London: Society for Promoting Christian Knowledge, 2004.

> Barker, a prominent (and controversial) Bible scholar and Methodist preacher, has focused her extensive research and writing on Israel's temples. A lengthy list of her publications is available at margaretbarker.com. The volume cited here is the most concise discussion of her views.

Brown, Matthew B. and Smith, Paul Thomas. *Symbols in Stone: Symbolism on the Early Temples of the Restoration.* American Fork, Utah: Covenant Communications, 1997.

Gaskill, Alonzo L. *The Lost Language of Symbolism: An Essential Guide to Recognizing and Interpreting the Symbols of the Gospel.* Salt Lake City: Deseret Book, 2003.

Gaskill, Alonzo L. *Sacred Symbols, Finding Meaning in Rituals and Ordinances.* Springville, Utah: Bonneville Books, 2011.

Lundquist, John M. *The Temple, Meeting Place of Heaven and Earth.* London: Thames and Hudson, Ltd., 2012.

Lundquist, a former member of the religion faculty at BYU, published this book as part of the Art and Imagination series.

Madsen, Truman G. *The Temple, Where Heaven Meets Earth.* Salt Lake City: Deseret Book, 2008.

McConkie, Joseph Fielding. *Gospel Symbolism.* Salt Lake City: Bookcraft, 1985.

Nibley, Hugh. *The Message of the Joseph Smith Papyri, an Egyptian Endowment.* Salt Lake City: Deseret Book, 1975.

Nibley discusses at length the long tradition of temple ceremonies in Egypt; an appendix contains excerpts from six apocryphal endowment-like writings from Jewish and early Christian authors.

Nibley, Hugh. *Temple and Cosmos: Beyond This Ignorant Present.* Salt Lake City: Deseret Book, 1992.

A collection of Nibley's extensive writings on the temple over a period of fifty years.

Ricks, Stephen D. and Nibley, Hugh. *Mormonism and Early Christianity.* Salt Lake City: Deseret Book, 1987.

Chapters related to temple worship in early Christianity are "Evangelium Quadraginta Dierum: The Forty-day Mission of Christ—the Forgotten Heritage," "The Early Christian Prayer Circle," "Baptism for the Dead in Ancient Times," "What is a Temple?" and "Christian Envy of the Temple."

Welch, John W. *Illuminating the Sermon at the Temple and Sermon on the Mount.* Provo, Utah: FARMS, 1999. Enlarged edition, Salt Lake City: Deseret Book, 1990.

Welch, John W. *The Sermon on the Mount in the Light of the Temple.* London: Ashgate Publishing Limited, 2009.

Bibliography

Asay, Carlos E. "The Temple Garment: An Outward Expression of an Inward Commitment." *Ensign*, Aug. 1997, 19.

Beck, Julie B. "Teaching the Doctrine of the Family." *Ensign*, March 2011.

Benson, Ezra Taft. *God, Family, Country.* Salt Lake City: Deseret Book, 1974.

_____. *The Teachings of Ezra Taft Benson*. Salt Lake City: Bookcraft, 1988.

_____. "What I Hope You Would Teach Your Children about the Temple." *Ensign*, May 1986, 6.

Black, Susan Easton. "I Have a Question." *Ensign*, December, 1988, 54.

Burton, Alma P. "Endowment." *Encyclopedia of Mormonism*. Daniel H. Ludlow, ed. Macmillan Pub., 1992, 1:454–56.

Clarke, J. Richard. "The Temple—What It Means to You." *New Era*, Apr. 1993, 4.

Drake, Pamela J. "Findings from the Fullerton Genealogy Study." Master's thesis. California State University Fullerton. 2000–2001. http://psych.fullerton.edu/genealogy/.

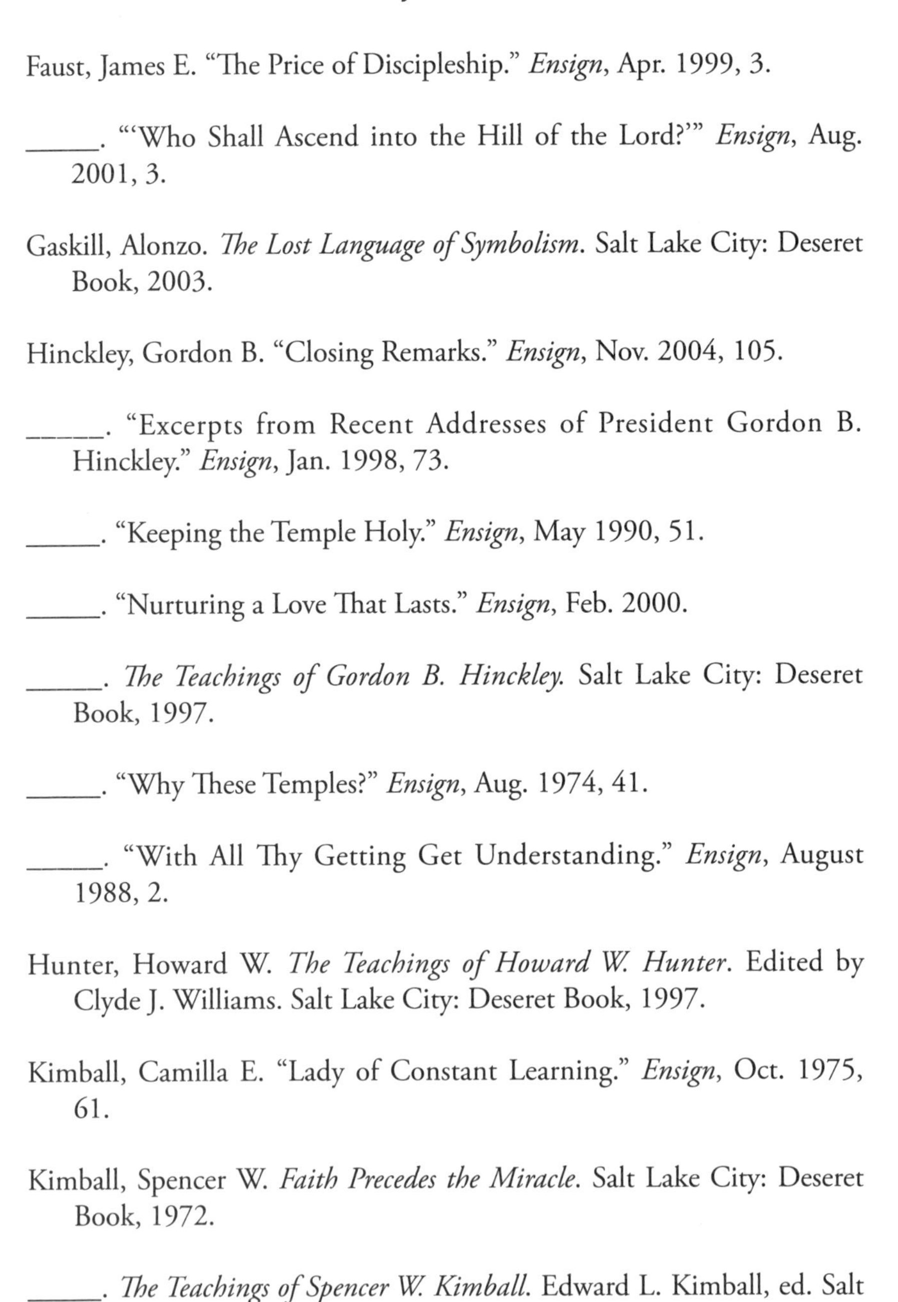

Faust, James E. "The Price of Discipleship." *Ensign*, Apr. 1999, 3.

_____. "'Who Shall Ascend into the Hill of the Lord?'" *Ensign*, Aug. 2001, 3.

Gaskill, Alonzo. *The Lost Language of Symbolism*. Salt Lake City: Deseret Book, 2003.

Hinckley, Gordon B. "Closing Remarks." *Ensign*, Nov. 2004, 105.

_____. "Excerpts from Recent Addresses of President Gordon B. Hinckley." *Ensign*, Jan. 1998, 73.

_____. "Keeping the Temple Holy." *Ensign*, May 1990, 51.

_____. "Nurturing a Love That Lasts." *Ensign*, Feb. 2000.

_____. *The Teachings of Gordon B. Hinckley.* Salt Lake City: Deseret Book, 1997.

_____. "Why These Temples?" *Ensign*, Aug. 1974, 41.

_____. "With All Thy Getting Get Understanding." *Ensign*, August 1988, 2.

Hunter, Howard W. *The Teachings of Howard W. Hunter*. Edited by Clyde J. Williams. Salt Lake City: Deseret Book, 1997.

Kimball, Camilla E. "Lady of Constant Learning." *Ensign*, Oct. 1975, 61.

Kimball, Spencer W. *Faith Precedes the Miracle*. Salt Lake City: Deseret Book, 1972.

_____. *The Teachings of Spencer W. Kimball*. Edward L. Kimball, ed. Salt Lake City: Deseret Book, 1982.

Lee, Harold B. *Decisions for Successful Living*. Salt Lake City: Deseret Book, 1973.

_____. *The Teachings of Harold B. Lee.* Clyde J. Williams, ed. Salt Lake City: Bookcraft, 1996.

Ludlow, Daniel H. *Encyclopedia of Mormonism*. 4 vols. New York: Macmillan, 1992.

Madsen, Truman G. *Radiant Life*. Salt Lake City: Bookcraft, 1994.

_____. "Who Shall Ascend into the Mountain of the Lord?": Three Biblical Temple Entrance Hymns." In *Reason, Revelation, and Faith: Essays in Honor of Truman G. Madsen*. Daniel C. Peterson and Stephen D. Ricks, eds. Provo, Utah: FARMS, 2002.

Marshall, Evelyn T. "Garments." *Encyclopedia of Mormonism.* Daniel H. Ludlow, ed. Macmillan Pub. 1992.

Maxwell, Neal A. "Lessons Learned from Laman and Lemuel." *Ensign*, Nov. 1999.

_____. *Notwithstanding My Weakness*. Salt Lake City: Deseret Book, 1981.

McConkie, Bruce R. *Mormon Doctrine*. Salt Lake City: Bookcraft, 1966.

_____. *The Mortal Messiah: From Bethlehem to Calvary.* Salt Lake City: Deseret Book, 1979.

McConkie, Joseph Fielding. *Gospel Symbolism*. Salt Lake City: Deseret Book, 1985.

Nibley, Hugh. *Temple and Cosmos: Beyond This Ignorant Present*. Salt Lake City: Deseret Book, 1992.

Parry, Donald W. In *Expressions of Faith: Testimonies of Latter-day Saint Scholars*. Susan Easton Black, ed. Salt Lake City: Deseret Book; and Provo, Utah: FARMS, 1996.

"Questions and Answers." *New Era*, Jan. 1994, 17.

Romney, Marion G. *Look to God and Live*. Salt Lake City: Deseret Book, 1971.

Scott, Richard G. "Temple Worship: The Source of Strength and Power in Times of Need." *Ensign*, May 2009, 43–44.

Simpson, Robert L. "The House of the Lord." *Ensign*, Nov. 1980, 10.

Smith, Joseph. *History of the Church of Jesus Christ of Latter-day Saints*. 7 vols. B. H. Roberts, ed. Salt Lake City: Deseret Book, 1958.

_____. *The Teachings of the Prophet Joseph Smith*. Joseph Fielding Smith, ed. Salt Lake City: Deseret Book, 1976.

Smith, Joseph Fielding. *Answers to Gospel Questions*. 5 vols. Salt Lake City: Deseret Book, 1963.

_____. *Church History and Modern Revelation*. Salt Lake City: Deseret Book, 1946.

_____. "Provo Temple Dedicatory Prayer." *Ensign*, Apr. 1972.

Smith, Joseph Fielding and McConkie, Bruce R. *Doctrines of Salvation*. Salt Lake City, Bookcraft, 1954.

Snow, Lorenzo. "Manti Utah Temple Dedicatory Prayer." May 21, 1888. http://www.ldschurchtemples.com/manti/prayer/.

Talmage, James E. *The House of the Lord*. Salt Lake City: Deseret Book, 1912.

Taylor, John. *The Gospel Kingdom: Selections from the Writings and Discourses of John Taylor*. Homer G. Durham, ed. Salt Lake City: Deseret Book, 1943.

Theological Dictionary of the New Testament. Gerhard Kittle, ed. Grand Rapids, MI: Eerdmans, 1983.

Times and Seasons. 6 vols.

Tucker, Robert A. "Temple Recommend." *Encyclopedia of Mormonism*. Daniel H. Ludlow, ed. Macmillan Pub. 1992, 4:1446.

Welch, John W. "New Testament Word Studies." *Ensign*, Apr. 1993, 28–30.

Whitney, Orson F. *Conference Report*, Apr. 1929, 110.

Widtsoe, John A. *Conference Report*, Apr. 1922, 96–97.

_____. "Looking Toward the Temple." *Ensign*, Jan. 1972.

_____. *Priesthood and Church Government*. Salt Lake City: Deseret Book, 1939.

_____. *A Rational Theology*. Salt Lake City: Deseret Book, 1937.

_____. *Utah Genealogical and Historical Magazine*. Apr. 1921, 63–64.

_____. "Why Symbols?" *Ensign*, Feb. 2007.

Winder, John R. Conference Report, Apr. 1903, 97.

Winkel, Richard H. "The Temple Is about Families." *Ensign*, Nov. 2006, 9–11.

Wirthlin, Joseph B. "Cultivating Divine Attributes." *Ensign*, Nov. 1998, 27.

_____. "Seeking the Good." *Ensign*, May 1992, 88.

Woodruff, Wilford. *The Discourses of Wilford Woodruff.* G. Homer Durham, ed. Salt Lake City: Bookcraft, 1946.

_____. *Teachings of the Presidents of the Church: Wilford Woodruff.* Salt Lake City: The Church of Jesus Christ of Latter-day Saints, 2004.

Young, Brigham. *Discourses of Brigham Young*. Edited by John A. Widtsoe. Salt Lake City: Deseret Book, 1976.

Young, Brigham. *Teachings of the Presidents of the Church: Brigham Young.* Salt Lake City: The Church of Jesus Christ of Latter-day Saints, 1997.

About the Author

Ed J. Pinegar

Ed J. Pinegar is the author of more than sixty nonfiction books, audio books, and talks. As well as being a retired dentist, he is a longtime teacher at Brigham Young University, the Orem Institute of Religion, the Provo MTC, BYU Education Week, and of seminary classes. He has served in many positions of leadership in The Church of Jesus Christ of Latter-day Saints. He and his wife, Pat, are the parents of eight, grandparents of thirty-five, and great-grandparents of eighteen. Ed and his wife live in Orem, Utah.